The Melting Pot Cuisine

America's Favorite Recipes
Part II

Entrees

Uma Aggarwal

iUniverse LLC
Bloomington

AMERICA'S FAVORITE RECIPES, PART II
The Melting Pot Cuisine

iUniverse books may be ordered through booksellers or by contacting:

iUniverse
1663 Liberty Drive
Bloomington, IN 47403
www.iuniverse.com
1-800-Authors (1-800-288-4677)

ISBN: 978-1-4759-7785-1 (sc)
ISBN: 978-1-4759-7786-8 (e)

Library of Congress Control Number: 2013903358

Printed in the United States of America.

iUniverse rev. date: 10/22/2013

Dedication

I dedicate this book to my late brother Mr. M.K.
Aggarwal who shared my passion of preserving
history and cherishing our traditions.

Acknowledgements

I would like to thank my daughter Aanshu and her husband Tapan, my daughter Tina and her husband Ravi and my son Arun and his wife Ruthe for their constant support and inspiration and for appreciating and enjoying my cooking. I definitely want to thank the Faculty Folk Gourmet Club of Michigan State University where I got my start and most of all my students at the Community College of Southern Nevada who made me feel like a great cook.

I would also like to thank my mother who believed that food becomes delicious only when seasoned correctly and her belief that a cook becomes a chef when he or she uses not just a great technique but cooks with passion and with fresh and pure ingredients. She also believed that we use spices not only for taste but also for their miraculous healing power and hidden wealth of health benefits.

Last, but not least my husband whose constant encouragement and faith that I can do it. His help in editing and photography is greatly appreciated. I also would like to thank my niece Ashima Gupta and my beautiful brilliant grand kids who brighten everyday of my life.

In the end I would like to thank all those great cooks out there in restaurants and on television food channels who are making cooking so much fun and for making it such a pleasure for all.

Preface

I came to the United States of America some forty-seven years ago as a new bride with new aspirations and dreams. In a new country with no family and friends, I was trying to find some ways to keep myself busy. My husband was on the teaching faculty of Michigan State University and had been living in the United States 5 years prior to my arrival. I quickly realized that he had become quite accustomed to American food. To become more proficient in local cooking I joined the "Faculty Folk International Gourmet Club" and started to experiment with dishes not only American but with dishes from all over the world. That kept me busy and I learned a lot about different cuisines and cultures. This also gave me an opportunity to entertain friends and keep myself both busy and happy.

Soon I started working as a chemist for the State of Michigan (Masters in Sciences). I entered couple of cooking contests and won first prize for my Chili that I never expected. Faculty Folk Gourmet Club also did fundraisers to raise funds for needy students and my food was very well received. My new friends and family enjoyed my food creations and this gave me confidence. I experimented with traditional American dishes and enhanced their flavors with Indian spices and flavors to make them unique and delicious. I carefully catalogued those recipes thinking that I may one day publish them. I have really come to love American Cuisine because of its wide array of flavors and ingredients. OVER THE YEARS I have learned to fuse THESE flavors WITH other lands… an American Salad Bowl, if you will.

I retired early and moved to Las Vegas to be near my children and grandchildren. My children are now grown and are successful Physicians and businessmen and THEY have developed an excellent palate over the years. They have encouraged me as I continue to pursue my passion for cooking. I started to teach cooking in the evening College of Southern Nevada. In this restaurant capital of the world I had the amazing opportunity to admire and taste great dishes of the world. There is a range of restaurants here from Michelin starred RESTAURANTS to Resort buffets; all showcasing exclusively symbolic dishes from different countries of the world that have become heart and soul of American Cuisine. A great revolution in American Cuisine has taken place over my lifetime. Americans have embraced other cultures' food from Andouille to Sushi. As a student of the culinary arts, I wanted to capture and describe how this process of transformation of the modest cuisine of the Pilgrims is shaping itself by gracefully incorporating the best of all the cuisines of the world. It is so important because 100 years from now nobody will be able to know how their present American Cuisine originated and what road it had to travel to get there. I feel very lucky that I can see this entire fusion-taking place right in front of my eyes.

Back in the early 1960's when I came to the United States of America, American Cuisine was still quite traditional and clearly showed clear reflections of the cuisines of the pilgrims, native

Indians and early European settlers. Except for French and Chinese or Mexican cuisines no other ethnic cuisine was making any significant visibility. People were just beginning to hear and taste other ethnic foods occasionally and with great caution. Gradually all this has changed.

As the European and Mediterranean immigrants made this country their home they opened authentic restaurants in order to preserve their identity and preserve their culture. Most of the Americans by nature are very adventurous and are inquisitive about other cultures and cuisines. They do not hesitate to try new dishes. They were and still are fascinated with these different cuisines and whatever they find delicious as well as healthy and easy to cook they try and if they like it they adapt it into their cuisine. This is how the present American cuisine is becoming a real melting pot and is continuing to do so. This spectacle of globalization of cuisines can only be seen in the United States of America because so many different cultures have migrated here in such a short period of time and made America their home

I am also writing this book with the hope that it will help all those naïve cooks and new immigrants who have come to this country like I did long ago. I feel that they will be able to learn and familiarize themselves with the new recipes of America's fast food restaurants, ethnic restaurants and America's traditional cuisine and can also get some instant information about the origin, history and contents of the food that they are eating and ordering in this new country.

In the end I am hoping that I will be able to do some Justice to the globalization of American cuisine in these books by giving the origin and history of those recipes that we so willingly have adapted into our cuisine. I am enjoying writing this series of books and I hope you will also enjoy reading and learning the origin and history of these wonderful recipes.

A beautiful display of Different kinds of Breads of American Cuisine

A few years ago I published "the exquisite World of Indian Cuisine" A wonderfully illustrated full color book with emphasis on the health benefits of the Indian spices used.

Last year, I published Part 1 of "America's favorite Recipes". This book has the most well liked and loved recipes of soups, appetizers, salads, dressings, breakfasts and dips.

This is part II of this series and enlists entrees that are becoming the heart and soul of America. Part III will have the side dishes, breads, desserts and drinks. I hope you will enjoy the three part series of this book and here I end my journey into the Cuisine of this great country the United States of America.

Table of Contents

Mexican Specialties

America's Favorite One Dish Meals

American Flag

Introduction

American Cuisine is as spectacular and diverse as its people. It is a melting pot of different cuisines exactly like this country and its people. No other country in the world has such varied fusion of different cuisines and cultures as America. From the very beginning of its existence, America has been a land of immigrants but the major influx of diverse cultures came here from middle of 20th century and is still continuing to this day. America is known to the whole world as a land of vast opportunities and is a country where dreams of an aspiring human mind can come true. Whether the dreams are personal or culinary, there is a chance for you to realize them.

The immigrants who come here also have an intense desire to preserve their identity and their roots in their new homeland. They try to present their cuisines to the people of this country with its real ethnic authenticity and beauty. Americans by nature are adventurous, courageous and ambitious and they honor, preserve and experience new and exciting cultures and other cuisines with an open mind. That is why all cultures as well as their cuisines are encouraged to flourish here with full glory and ultimately graciously merge and fuse with the local American tastes.

Early Native Americans utilized a number of cooking methods that were blended with cooking methods of early European English settlers to form the basis of American Cuisine today. Grilling meats was common. Spit roasting over a pit fire was common as well. In comparison to the Northern colonies, the Southern colonies of Native Indians were quite diverse in their agricultural diet. Native Americans taught the early settlers the importance of three native foods that were so vital to their existence, Corn, Beans and Squash. Even to this day these foods are an integral part of our Cuisine. They are clearly visible especially on Thanks giving dinner Grits and hoping John in the South, Tortilla and pinto beans in Southwest, Baked beans and Succotash in the Northeast and Pumpkin Pie all over the United States.

The slaves and poor of the south often ate a similar diet, which consisted of many of the indigenous new world crops. Salted or smoked pork often supplemented the vegetable diet. The diet of the uplands often included cabbage, string beans and white potatoes. The lowlands, which included much of the Acadian French regions of Louisiana and the surrounding area, included a varied diet heavily influenced by Africans and Caribbean's rather than just the French. In addition, unlike the uplands, the lowlands subsistence of protein came mostly from coastal seafood and game meats. Much of the diet involved the use of peppers, as it still does today.

Foods like cornbread, turkey, cranberry, blueberry, hominy and mush have been adopted into the cuisine of the United States from Native American groups. In the Northwest of what is now the United States, Native Americans used salmon and other fish, seafood, mushrooms, berries, and meats such as deer, duck, and rabbit. South Carolina has 2 major cuisines with their own histories but both styles start their cooking mostly using roux-a sauce prepared by cooking the flour in butter anywhere from light to gold. Both have rich histories, The Creole cuisine with its rich array of courses clearly showing its close ties with European aristocrats. The influences of classical and regional French, Spanish, German and Italian cooking are readily apparent in Creole cuisine. The Spanish, who actually played host to this new adventure, gave Creole food its spice, many great cooks and paella, which was the forefather of Louisiana's jambalaya.

Cajun cuisine is characterized by the use of wild game, Seafood wild vegetation and hot spices. Truly remarkable are the variations that have resulted by cooking with ingredients in black iron pots of the Cajuns. Cajuns are the French refugees who got deported from New Brunswick and Nova Scotia to settle in Louisiana USA. It is a rustic cuisine where French, Native American, Caribbean, Spanish, Italian, Portuguese, and African culinary influences can be detected. Native Africans influenced the traditional American cuisine in a major way. They brought with them some amazing cooking techniques especially Barbecuing. American food is unimaginable without it. Their techniques of smoking meats, frying grains, and legumes into fritters, Cooking leafy vegetables and okra and making up hot spicy sauces have no parallel in the culinary world.

The delicious Pork and beef preparations were introduced by the Spanish but were modified to suit the local pallet. Where as German Immigrants brought with them their staple and most beloved foods like sausages and the Hamburgers and these two made a permanent impact on the Nation's culinary world and have become the heart and soul of America. Germans also brought with them beer to Milwaukee and that this town the beer capital of the country. While the earliest cuisine of the United States was influenced by indigenous American Indians, the over all culture of the nation, its gastronomy and the growing culinary arts became evermore influenced by its changing ethnic mix and immigrant patterns from the 18th and 19th centuries unto the present. Major migration waves of English, Irish, Germanic, Scandinavian, and others from northwestern Europe occurred from 1815-1915. From early 1900 to present occurred the migration of Polish, Russian, Japanese, Cuban, Chinese, Vietnamese, Indians and Lebanese.

In this book I have captured the best of all the major cuisines that have become the mainstream food of America and its people. I came to this country about 50 years ago and I have tried to combine here recipes that are supposed to be originally American (developed by the pilgrims and the early settlers of America) and the main stream classic of all major cultures that keep merging and are becoming part of the cuisine of this beautiful country. Here is a collection of recipes that are Americanized French, Italian, Indian, German, Chinese, Mexican, Vietnamese, and Korean and in them you see the reflection of cultures of their country. The recipes have been written by keeping in mind the health aspects of ingredients used and with the concept that the average household does have great constraints of time.

"American cooking" loosely defines a collection of traditional dishes that have gained popularity across the USA. Here listed are the recipes that you see on a menu of the ethnic restaurants of the country and are also becoming integral part of our daily meal at home too. For new immigrants this book would familiarize them at a glance with the local as well as the most popular and liked recipes of this country. All newcomers will get to know what to order and what that recipe will offer to them whenever, they go to an ethnic restaurant or a local friend's house. America's best recipes are the product of fusion of some of the best European and Asian recipes and they signify our basic existence as the melting pot of different cuisines and cultures. You cannot see this phenomenon taking place anywhere else. This is by far the best cuisine there is because America was built on a cuisine that uses best wholesome, fresh and FDA approved ingredients. It was very hard for me to narrow down my favorites but If I have missed some it is not intentional in the least. We are a nation of great Presidents like Thomas Jefferson who were also agriculturists and great thinkers they believed in bringing in any unique plant, ingredient or a idea from anywhere in the world and adapting it to make this country the best country in the world. You have to agree that Americans have always been willing to embrace the new and the different on their plates. It also means we're insatiably curious and fiercely proud about food.

Like Virginia Woolf said "One can not think well, work well, love well or sleep well if one has not dined well". Never before – and in no other country – have as many varied ethnic groups have migrated and fused together as they have in the United States". Its basic idea presents the whole nation as one large pot. Whether to apply the term "melting pot" or the term "salad bowl" to the American multi ethnicity is your own perspective. I have enjoyed my journey into this Global spectacle of cuisines and I hope you will too.

Main Dishes Or Entrees

The beautiful Saguaro cactus in bloom, Scottsdale, AZ, U.S.A

American Specialties

Beef

A platter of beef nibblers

Beef is the culinary name for meat from bovine, especially domestic cattle. It can be harvested from cows, bulls, heifers or steers. It is one of the principal meats used in the cuisine of the North America, Australia, Argentina, Brazil, Europe, Middle East (including Pakistan and Afghanistan), Africa, parts of East Asia and Southeast Asia. Beef is the third most widely consumed meat in the world, accounting for meat production worldwide, after pork and poultry respectively. In absolute numbers, the United States, Brazil and People's Republic of China are the world's three largest consumers of beef. On per capita basis Argentina comes first followed by US and EU is the 3rd.The flesh of bovines has been eaten by hunters from prehistoric times. Domestication of cattle occurred around 8000 BC, providing ready access to beef, milk and leather. The world's largest exporters of beef are Brazil, Australia and Untied States. Beef production is also important to the economics of Paraguay, Argentina, Ireland, Mexico, New Zealand, Nicaragua, Russia and Uruguay. Beef meat is hearty, deeply flavored and more satisfying than veal or pork.

Romans already knew that beef from steer tasted better and accordingly castrated heifers to obtain firmer and more flavorful meat. Steer beef is lighter in color, firmer without being chewy, and contains better marbling. The tenderest cuts are the tenderloins, but most flavorful are strip loin and rib. Tenderloins freeze well, whereas strip loins and ribs do not, due to their muscle structure. Japanese Kobe and Matsuzake beef are famous for their tenderness, rich taste and flavor, but can only be enjoyed by the wealthy and has led some cattle ranchers in America to raise their animals according to the Kobe protocol.

Beef or the cow meat comes in many different kinds of cuts and each cut has its own special quality. The rib area is used for the most prized steaks like rib eye steaks and they are costly. Similarly Loin is divided into 3 separate types: Short loin, sirloin and tenderloin. These are some of the best steaks there are for example the T-bone steak, Porterhouse steak and Filet mignon. Cuts of lower quality like plate and flank running along the underside of the cow are used to make corned beef, beef jerky, hamburgers and kebobs. The brisket and fore shank are the cuts that found in the front lower half of the cow and are used in the production of corned beef. The round known as rump is found at the rear of the cow. It is supposed to be lean but fairly tough useful only for boiling and stewing.

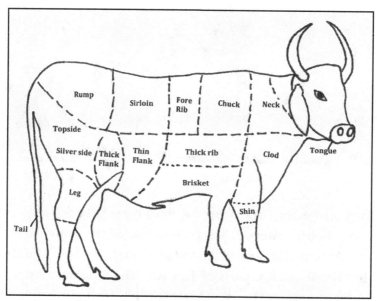

The diagram showing different cuts of Beef.

Major consumers of beef are Britons, Americans, Australians and Argentineans, Japanese and wealthy continental Europeans. Whole specialty tender cuts like rib, roasted strip loin or tenderloin is often served for ceremonial dinners with sauces like Hollandaise, Choron, Mousseline, Béarnaise or Bordelaise.

Filet Mignon

Ingredients

Marinade for the steaks
 ¼-Cup Olive oil
 1/2-Cup Soy sauce
 2-Tbsp Brown sugar
 1-Tbsp Grated ginger
 ½- tsp Roasted cumin powder
 1-Tbsp Lemon juice
 1- Tbsp Tomato sauce
 ¼-tsp Dried rosemary
 2-tsp Onion powder
 ½-tsp Cayenne pepper
 2-(8-Oz) Fillet mignon steaks

For Gravy
 2-Tbsp Olive oil
 2-Large shallots, minced
 1-Cup Assorted mushrooms
    chopped
 1-tsp Minced garlic
 ½-Cup Marsala or Cabernet or
    any dry wine
 1 ½-Cups Beef broth
 1 ½-Tbsp Chopped fresh
    rosemary leaves
 1 ½- 2Tbsp Flour
 3-Tbsp Melted butter
 Salt and freshly ground black
    pepper
 1/8 –tsp Garammasala

This cut of the meat is obtained from the small end of the tenderloin on the back rib cage of the animal and is not toughened by exercise making it extremely tender. Sometimes filet mignon is sold in the grocery stores wrapped around with a piece of bacon and pinned to the meat by a toothpick. High heat is the usual method of cooking it. It can be grilled, fried, broiled or roasted. It is then slow cooked for a while until it is cooked through, but it is sometimes served rarer than other meats.

It is then cut into 2 inch pieces and served with cognac cream sauce or any other sauce of your choice.

Filet mignon is so tender that it melts in your mouth and literally can be cut with a fork. Filet mignon when coked can be easily affordable but could be quite costly when dining out.

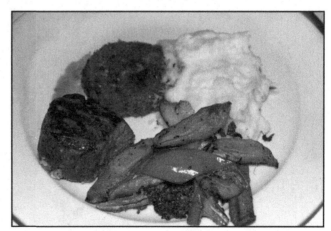

Filet Mignon with roasted vegetables

Method

1. Mix the ingredients of the marinade in a zip loc bag and transfer the fillet mignon into the bag. Seal ends and shake the bag. Refrigerate the fillets in the bag for an hour at least.

2. Oil the grill grate and place the steaks on the grill. Cook each side for 2-3 minutes or longer depending on the thickness of the steak. Cut in the middle to see if it is done.

Gravy

1. In a skillet heat 2- tablespoons of oil over medium-high heat. Add the shallots and cook until light brown and then add the mushrooms and garlic. Cook until all the moisture is gone.

2. Add the wine and scrape up the brown bits that cling to the bottom of the pan with a wooden spoon. Cook about 2 minutes.

3. Stir in the beef broth and rosemary. Whisk in the flour until smooth. Reduce the heat to a simmer and cook, stirring occasionally, until the sauce has thickened slightly.

4. Remove the pan from the heat and stir in the butter until smooth. Season with salt and pepper, to taste and serve the gravy.

5. Cutting across the grain, slice the steak into 1/4-inch thick slices and arrange on a platter. Pour the sauce into a serving bowl and serve alongside the meat. Sprinkle Garammasala to flavor the steak if you wish.

6. Serves 2-4.

French Beef Bourguignon

Ingredients

½- Cup All-Purpose flour
1-tsp Salt
1-tsp Ground black pepper
½-Lb Bacon
2- Lbs Cubed stew meat
4-Tbsp Butter
1-Onion chopped
1-tsp Minced ginger
2-Carrots, peeled and sliced into
    ½-inch pieces
1-Lb Mushroom sliced
1- Red pepper, diced
3-Garlic cloves minced
¼-Cup Tomato sauce
2-Cups Red wine
Couple of small bay leaves
3- Tbsp Chopped fresh parsley
1-Tbsp Chopped fresh Thyme
2-Cups Chicken -stock
2-Tbsp Heavy cream
1- Lb White pearl onion, peeled
¼- tsp Garammasala

It is a stew prepared with beef braised in red wine traditionally red Burgundy, beef broth generally flavored with garlic, onions and a bouquet garni, with pearl onions and mushrooms added towards the end of cooking. Beef bourguignon is one of many examples of peasant dishes being slowly refined into haute cuisine. Most likely, the particular method of slowly simmering the beef in wine originated as a means of tenderizing cuts of meat that would have been too tough to cook any other way. Over time, the dish became a standard of French cuisine. The authentic beef bourguignon has undergone subtle changes. Julia Child's Mastering the Art of French Cooking describes the dish (sauté de boeuf à la Bourguignon), as "certainly one of the most delicious beef dishes concocted by man." Universally enjoyed, this slow-cooked beef stew is the ultimate comfort food.

Beef Bourguignon with Vegetables

Method

1. In a small bowl, combine the flour, salt and ground black pepper.

2. Coat the beef cubes with the above mixture.

3. Cook bacon in cast iron pot over medium high heat. Discard the bacon fat and set it aside.

4. Add the butter to the same pot and melt it. Add the floured beef cubes and brown well on all sides.

5. Add the onion, ginger, carrots, mushrooms, red pepper, and garlic to it.

6. Sauté for 5 to 10 minutes, or until onion is tender.

7. Add the tomato sauce, 1 ½-cups wine, bay leaf, parsley, and thyme. Cook on the stove for ½ an hour stirring and then add 1 cup of chicken broth.

8. Bake, covered, at 350° F for 2 hours. Remove cover and add the pearl onions. Bake for 30 more minutes, adding remaining wine and chicken broth and cream.

9. Garnish with parsley, garammasala and cooked crumbled bacon and garammasala.

10. Serve on a platter sprinkled with parsley, pan seared potatoes on the side and with noodles or rice. It makes a great presentation.

11. Serves 6-8.

Prime Rib Roast

Ingredients
Beef prime rib roast (8-9 lbs)
¼ Cup Olive oil
Fresh coarse-ground black
    pepper, as needed

Marinade
3-tsp Grated fresh ginger root
1/3-Cup Orange marmalade
2- Cloves garlic, minced
1-Tbsp Worcestershire sauce
2-Tbsp Brown sugar
1 Tbsp Onion powder
1-tsp Mustard powder
1 – Cup Beer

For Gravy
2-Tbsp Softened butter
2- Tbsp Chopped canned
    mushrooms
2-Tbsp All purpose flour
2-Clove garlic minced
½- tsp Hot pepper sauce
1- Cup Beef broth
½-Cup cream
Salt and garamamasala to flavor

This cut comes from around the rib cage of the cow whereas most of the prime cuts come from the lower part of the rib cage. Use a digital thermometer to cook a perfect prime rib that should be pink medium rare, because at this point the meat flavor is at its best.

Method

1. Remove the prime rib from the refrigerator and place in the pan and prick it well with fork all over.

2. Mix the ingredients of the marinade and pour over the roast. Shake it well and put it back in the refrigerator for at least 2 hours.

3. Preheat the oven to 400° F. When the oven is hot, put the roast in after basting it with olive oil and fresh black pepper. Insert a meat thermometer into the roast making sure it does not touch the bone. Cover the roast with foil completely going around the pan too. Cook for an hour.

4. Remove the foil baste it again and turn the oven down to 325° F. Cook for one more hour. The temp of the thermometer should read 140°F for medium rare and 170°F for well done.

5. Transfer to a large platter, and loosely cover with foil for 30 minutes before serving. Cutting into the meat too early will cause a significant loss of juices.

6. Prepare the gravy by heating the butter in a small saucepan and add the mushrooms. Fry

until the mushrooms are lightly brown, add the flour, salt and pepper to taste and fry until the flour is bubbling. Add the garlic. Fry a minute.

7. Add the hot sauce and beef broth and stir until the gravy is bubbling and add the cream and stir until thickened. Pour over the roast when serving. Flavor with garamasala.

8. Serves 6-8.

Beef Wellington

Ingredients

1-Lb Beef fillet
Dijon mustard for brushing meat
1-tsp Chopped ginger
½-tsp Garammasala
1-Lb Flat mushrooms
Salt to taste
1-Tbsp Olive oil
½-tsp Onion powder
½-tsp Cayenne pepper
Slices Parma ham or substitute
    with Prosciutto
½- Lb Puff pastry
2- Egg yolks
4-Tbsp Butter
6-8 Potatoes
1-Clove garlic, crushed
½- tsp Dry thyme
Salt, Black pepper and Cayenne
    pepper
2-Tbsp-All-Purpose flour
1-Cup Beef broth
½-Cup Red wine

A national hero for defeating Napoleon at Waterloo in 1815, Arthur Wellesley was made the first Duke of Wellington. He loved a dish of beef, mushrooms, truffles, Madeira wine, and pâté cooked in pastry, which has been named in his honor. Beef Wellington is a preparation of fillet steak coated with pâté and duxelles (mushroom puree). It is then wrapped in puff pastry and baked. Some recipes include wrapping the coated meat in a crepe to retain the moisture that way it prevents the pastry from getting soggy.

Whole tenderloin may be wrapped and baked, and then sliced for serving, or the tenderloin may be sliced into individual portions prior to wrapping and baking. Many spices may be added to enhance the flavor and some examples are curry, allspice, any grilling mix or ginger.

Method

1. Pre-heat the oven to 400°F.

2. Heat oil in a large pan and sear the beef fillet to brown each side. Let it cool and then brush it with the mustard, chopped ginger and sprinkle of Garammasala.

3. Chop the mushrooms in a food processor to make a puree. Cook the puree in a hot pan with 1-teaspoon of oil. Sprinkle salt, onion powder and cayenne pepper till all of the moisture is gone. Set it aside to cool.

4. Lay four slices of ham down on a large piece of cling film, slightly overlapping, then brush with mushroom mixture.

5. Put the beef in the middle of the ham and roll the ham around the beef using the cling film. Twist the ends of the cling film to tighten the roll then refrigerate it for 15 minutes to let it set.

6. Take out the beef roll from the refrigerator and remove the cling wrap.

7. Roll down your puff pastry and then brush the edges with egg wash. Wrap pastry over the beef completely covering it. Cut off any excess pieces. Eggs wash the top. Put the rolls back in the fridge for 5 minutes.

8. Remove from frig and egg wash again. Bake for 35-40 minutes. Let it cool for 10 minutes before slicing.

9. Boil the potatoes in salted water for 5 minutes. Quarter them and leave the skin on. Sauté in 2- tablespoon of butter with the garlic and thyme, until browned and cooked through. Season with salt and pepper.

10. Heat remaining 2-Tbsp of butter and fry the flour until light brown and add the beef stock and then the wine and stir to make the sauce.

11. Serve hearty slices of the Wellington alongside the sautéed potatoes. Serve with the white sauce or any other sauce of your choice.

12. Serves 4 or more.

Ingredients

- 2 ½-Lb Lean ground beef
- 2- Eggs Beaten
- ¾-Cup Quick cooked oatmeal
- 1/3-Cup Milk
- ½-tsp Pepper
- 1-tsp Salt
- 1-tsp Garlic powder
- 1-Cup Chopped onion
- ½-Cup Chopped celery
- 3-Tbsp All-purpose flour, divided
- 2-tsp Olive oil
- ¾- Cup Water
- 1-Tbsp Ketchup
- 2-tsp Worcestershire sauce
- 1-Cup Beef Broth (1-tsp Beef bouillon granules dissolved in 1-Cup of water)
- 1-Medium onion, quartered and sliced
- 1-4Oz. Can mushroom stems and pieces, drained

Note: In step 2 of the method I usually add 1 tsp/ea of chopped ginger, garlic, green chilies and fry them along with the onions and add ½ tsp of cumin powder and Garammasala. Mix this mixture into the meat mixture before making it into a patty. The spices really add a lot of extra flavor to the patty.

Salisbury Steak is nothing but a fried or broiled lean ground beef patty mixed with egg, breadcrumbs, onions, and seasonings.

It was very common in the 60's and is starting to make a come back now. Hamburger steak is a similar product, but differs in ingredients. H. Salisbury, a nineteenth-century English nutritionist from England who was an American physician (1823–1905) is known to be the inventor of this dish. It is still on the menus of some restaurants around the country but not on top of their menu as it used to be. Traditionally it is served with gravy, mashed potatoes and noodles. Add buttered corn and a salad for a complete meal.

Method

1. In a small bowl, combine the meat, eggs, oatmeal, milk, salt, garlic powder and pepper. Mix well. Set it aside.

2. Fry the onions and the celery in little oil until transparent and mix them into the meat mixture.

3. Shape into patties. Dredge them in 2 tablespoons flour. In a small skillet, brown patties on both sides in oil, drain the oil and set the patties aside.

4. Add the remaining flour to the skillet; whisk in water until smooth. Stir in the ketchup, Worcestershire sauce and add the mushrooms and onions. Bring to a boil. Return patties to the pan. Reduce heat; cover and simmer them in the gravy for 15-20 minutes or until beef is no longer pink. Serve gravy over patties.

5. Serve them with delicious mashed potatoes.

6. Serve 4-6

Beef and Rice Stuffed Bell Peppers

Ingredients

For the sauce

2-Tbsp Olive oil

1-Onion Chopped

2-Cloves garlic minced

2 ½- Cups Tomato sauce

1-Cup Beef broth

1-Tbsp Balsamic vinegar

2-Tbsp Heavy cream

Salt, black pepper and Red pepper flakes to taste

For the Peppers

1 ½-lb Lean ground beef

3-Cloves Garlic, minced very fine

1-Tbsp Chopped ginger

1-Can (10 Oz) Diced tomatoes drained

2-tsp Salt and black pepper to taste

Pinch cayenne pepper

2-Cup Cooked rice

4-Large Red bell peppers

1-Cup Finely grated Parmesan cheese

¼-Cup Chopped Italian parsley

Stuffed peppers is a dish that exists in different names and forms around the world. In American cuisine they are typically filled with a stuffing such as ground beef mixed with breadcrumbs or cooked rice, eggs, herbs and spices (especially paprika, parsley and cheese. In some parts of the United States, this dish is sometimes referred to as "stuffed mangoes" despite having no actual mangoes as an ingredient. In Indian cuisine stuffed peppers are served as a vegetable accompaniment in a meal and are stuffed with rice or mashed potatoes.

This recipe of stuffed bell peppers makes a great use of leftover rice and it is well liked because it gives you -meat, vegetable, and starch all in one delicious, package.

Method

1. Add the olive oil to a saucepan, and lightly brown the onions with a large pinch of salt over medium-high heat. Remove half and reserve for the stuffing.

2. Add the garlic and cook for a minutes. Add the tomato sauce, broth and vinegar and bring to a simmer. Add the cream and season with salt and peppers. Pour the sauce into the bottom of a large deep casserole dish.

3. Fry the ground beef till it is brown and drain the fat. Add the reserved onions, garlic and ginger and cook until it is sizzling. Add the tomatoes and fry for 5 minutes or until it is no longer watery. Add the salt, black pepper, cayenne pepper and cooked rice and mix until everything is combined. Set aside the filling.

4. Place the bell peppers in boiling water for a minute, take them out and cut the bell peppers in half lengthwise. Use a spoon to remove the stem; seeds and white membrane from each pepper half.

5. Place them in the casserole dish with the sauce in it and fill each pepper-half with the stuffing.

6. Top the filling with sprinkle of grated cheese. Cover with foil and bake for 15 minutes at 425° F.

7. Remove foil and bake uncovered until the peppers are tender. Exact cooking time will depend on size, shape and thickness of the peppers.

8. Let it rest for 10 minutes before serving. Serve with the sauce spooned over the top and sprinkle of parsley.

9. Serves 4-6

Corned Beef and Cabbage

Ingredients

3-Lbs Corned beef brisket
  cooked with spices
2-Tbsp Yellow mustard
1-12 Oz, Can beer
¼- Cup Brown sugar
1-Cup Water
2-Onions Chopped
4- Small Red potatoes
4-Carrots, peeled and cut into
  3-inch pieces
1-Stalk Celery only tender parts
  Chopped
1-tsp Chopped garlic and ginger/
  ea
1-Large head cabbage, cut into
  small wedges
2-Tbsp Butter
2-Tbsp All Purpose flour
¼-tsp Garammasala

Corned beef is a type of salt cured beef product. The term comes not from the grain corn, but from the treatment of the meat with "corns" of salt. Anything wet-cured in spiced brine becomes more supple and tender due to the brining. Nowadays corned beef is usually made from brisket or round steak.

In the U.S. and Canada, consumption of corned beef is often associated with Saint Patrick's Day. Corned beef is not an Irish national dish, and its connection with Saint Patrick's Day specifically originated as part of Irish-American culture. In the U.S., corned beef is often purchased from ready to eat delicatessens. It is the key ingredient in the grilled Reuben sandwich, consisting of corned beef, Swiss cheese, sauerkraut, and Thousand Island or Russian dressing on rye bread. Corned beef and cabbage became popular in the U.S. when Irish immigrants in the northeast started using corned beef instead of pork in beef with cabbage dish. This substitution was likely due to the low cost of corned beef in the U.S.

Corned beef hash is commonly served with eggs for breakfast. Smoking corned beef, typically with a generally similar spice mix as the hash produces smoked meat ("smoked beef") such as Pastrami. Pastrami too makes great sandwiches. Simmered cabbage, carrots and potatoes with corned beef makes a traditional centerpiece dish for many on St. Patrick's Day.

Method

1. Rinse corned beef in cold water and pat dry.

2. Sprinkle the spices from the spice packet (that came with the corned beef or prepare your own mix of spices) and the mustard over the brisket. Place it in a large pot or Dutch oven and cover with beer.

3. Mix sugar with water and add it to the pot. Cover the pot and bring the contents to a boil, reduce to a simmer until tender about 2 hours. Add more water if needed.

4. Add the whole potatoes, celery, onions and carrots, ginger, garlic and cook until the vegetables are almost tender. Remove the brisket from the pot and let it rest in the warm oven. Add cabbage to the pot and cook till the cabbage wilts (15-20 minutes).

5. To serve, remove brisket from the oven and cut corned beef across grain into thin slices. Remove vegetables from cooking pot with slotted spoon and serve with corned beef. Strain the cooking fluid and set aside.

6. Prepare gravy with the cooking juices by frying in 2 Tablespoons of all-purpose flour in 2- tablespoons of butter until light brown. Slowly add the cooking fluid to make the sauce to go over the meat and vegetables. Season with garammasala and Serve it with mustard on the side.

7. Serves 8.

Pot Roast

Ingredients

- 1-tsp Olive oil
- 1- (3Lb) Boneless chuck roast, trimmed
- 1-tsp Salt
- ¼-tsp Freshly ground black pepper
- 1-tsp Ginger powder
- 2-Cups Coarsely chopped onion
- 1-Cup Dry red wine
- 4-Thyme sprigs
- 3-Garlic cloves, chopped
- 1- (14 Oz.) Can Beef broth
- 1- Can Tomato sauce
- 2-Bay leaves
- 2-Dried whole red chili peppers (optional)
- 4-Large carrots, peeled and cut diagonally into 1-inch pieces
- 1-Stalk Celery chopped
- 2-Lb potatoes, peeled and cut into 2-inch pieces
- 2-Tbsp Butter
- 2-Tbsp All purpose flour
- ¼-tsp garammasala

The term "pot roast" seems to date in print to 1881 and the term evolved from the New England's colonial-era boiled dinner of United States. Pot roast is a braised beef dish and is typically made by browning a roast-sized piece of beef and slow cooking it in a covered pan. The concept of braising comes from the French cuisine since tougher cuts are unsuitable for oven roasting due to the toughness of the fibers, they are made tender and flavorsome by slow braising technique. As with all braises, slow cooking tenderizes, while the liquid exchanges its flavor with that of the meat, resulting in tender, succulent preparation. Pot roast in North America (also known as Yankee pot roast) is often served with carrots and/or potatoes as well as other vegetables such as onions simmered in the cooking liquid. Beef brisket is also used as a pot roast sometimes because it is a fabulous cut of meat. It is located between the shoulders and the forelegs of the steer; these muscles get a workout and they are also well marbled with fat. So they are highly flavorful and perfect for slow braises. Long cooking time is needed to melt the connective tissue. Upon serving, the meat is cut against the grain, helping it to cut and part easily.

Method

1. Preheat oven to 350° F. Heat olive oil in a large Dutch oven over medium-high heat.

2. Sprinkle chuck roast with salt and pepper, and ginger powder. Add roast to the pan and cook 5 minutes, turning to brown on all sides. Remove and set aside.

3. Add chopped onion to the pan and fry until tender. Return browned roast to pan and add the red wine, thyme sprigs, chopped garlic, beef broth, tomato sauce, dry red whole chili peppers and bay leaves to pan; bring to a simmer. Cover pan and bake at 350° F for 1 ½-hours or until the roast is almost tender.

4. Add carrots, celery and potatoes to pan. Cover and bake an additional 1 hour or until vegetables are tender. Remove thyme sprigs, bay leaves and red chilies from pan and discard them. Remove the meat and shred with meat with forks and also remove the vegetables and strain the liquid.

5. Heat 2 tablespoons of butter and add the flour. Stir until rich brown color is reached and add the cooking liquid slowly to make the sauce of desired consistency.

6. Serve roast with vegetable mixture. Garnish with parsley and garammasala if desired. Serve the roast with the gravy.

7. Serves 8-10.

Beef Stroganoff

Ingredients

2-Lb Beef chuck roast

½-tsp Salt

½-tsp Ground black pepper

½-Cup Butter

4-Green onions, sliced (white parts only)

1-Tbsp Chopped garlic

1-tsp Chopped ginger

1-tsp Green chilies mild chopped

4-Tbsp All-purpose flour

1-10.5Oz Can Beef broth

1-tsp Prepared mustard

½-CupTomato sauce

1-(6 Oz) Can Sliced mushrooms, drained

1/3-Cup Sour cream

1/3-Cup White wine

Salt and Black pepper and red pepper to taste

¼-tsp Garammasala

1-Tbsp Chopped cilantro

Beef Stroganoff seems to be invented in the 1890s by a chef working for a Russian general Count Pavel Stroganov. It became popular in the U.S. in the 1950s by the servicemen returning from Europe and China after WWII. Beef Stroganoff is basically tender cuts of beef, such as tenderloin or top sirloin strips and mushrooms cooked in a sour cream sauce and served over noodles, rice, or even French fries. For a quick version you can use ground beef instead of beef strips. You can also easily substitute yogurt for sour cream and leave out the mushrooms entirely.

From its origin in 19th-century Russia, with considerable variation from the original recipe it has become quite popular around the world. A recipe very similar to that commonly found in the USA is also popular in UK and Australia, but here it is generally served with rice. British pubs usually serve this dish in a creamy white wine sauce whereas the 'authentic' versions are red stews with a scoop of sour cream separately served on top.

Stroganoff is also popular in the Nordic countries. In Sweden, a common variant is korv-stroganoff (sausage stroganoff) that uses the local falukorv sausage as a substitute for the beef. In Finland, the dish is called makkara stroganoff, Makkara meaning any kind of sausage. Stroganoff's popularity extends to Japan, where it is most commonly served with white rice, sometimes seasoned with parsley and butter. Its popularity increased dramatically with the introduction of "instant sauce cubes" available in U.S. supermarkets. These are cubes of dried seasoning and thickening agents that can be added to water, onion, beef, and mushrooms to make a stroganoff-style sauce. Additionally, Japanese home recipe for Stroganoff frequently calls for "non-traditional" Japanese ingredients, such as small amounts of soy sauce.

Beef Stroganoff is also very popular in China and Portugal, under the name estrogonofe. The Brazilian variant includes diced beef or strips of beef (usually filet mignon) with tomato sauce, onions, mushrooms and heavy whipping cream. Stroganoff is also often made with strips of chicken breast rather than beef (also called fricassee in some restaurants in Brazil). It is commonly served with crisp potato straws, as in Russia, but with the addition of white rice. Sometimes one can also see creative servings of estrogonofe (as pronounced in Russian), as a crepe-filling with a topping of baked potatoes, or served on top of pizzas. Many recipes and variations exist: with or without wine, with canned sweet corn, with ketchup instead of tomato sauce, etc.

Beef Stroganoff is popular in Iran, where it is made with strips of lean beef fried with onion and mushroom, then further cooked in whipped cream and topped with crisp potato straws. Here is an American version:

Method

1. Remove any fat from the roast and cut into strips ½-inch thick by 2 inches long. Season with ½- teaspoon salt and pepper.

2. In a large skillet over medium heat, melt 2-tablespoons of the butter and brown the beef strips quickly. Remove and set aside. Add the onions, ginger, garlic, and green chilies and cook slowly for 3 to 5 minutes then add the beef strips. Stir well. Set aside

3. In a saucepan heat remaining butter. Stir in the flour. Fry till it reaches a light brown color. Pour in beef broth and bring to a boil, stirring constantly. Lower the heat and stir in mustard. Add the Beef strips and onion mixture. Mix everything together, Cover and simmer until the meat is tender. Add the tomato sauce and simmer for 2 minutes more.

4. Five minutes before serving, stir in the mushrooms, sour cream, and white wine. Heat briefly, add salt, peppers and garammasala to taste and sprinkle Chopped cilantro.

5. Serve with noodles or rice or any other staple of your choice.

6. Serves 4-6

Ingredients

- 4- Beef top loin steaks, cut ½ - to ¾-inch
- ½-Cup prepared vinegar and oil dressing (By mixing 2 Tbsp each of vinegar and dressing)
- ½- Cup Dark beer
- ¾-tsp Cinnamon
- 2-Cloves Minced garlic
- ½-tsp Cumin and chili powder
- 4-Large red Sweet peppers
- 1- 11 Oz Can whole kernel corn, drained
- 1-Small green chili pepper, seeded and thinly sliced
- 2-Tomatillos, each cut into quarters
- 2-Tbsp Fresh cilantro, minced lime for garnish

Each harvest season in southwest New Mexico the green chilies make their grand entrance, spreading their flavor into all types of steak dishes. Limejuice or vinegar tenderizes the steak while garlic, chilies and red pepper flakes make them a little spicy. Meat dishes when cooked over hot coals or broiled after they have been treated with a marinade like that become devour-ably tasty. Prepare a vegetable kabob and corn on the cob and add a great home-style condiment to your steak dishes, making a true southwestern comfort meal. The meal is no doubt called "Southwest Painter's Palette".

Prepare this special hot preparation and add a southwest flair to your meals with these southwestern chili condiments and keep your taste buds happy.

Method

1. Place steaks with dressing and beer in plastic bag, turning to coat. Close bag securely. Marinate in refrigerator 4 hours or overnight, turning occasionally.

2. Prepare the spice mixture by mixing cinnamon, minced garlic, cumin, and chili powder; set aside.

3. Preheat broiler. Adjust oven rack so peppers on baking sheet will be 4-5 inches from the element. Broil peppers, turning often until charred. Carefully remove peppers to brown paper bag to cool.

4. Over a bowl to catch juices, gently remove charred pepper skin with fingers. De stem, seed and slice into long thin strips. Arrange on individual serving plates in spoke-fashion.

5. Prepare the corn mixture by combining pepper juices, corn, chili pepper, tomatillos and cilantro in a saucepan. Heat on stove top on medium heat, stirring occasionally until heated through, about 5-8 minutes. Set it aside.

6. Remove steaks from marinade; discard marinade. Sprinkle steaks evenly with spices mixture.

7. Place steaks on rack in broiler pan so surface of beef is 4-5 inches from the heating element. Broil 6 minutes for rare or to desired doneness, turning once.

8. Place steak in center of roasted pepper arrangement. Spoon 2 tablespoons corn mixture on each steak.

9. Garnish with a lime slice. Serve with remaining corn mixture. Serve the steak with your favorite bread and salad.

10. Serves 4.

Basic Meatloaf

Ingredients

- 1-Cup Italian seasoned breadcrumbs
- ¼-Cup Milk or beef broth
- 2-Large eggs
- 2 to 3 Tbsp Chopped fresh parsley
- 1-tsp Salt
- ½ to 1-tsp Freshly ground pepper
- 2- 4 Minced garlic cloves
- ¼- Cup grated onion
- 1-Tbsp Chopped ginger
- 2-Tbsp Ketchup
- 1-Tb Worcestershire sauce (optional)
- 1-Lb Lean ground beef
- ½- Lb Ground pork
- 1-10 Oz - package frozen spinach
- 1-Tbsp Chopped green chilies
- ½-Cup grated Mozzarella cheese
- ½-Cup freshly grated Parmesan cheese
- ½ cup Ketchup
- 2-Tbsp brown sugar

Meatloaf is a dish of ground meat formed into a loaf shape and baked or smoked. The meat loaf is formed by either shaping it in a loaf pan, or by hand on a flat baking pan. It is usually made from ground beef although lamb, pork, veal, venison pork, veal, venison, and poultry or a combination is also used. Meatloaf is a traditional German, Belgian and Dutch dish, and it is a cousin to the Italian meatball. American meatloaf has its origins in scrapple, a mixture of ground pork and cornmeal served by German-Americans in Pennsylvania since Colonial times. However, meatloaf in the contemporary American sense did not seem to appear in cookbooks until the late 19th century. Meatloaf is usually served warm, with mashed potatoes, gravy, vegetables or other side dishes. Leftovers are sliced and used for making sandwiches, because meatloaf tastes good even when it is cold.

Method

1. Combine bread crumbs in a large bowl with milk or beef broth, eggs, parsley, salt, pepper and half garlic, 2 tablespoons ketchup, onion, ginger and stir well to combine. Add meat(pork and beef) and blend well withw the ingredients and set it aside.

2. Fry the spinach in 1 Tbsp of oil with remaining minced garlic and green chilies. Add some salt and pepper stir until most of the moisture is gone. Cool it, mix with the cheeses and set it aside.

3. Place beef mixture on waxed paper and pat into 12/8- inch rectangle. Spread spinach filling

over beef, leaving 3/4-inch border about edges. Starting at short end, roll up jelly- roll fashion. Press beef mixture over spinach filling at both ends to seal. Place seam side down on rack in open roasting pan.

4. Bake 40 to 50 minutes at 375°F. After about 30 minute top the meat loaf with mixture of ½- cup of ketchup and brown sugar.

5. Serve it with brown gravy and mashed potatoes or home fries or baked potatoes and greens or green beans.

6. Serves 4.

Note: Optional toppings: Drape bacon (cut in half to make short pieces) over the meat loaf, if desired before baking.

Decorated Cow in a conservatory

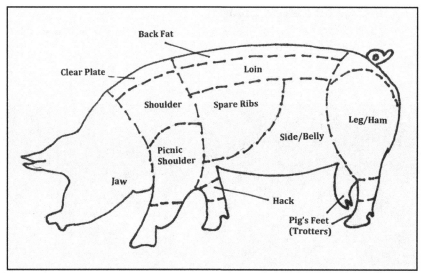

Diagram depicting different cuts of Pork.

Pork

A wood carving of Pig

Since pigs first arrived with the early settlers, Americans have used pork in an endless array of recipes. American food just wouldn't be the same without pork.

Pork is one of the most widely consumed meats in the world. Whole roast pig is a popular item in Pacific Island cuisine. It is also the most popular meat in Scandinavia, Germany, and France. The shoulder, loin, tenderloin ((refers to the psoas major), leg, side, spare rib, shoulder, and hock all provide very tender and lean meat. Pork is the meat of hogs usually butchered before they are one year old but of course with some exceptions. The most popular cut from the loin is the pork chop. Pork chops are the strip of meat that runs from the pig's hip to shoulder. Depending on where they originate pork roast is technically called the loin cut. They are the most popular of all pork cuts and justifiably so lean, tasty and easy to cook. Pork is eaten in several forms, including cooked (as roast pork), cured as with bacon, prosciutto and pancetta, baked, stuffed, pulled and grilled and more.

Below are few American Favorites.

Pork Tenderloin

Ingredients

- 1- to 3 ½- Lb Pork tenderloin
- 1-Oz-Envelope dry onion soup mix
- 8-Cups Cold water
- ¾- Cup Red wine
- 2-Tbsp Brown sugar
- 1-Tbsp Salt
- 3-Tbsp Soy sauce
- 1-Tbsp Apricot preserve
- 4- Slices uncooked bacon pureed
- 1-Tbsp Chopped fresh rosemary
- 3-Tbsp Minced garlic
- 1½-Cup Bread crumbs
- 2-Tbsp Fresh parsley
- 3-Tbsp Melted butter
- Salt and freshly ground black pepper to taste

Pork tenderloins are the most popular cuts of pork as they're lean, tender, and boneless and are one of the leanest meats available. Fresh uncured pork tenderloin is easy and quite fast to prepare. Having pork tenderloins on hand means you can whip up a meal quickly for two or more with little effort. It is a lean source of protein and can be grilled, roasted or pan-seared. Pair the pork with roasted broccoli with garlic or mashed potatoes to make a nice meal.

Whether serving grilled, roasted, or stuffed, pork tenderloins pairs very well with a variety of flavors of fruity chutneys to savory marinades.

Method

1. Place pork tenderloin in a slow cooker with the contents of the soup packet, water, wine, brown sugar, salt and soy sauce over the top, turning the pork to coat and cook on slow heat for 2 hrs.

2. Remove from the liquids. In a nonstick frying pan fry the pork on both sides about 10 minutes. Set aside to cool.

3. Mix together the apricot preserve, 2 tablespoon of the bacon puree, chopped garlic, chopped rosemary and spread the mixture on top of the roast.

4. Mix together breadcrumbs with melted butter, ½ teaspoon each of salt and black pepper, chopped parsley and press the mixture on top of the roast so that the crumbs adhere to the surface of the roast.

5. Set the roast on a wire rack inside a baking dish at the bottom of the oven and set the temp at 425° F. Bake for 10 minutes and then reduce the temp to 350° F and cook until the inside temp is 145°F or another 25 minutes or more and cover the top with the foil if the crust starts to brown too deeply. Serve it with your favorite vegetables and bread.

6. Serve it with fresh rolls, small red potatoes and salad.

7. Serves 6 or more.

Baked Country Ham

Ingredients

8- to-11 Lb Country ham

10- Bay leaves

2-Tbsp Mustard seeds

3-Cups Cider vinegar or apple juice or cola (If using apple juice or cola then do not use brown sugar or molasses for glaze)

24-Whole cloves

1-Cup Dark brown sugar or 1-cup molasses

Country hams are an old tradition in the American South. Fresh pork legs are salt-cured, sometimes smoked, and then dry aged for several months. Because the meat can be very salty, country hams must be soaked in water for a time to remove excess salt. Baked country ham is the perfect centerpiece for any family celebration. Leftovers are great for breakfast with red-eye gravy or served as a sandwich in buttermilk biscuits.

Southerners usually fry country ham slices to serve for breakfast or supper. A smaller slice of fried country ham is often placed between a split biscuit and served as a delicacy known as "Country Ham Biscuit". A boiled whole or half country ham is usually served for large family gatherings such as Easter, Thanksgiving or Christmas. Boiled country ham pieces can also be served between a biscuit or roll at parties as an appetizer.

Method

1. Place the ham under warm running water and scrape any surface mold, seasonings or any other matter from the ham with a stiff brush.

2. Place the ham in an 8-gallon stockpot and fill it with enough water to cover the ham. Let the ham soak for 24 hours, changing the water as often as possible, ideally once every 6 hours. Change the water one final time and transfer the pot to a stovetop.

3. Add the bay leaves, mustard seeds, and vinegar and bring to a boil over high heat. Lower the

heat to medium and simmer for 2 hours, adding fresh water as necessary. Preheat the oven to 375°F (190°C).

4. Remove the ham from the stockpot and turn off the heat. When the ham is cool enough to handle, use a sharp knife to shave off the skin (but not the fat) from the ham. Score the surface of the ham—meaning fat and any exposed flesh—in a diagonal pattern place a single clove in the center of each scored diamond. Pat the ham thoroughly on all sides with the brown sugar.

5. Place the ham on a rack in a 9-by-13-inch roasting pan and bake for 45 minutes to 1 hour, or until the fat has crisped and the sugar has melted into a nice glaze. Let the ham rest on the rack for 15 minutes. Transfer to a cutting board, carve and serve.

6. Serves 10-12.

• •

Note: Below are few optional Glazes to use with Country Ham.

Pineapple and brown sugar glaze
Method
1. After ham has cooled in water remove the rind from the ham and the fat.
2. Mix one small can crushed pineapple and 2/3- Cup brown sugar and mix until smooth.
3. Pour over fat of ham, then garnish with one small can of slice pineapple and cherries. Bake in a hot oven at 400°F for 20 minutes or until golden brown.

Honey glaze
   1-Tbsp Garlic powder
   ¼- Cup Orange juice
   ¼-Cup Honey
   1-tsp prepared mustard.
   2-Tbsp Butter
   ½-tsp Thyme
   ½ -Cup Chicken broth

Method
1. Remove skin from cooked ham.
2. Sprinkle garlic powder on the top of the ham that is covered with fat.
3. Mix the remaining ingredients and brush over ham. Add the chicken broth to the pan.
4. Broil fat side up for 14 to 15 minutes and serve.
5. Strain the pan juices into a saucepan. Reduce until slightly thickened.
6. Serve over the sliced ham.

• •

Barbecue Spare Ribs

Ingredients

2-3 Lb pork spare ribs
¼-Cup Soy sauce
½-Cup Brown sugar
¼-Cup Ketchup
1-Tbsp Hoi sin sauce (An Asian bean fermented sauce)
2-Tbsp White vinegar
1-Tbsp Sake (Japanese Beverage)
2-Cloves garlic, minced
2-Tbsp Chili sauce
1/2-tsp Dry mustard
2-Tbsp Pork stock
Freshly ground black pepper and salt

Note: Serve warm with Parmesan cheese and a loaf of crusty bread.

Barbecued Spare Ribs are a classic American barbecue meal, made from pork.

The technique of barbecuing meats originated in the late 1800s by the Western cattle ranchers. On these ranches cowboys were offered the cheapest cuts of meat, often brisket and they were tough and stringy and required hours of cooking to make it edible. Cooking the meat on the open fire was the easiest, simple and foolproof way of making it edible and was practically a non-brainer. We really want to thank those helpless cowboys for providing us with one of the best ways of cooking meat known to man – the barbeque. There are so many BBQ ribs recipes that it is difficult to pick one but here is a great recipe. If you choose not to barbecue it is a great recipe to cook in the oven too. It will also give you a distinct Asian flavor, featuring soy sauce, rice vinegar, and garlic.

Method

1. Place spare ribs in a large baking dish in one layer. In a small bowl, combine the remaining ingredients. Pour over spare ribs and coat on both sides. Marinate overnight, basting occasionally.

2. Preheat the oven to 375°F. Place a large, shallow roasting pan on the oven bottom. Fill with ½-inch water. Place spare ribs on a roasting rack.

3. Roast ribs for 45 minutes.

4. Raise oven temperature to 450°F, and roast for 15 more minutes.

5. Serve hot or cold.

6. Serves 4-6

Ingredients

- 6-Large pork chops, about 1 ½-inch thick
- 1-tsp Garlic powder
- Fresh Ground black pepper to taste
- 2-Eggs well beaten
- ½-Cup Flour
- 1-Cup Seasoned breadcrumbs
- 2-Tbsp Vegetable oil
- 2-Tbsp Butter
- 1-Large yellow onion, sliced
- 2-Tbsp Brown sugar
- ¼-tsp Cinnamon powder
- ¼-tsp Nutmeg powder
- Salt and pepper to taste
- 2-Green tart apples peeled and chopped

A pork chop is a cut of pork (a meat chop) cut perpendicularly to the spine of the pig and usually containing a rib or part of a vertebra and is served as an individual portion. Pork chops are suitable for roasting, grilling, or frying, Smothered pork chops are a southern comfort classic featuring pan-fried chops, covered in a simple, but super savory onion gravy. This smothered pork chop recipe is great over rice, which soaks up the delicious sauce.

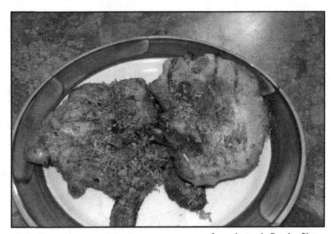

Smothered Pork Chop

Method

1. Season pork chops on both sides with garlic powder and pepper. Coat the chops in flour, dip them in beaten eggs and coat them with breadcrumbs.

2. Heat the oil in a large frying pan over medium to high flame. When the oil is hot, brown the pork chops well, about 5 minutes per side. Cover the pan and bake them at 350°F in the oven until the pork reaches your desired level of doneness.

3. In a small bowl, combine brown sugar, salt and pepper, cinnamon and nutmeg. Add butter to skillet and brown the sliced onion and stir in brown sugar mixture and apples. Cover and cook until apples are just tender. Remove apples with a slotted spoon and arrange on top of chops. Keep warm in the preheated oven.

4. Continue cooking remaining sauce uncovered in skillet, until thickened slightly. Spoon sauce over apples and chops.

5. Makes 4-6 Serving.

Note: Try serving the pork chops over rice with mushroom soup gravy.

Oven Roasted Pork Loin

Ingredients

1-4Lb Boneless pork loin with
  fat left on
1- Tbsp Salt
1-tsp Black Pepper
4-Tbsp Olive oil
1-tsp Onion powder
1 ½- tsp Garlic powder
2-tsp Dried thyme or 2
  teaspoons minced fresh
  thyme leaves
1-tsp Dried basil or 2 teaspoons
  fresh basil leaves
1-tsp Cumin powder
8-10 Medium potatoes
2-tsp Dried rosemary or 2
  teaspoons minced fresh
  rosemary
2-Tbsp Fresh chives

For the Sauce

½-Cup Apple cider vinegar
2- Tbsp Worcestershire sauce
1-Cup Ketchup
2-Tbsp Brown sugar
1-Large onion Sliced
2- Cloves garlic
1-tsp Mustard powder

This is a great meal to make for a nice family dinner or when you have company over. It is also a great make a head recipe that always turns out beautifully. Serve it with a vegetable side dish and your favorite salad for an extra special dinner. Tuscans call pork loin arista, a word that comes from the Greek aristos, meaning "the best" (Greek bishops visiting Florence in 1450 declared it so). In Tuscany if the grilled steak known as "bistecca alla fiorentina" is the king of meats then pork loin is surely the queen. It is usually cooked on a spit studded with garlic and rosemary but roasting in the oven is also a great alternative. Cooking it covered for the first two hours is the secret to making the meat tender and delicious. In Italian cuisine, thin overlapping slices of this pork are often served surrounded by roasted potatoes. This oven roasted spiced pork is "fork-tender". Sometimes it is shredded and blended with a homemade barbecue sauce or your favorite purchased barbecue sauce and it is then served on soft buns with slaw and beans on the side. Pork cooked this way makes mouthwatering delicious sandwiches. Serve extra barbecue sauce for these sandwiches.

Method

1. Preheat oven to 475° F.

2. Place the pork loin on a rack in a roasting pan. Combine 2-tablespoons of olive oil, salt and pepper, 1-tsp of garlic powder 1-teaspoon of onion powder, 1-teaspoon of thyme, basil leaves and cumin powder and rub the mixture on the roast. Place pork loin in a shallow roasting pan.

3. Meanwhile, peel and quarter the potatoes; cook in boiling water for about 10 minutes. Drain, let cool, and place potatoes in a large bowl; toss with remaining olive oil, remaining thyme, ½- teaspoon garlic powder, rosemary, chives and garnish with salt and pepper and set them aside.

4. Roast the pork for 30 minutes and then reduce the heat to 425 °F and place potatoes around pork loin. Roast for an additional hour. Test for doneness of pork using an instant-read thermometer. When the internal temperature of the roast reaches 155 °F, remove the roast and potatoes from the oven. Allow the roast to sit for about 20 minutes before carving. It will continue to cook while it rests.

5. Serve with the roasted potatoes and another vegetable side dish and extra salad and it makes an excellent meal.

6. Meanwhile prepare the barbecue sauce by mixing together apple cider vinegar, onions, ketchup, Worcestershire sauce, brown sugar, onions, garlic and mustard powder, Cook on medium heat until thickened about 10-15 minutes and serve it on the pork.

7. Serves 6-8.

Pork Chops with Cider Braised Sauerkraut

Ingredients

2-Slices of bacon, chopped

4-Tbsp Olive oil

1- Onion, thinly sliced

1 ½- tsp Caraway seeds

¼-tsp Celery seeds

1- Cup Apple juice or Riesling wine

3- Cups Sauerkraut, rinsed and drained

1-Apple sliced

2-Cloves garlic chopped

4- Pork chops, about 1-inch-thick

Salt and pepper

4 –Tbsp Fresh dill, chopped

Give yourself plenty of time to prepare and cook this dish but rest assured it is definitely worth the time and the effort! Serve with hot German potato salad and red cabbage. The combination of pork and sauerkraut originated in Germany, but can be found all over the world. Sauerkraut is shredded cabbage that has been fermented and pickled. Cooking pork in your Crock-Pot results in a tender piece of meat that is both flavorful and moist. Sauerkraut lends additional flavor and increases the juiciness of the meat. Traditionally served with green beans, mashed potatoes or noodles, this slow-cooked dish pairs well with any type of vegetable side dish you enjoy.

Method

1. Add the chopped bacon to a heavy saucepan set over medium heat. Cook, stirring often, until bacon is crisp. Remove the bacon, crumble it and set it aside.

2. Heat 2 tablespoons of oil in a pan and add onion, caraway seeds and celery seeds and cook, stirring occasionally, until the onion is golden. Pour in the Riesling wine and the sauerkraut, sliced apple and crushed garlic. Stir well, and then reduce heat to low, cover the saucepan, and simmer gently for 20 minutes.

3. With about 10 minutes left, season both sides of the pork chops with salt and pepper. Pour the remaining oil into a heavy skillet set over medium-high heat. When simmering, add the chops and cook for about four minutes on each side. Check to see if they are done using a meat

thermometer (about 140° F). Cook longer if not done. Remove from the skillet and let rest for a few minutes.

4. Mix two tablespoons of the fresh dill into the sauerkraut mixture. Divide the sauerkraut between four plates. Top each with a pork chop, and then garnish with the remaining fresh dill and crumbled bacon and serve.

5. Serves 4.

Stuffed Pork Tenderloin with Mushrooms/White Sauce

Ingredients

2-Pork tenderloins, 1 ½-lbs each
6-Oz. Frozen spinach
2-Tbsp Butter
1-tsp Chopped garlic
1-tsp Chopped ginger
1-tsp Chopped green chilies
3-Cup Chopped shiitake
   mushrooms
2-Tbsp Chopped sun-dried
   tomatoes
Salt and Pepper to taste
2- Cups Soft bread crumbs
4-Oz. Goat Cheese
4-Oz Cream Cheese
2- Tbsp Olive oil
½-Large yellow onion, diced
1 tsp Thyme
2-Tbsp All purpose flour
1- Cup Chicken stock
½-Cup Riesling wine
2- Tbsp. Dijon mustard
Milk as needed

It is juicy and tender and you would like to make it again and again. This dish is one of those recipes that seem very impressive to your dinner guests, when in fact it is quite simple and easy to prepare.

Sliced Stuffed Pork Tenderloin with gravy, Corn and Rolls

Method

1. Make a lengthwise slit down the center of each piece of tenderloin but to ½- in. of bottom. Open them so meat lies flat. Cover with plastic wrap; flatten to ¼--in. to ½-in. thickness. Remove plastic wrap.

2. Thaw the spinach and squeeze out all of the excess water. Heat up 2- tablespoon of butter in a pan on medium heat. Toss in the chopped garlic, ginger and green chilies and let it cook for about 1 minute. Don't let the garlic brown. Now add 3- Cups mushrooms, the chopped sun-dried tomatoes, spinach, and season with salt and pepper and let it cook for about 2-3 minutes. Add the bread- crumbs and mix it well.

3. Put the mixture into a bowl, and add the cream cheese and goat cheese and set it aside.

4. Spoon half of the stuffing down center of each piece of tenderloin. Close and tie the two sides several times with kitchen string and secure ends with toothpicks. Sprinkle each roast with ½- teaspoon salt and ¼- teaspoon pepper.

5. Place tenderloins on a rack in a shallow roasting pan. Bake, uncovered, at 425°F for 35-45 minutes or until a thermometer inserted in pork reads 145° F. Let stand for 5 minutes before slicing and prepare the Dijon mustard sauce.

6. Sauté the onion in the olive oil using a skillet or sauce- pan.

7. Cook until the onion becomes translucent. Add the thyme and mix well. Add the flour and brown it a little.

8. Add the stock and mix in wine. Add Dijon mustard. Stir to cook until the gravy thickens. If this becomes too thick, you can add a little milk to create the desired consistency.

9. Pour the sauce on the plate and place the sliced pork on the sauce.

10. Add some vegetables sautéed in butter on the side and serve.

11. Serves 6-8.

Honey Mustard Barbecue Pork Chops

Ingredients
1/3- Cup Honey
3-Tbsp Orange juice
1-Tbsp Apple cider vinegar
1-tsp White wine
1-tsp Worcestershire sauce
2-tsp Onion powder, or to taste
¼- tsp Dried tarragon
3-Tbsp Dijon mustard
1-tsp Ginger powder
2- Garlic cloves crushed
8, 4-¾ -Inch pork chops
    about 6 Oz. each

Honey and mustard are such a good combination in all kinds of recipes but it works well with pork recipes. This is a simple, but very delicious honey mustard pork chops recipe and is quick to make. There is no slicing or dicing required and the result is great tasting pork chops.

It really seems very apparent that we Americans have used pork in such endless array of ways in our daily lives that our food just wouldn't be the same without pork.

Method
1. Place honey, orange juice, vinegar, wine, Worcestershire sauce, onion powder, tarragon, mustard, ginger powder, garlic cloves, in a large reseal able plastic bag.

2. Slice each chop down the center horizontally, cutting not quite through. Open flat to resemble a butterfly. Place chops in the plastic bag, and marinate in the refrigerator for at least 2 hours.

3. Preheat grill on high heat. Lightly oil grill grate. Place chops on grill, and keep basting with marinade. Cook chops for 6 to 8 minutes, or until the thermometer reads 145°F turning to desired doneness.

4. Serve with any staple like rice, or bread or couscous and potatoes. They are delicious.

5. Serves 4-6.

Pork Shoulder Roast

Ingredients

Rub

  2-tsp Whole black peppercorns
  2-tsp Mustard seed
  2-Tbsp Light brown sugar
  2-Tbsp Red wine vinegar
  1-tsp paprika/crushed red pepper
  1-tsp Garlic powder
  1-tsp Onion powder
  1-tsp ginger powder
  1-Tbsp Kosher salt

Roast

  1- 3 ½-4 Lb Boneless pork
     shoulder
  2-Tbsp Olive oil
  3 Large cooking apples
  1 Medium onion

Glaze

  ½- Cup Light brown sugar
  2-Tbsp chopped onions
  ¼- Cup Ketchup
  ¼- Cup Corn syrup (preferably
     dark)
  2-Tbsp Brown mustard
  1-Cup/Wine/ Rum/ Bourbon

Gravy

  Roasted apple and onions from
     under roast
  Water as needed
  Freshly ground salt and pepper

This pork roast recipe may become one of your most liked recipes. The secret is to let the rub soak into the meat overnight or at least for many hours and then smear the roast with a spice rub made from dried chilies, brown sugar, kosher salt and a few other ingredients listed below. Roast it first at a very high temperature to brown the outside, and then finish it at a very low temperature, to maximize juiciness. Serve it with carrots butter-steamed in a cooker with cream and olives. Add sautéed kale or a frisee salad and bread to round out the menu. Excellent example of inexpensive cut of meat changed into a glorious showstopper.

Method

1. Make the marinade: Grind peppercorns and mustard seed in coffee grinder and place them in small bowl. Add remaining ingredients. Rub pork shoulder with the paste and wrap in plastic.

2. Place in refrigerate overnight if possible. Remove from the Refrigerator and let meat stand at room temperature 30-45 minutes. Season with Kosher salt. Set aside.

3. Place the chopped and peeled apples and sliced onions in a roasting pan. Toss them with a little olive oil and salt and place the pork roast on top of the mixture of apples and onions. Roast at 500° F for 30 minutes and then cook over low heat at 250° F for 2 hrs.

4. Mix together Brown sugar, chopped onion, Ketchup, dark corn syrup and Brown mustard, and wine and glaze the pork while it is cooking

in the oven with this mixture every 20 minutes for the remainder of cooking time. Remove roast from oven, cover with foil, and let stand 20 minutes before slicing.

5. Puree the apples and onions with half cup of water. Add more water if needed to make it of pouring consistency and strain it. Adjust the seasoning with salt and pepper and serve with the Sliced pork.

6. Serves 6 to 8.

Pork Leg Roast

Ingredients

- 1 leg of pork, approximately 10 pounds
- 2-Tbsp Coriander seeds
- 1-Tbsp Coriander powder
- 1-Tbsp Cumin powder
- 1-Tbsp Chili pepper flakes
- Salt and pepper
- 1-tsp Rosemary
- 1-tsp Sage
- 4-Tbsp Olive oil
- 10- Cloves garlic
- 1- Cup Brown sugar
- 1/4- Cup apple cider vinegar/1-Cup wine/ 1-Cup beer
- 1-tsp Dry mustard
- 2-Lb Small potatoes, cut into quarters
- 4- Carrots peeled, sliced diagonally into 2 inch pieces
- 1-Small onion sliced
- 1-Tbsp garlic salt
- 1- tsp cayenne pepper or paprika
- 1-Tbsp Olive oil

Roasted leg of pork is probably one of the best pork roasts you'll ever eat. The secret is in the slow roasting. Remember to put a drip pan under the roast so you can catch the juices. Using the drippings from the roasted meat will provide great flavor when making a stock, gravy or sauce. Keep some water in the pan so it doesn't dry out and you can baste the pork leg while it cooks. It will make a spectacular holiday roast for any family even a family with a tight budget. For a crisp surface on your roast, be sure the oven is fully preheated before you place the roast in the oven. Do not cover the meat while roasting.

Method

1. Roast the spices in a skillet until aromatic and grind them. Peel the skin off of the roast.

2. Gently rub the spice mixture on the fat layer. Make incisions all over the fat layer. Pull the skin back over the pork. Refrigerate overnight.

3. Mix the dry rosemary leaves and sage leaves and crushed garlic into the olive oil and brush it gently over the roast.

4. Place pork roast in preheated oven at 450° F for 30 minutes and reduce the temp to 325°F and bake for another 3-3 ½-hrs until the internal temp reaches 155° F.

5. Meanwhile, mix together Brown sugar, apple cider, and dry mustard and brush over pork leg during the last 30 minutes of cooking to form a crust.

6. During the last hour of cooking peel the potatoes and carrots and diagonally slice them. Transfer them into a shallow baking pan and sprinkle and coat them with cayenne pepper, garlic salt, sliced onions and olive oil.

7. Bake them along with the roast during the last hour and serve with the roast. Makes an excellent side dish.

8. Serves 6-8

Oven Roasted Pulled Pork

Ingredients

3-4 Lbs Pork roast, Boston butt or pork shoulder

2-Tbsp Spice mix (Ground roasted cumin, coriander, fennel)

1-tsp Ginger powder

1-tsp Red pepper

Black pepper and salt to taste

¾- Cup apple cider vinegar /Pine apple Juice/Beer/ Dr pepper

¼-Cup Brown sugar

¼-Cup Tomato sauce

2-Large clove garlic

1-Cup Sliced red onion

½ -tsp thyme

Pulled pork is prepared when shoulder cut or mixed cuts of pork is barbecued or cooked using any slow cooking method. With slow cooking at low temperatures, the meat becomes tender enough that it can be shredded in small pieces. It is prepared in different ways in different parts of the world. In the United States, pulled pork is commonly slow-cooked by a smoking method but slow cooking in domestic oven is also quite common.

Pulled pork is prepared from different parts of the pig all over the country. In Tennessee it is typically made from a mixture of the blade shoulder and arm shoulder meat and served with a tomato-based barbecue sauce. In North Carolina, either a whole-pig, mixed-cuts of the pig or the shoulder-cut alone are commonly used and are served with or without a sauce. Italian version of pulled pork is called Porchetta (Pork roast made with herbs and large amount of salt). While Mexican version is called Cochinita (baby pig) pibil (buried) –This preparation is slow roasted in a pit with a fire under it. Cochinita is of Mayan origin from the Yucatan peninsula. The traditional cochinita is prepared by marinating the meat in strongly tart citrus fruit juice (bitter oranges called Seville) and coloring the dish with annatto seeds. These seeds give the sauce a bright red color and the seeds also flavor the meat as it is roasting wrapped in banana leaves buried in a pit.

Method

1. Trim pork roast of excess fat and season it with spice mix, ginger powder, red pepper, salt and pepper.

2. Place in a slow cooker or Crock-Pot and pour vinegar over roast and make sure the vinegar reaches all sides.

3. Add brown sugar, tomato sauce, garlic, sliced onion and thyme. Cook on low heat for 10 to 12 hours or until roast is tender enough to pull apart with your fingers.

4. Remove the roast and shred pork roast into small pieces and store it in a bowl. Pour the remaining liquid into a strainer and cook the liquid in a small saucepan on low heat until reduced to about 1 cup.

5. Mix the liquid into the shredded pieces of pork in the bowl. Adjust the seasonings with a little Worcestershire sauce and ketchup or barbecue sauce of your choice and serve on the sandwich buns to make pork sandwiches. Serve them with Cole slaw or with cooked vegetables or French fries or onion rings on the side if you want to make a meal out of it.

6. Serves 6.

Turkey

Turkey had directly influenced the lifestyles of Native Americans and it continued to do so with the new European Immigrants and their descendants. It was the largest ground–nesting bird found by the Pilgrims when they arrived in this country.

Turkey meat was one of the staple foods in the Native American diet. It is low in fat and high in protein, making it healthier than many other types of meat and has become one of most favorite meats consumed in modern America. Turkey was most-associated with Thanksgiving and Christmas, making winter the prime season for turkey farmers. In 1935, the per capita consumption of turkey was only 1.7 pounds/per person. Today, turkey has been recognized as a lean substitute for red meat. Aggressive marketing by turkey farmers by advertising and availability of parts rather than the necessity of cooking a whole bird has increased consumption to 20 pounds per person per year, with 74 percent of the consumption being in sliced turkey meat (the most favored deli meat after ham) in sandwiches.

It is a native bird with a proud demeanor and protective instincts. The wild turkey was Benjamin Franklin's choice for the national bird.

Whole Roasted Turkey

Ingredients

- 6-Tbsp Butter, divided for basting before and after roasting
- 1- 12 lb Whole turkey
- 3- Cloves minced garlic
- 2-Chopped Fresh rosemary
- 2-Tbsp Dried minced onion
- 1-Tbsp Chopped fresh basil
- 1-tsp Ground black pepper
- ½-Cup Butter
- 2- large onions, peeled and chopped
- 4-Carrots, peeled and chopped
- 2-Stalks celery, chopped
- 2-Sprigs fresh thyme
- 1-Bay leaf
- 6-Cups Soft bread cubes (crust removed)
- 2-Tbsp Dried parsley
- Salt and pepper to taste
- 1-Cup Dry white wine

Although Thanksgiving celebrations dated back to the first European settlements in America, it was not until the 1860s that Abraham Lincoln declared the last Thursday of November to be a national holiday. In 1621, Plymouth colonists and Wampanoag Indians shared a harvest feast together and it was acknowledged as one of the first celebrations of their friendship together. The early settlers offered a prayer of thanks to the almighty for surviving and making it in the new land and celebrated this event with a three-day feast sometimes between September 21 and November 11 with the native Indians that year. The Pilgrims were joined by approximately 90 of the local Wampanoag tribe, including Chief Massasoit, in this meeting. They ate fowl and deer for certain and most likely also ate berries, fish, clams, plums, and boiled pumpkin. Gradually over period of time turkey dinner became a tradition and a symbol of Thanksgiving. This time was declared as a U.S. holiday in 1860 by Abraham Lincoln to commemorate the good harvest of the Pilgrims in 1621.

Whole Roasted Turkey

Method

1. Rub the turkey inside and out with the kosher salt. Place the bird in a large stockpot, and cover with cold water. Place it in the refrigerator, and allow the turkey to soak in the salt and water mixture for 12 hours, or overnight.

2. Preheat oven to 350° F (175° C). Rinse and wash turkey. Clean the body cavity and discard the giblets, or add to pan if they are anyone's favorites and discard the brine.

3. Place turkey in a Dutch oven or roasting pan. Separate the skin over the breast to make little pockets. Insert crushed garlic into them. Melt 3 tablespoons of the butter and add chopped rosemary, dried minced onion, fresh basil, and black pepper. Mix this mixture well and rub it or inject it with a syringe into the breast meat on both sides between the skin and breast meat. This makes for very juicy breast meat.

4. Prepare the stuffing by melting ½ cup of the butter in a saucepan and fry the ½ of the chopped - onion, ½- the carrots, ½- the celery, 1 sprig of thyme, and the bay leaf. Add the bread cubes and dry parsley and mix well. Add salt and pepper to taste.

5. Stuff the turkey cavity with stuffing. Scatter the remaining vegetables and remaining thyme around the bottom of the roasting pan, and cover with 1-cup of the white wine.

6. Cover the turkey with foil, and bake in the preheated oven 3 ½- to 4 hours. Remove the foil last half hour of cooking to baste the turkey with the remaining melted butter so the turkey will brown nicely. Allow the bird to stand about 30 minutes before carving. Serve it with stuffing. Carve and serve with stuffing, mashed potatoes, cranberry sauce, creamed corn, corn bread and turkey gravy.

7. Serves 12-15.

Note: Any stuffing of your choice can be used.

Herb Roasted Turkey Breast

Ingredients

- 1-Whole breast, 6 ½- to 7 pounds
- 1-Tbsp Minced garlic (3 cloves)
- 2-tsp Dry mustard
- 1-Tbsp Chopped fresh rosemary leaves
- 1-Tbsp Chopped fresh sage leaves
- 1-tsp Chopped fresh thyme leaves
- 2-tsp Kosher salt
- 1-tsp Freshly ground black pepper
- 2-Tbsp Good olive oil or melted butter
- 2-Tbsp Freshly squeezed lemon juice
- 1-Cup Dry white wine or chicken broth

Herb roasted turkey breast is a wonderful substitute for special occasions like Thanks giving or for a Sunday dinner. It is especially favorable because you do not have to worry about the leftovers. This is the way I fix my Thanksgiving dinner. Prepare all the trimmings and the stuffing on the side and give yourself time to enjoy family and friends.

Method

1. Preheat the oven to 325° F. Place the turkey breast, skin side up, on a rack in a roasting pan.

2. In a small bowl, combine the garlic, mustard, herbs, salt, pepper, olive oil, and lemon juice to make a paste. Loosen the skin from the meat gently with your fingers and smear half of the paste directly on the meat. Spread the remaining paste evenly on the skin. Pour the wine into the bottom of the roasting pan.

3. Roast the turkey for 1 ¾- to 2 hours, until the skin is golden brown and an instant-read thermometer registers 165° F when inserted into the thickest and meatiest areas of the breast. If the skin is over-browning, cover the breast loosely with aluminum foil. When the turkey is done, cover with foil and allow it to rest at room temperature for 15 minutes. Slice and serve with the pan juices spooned over the turkey along with your trimmings, or prepare gravy by using pan juices.

4. Serves 6-8

Roasted Turkey Breast Tenderloins and Vegetables

Ingredients

- 1-tsp Dill weed
- 1-tsp Dried thyme
- 1-tsp Dried oregano
- 1-tsp Dried minced onion
- ¾-tsp Salt
- ¼- tsp Pepper
- 1-Tbsp Olive oil
- 4-Turkey breast tenderloins (5 Oz each)
- ¼- Cup Butter, melted
- 3-Cups Fresh baby carrots
- 4-Celery ribs cut into 2-inch pieces
- 2-Medium onions cut into wedges
- 2-tsp Cornstarch
- ½-Cup Cream
- ¼- Cup Water

Classic flavors come together quickly with this family pleasing roasted turkey, vegetables and gravy. You do not even have to prepare a veggie side dish, because it's all there and cooked together. Alternately you can cook the turkey tenderloin and the vegetables also in the slow cooker and cook till the meat thermometer reads 170° F.

Method

1. In a small bowl, combine the first six ingredients. Combine 2 teaspoons of the seasoning mixture with butter; toss with vegetables. Transfer to a roasting pan. Bake, uncovered, at 425°F for 15 minutes.

2. Meanwhile, rub oil over turkey; sprinkle with remaining seasoning mixture. Move vegetables to edges of pan and place turkey in the center.

3. Bake, uncovered, at 425°F for 20-25 minutes or until a meat thermometer reads 170°C and vegetables are tender.

4. Transfer turkey and vegetables to a serving platter and keep warm.

5. Pour cooking juices into a small saucepan. Combine cornstarch with water to make a paste and add cream until smooth, gradually stir the mixture into the pan. Bring to a boil, cook and stir for 2 minutes or until thickened. Serve with turkey and vegetables.

6. Serves 4 or more.

Turkey Meat loaf

Ingredients

8 Oz. Can tomato sauce

2- tsp Worcestershire sauce

2- Lbs Fresh lean ground turkey

½-Cup Dry breadcrumbs

1-Egg white, slightly beaten

¾-tsp Dried oregano leaves

1-Tbsp Olive oil

½-Finely chopped onion

1-Tbsp Chopped ginger and
   garlic each

1-Tbsp Hot or Mild chopped
   green pepper

½ tsp Salt and pepper/ each

2-(9-oz.) Pkgs Frozen chopped
   spinach, thawed, well drained

¼-Cup Shredded low-
   fat Swiss cheese

Meatloaf is probably the ultimate American comfort food. One of the perks of making a "turkey meatloaf" is that it is lot more healthier than a regular good old fashion meatloaf and still tastes great. Meatloaf basically belongs to a European cuisine and has been enjoyed by the people of mainland Europe for many centuries. As the name suggests, meatloaf is prepared by using different varieties of meat and resembles a common bread loaf. A Turkey meatloaf usually contains one or more types of meat, vegetables and spices that are grounded and added to it. The meatloaf gets its shape, like a bread loaf, as a result of the baking pan in which it is baked. The meatloaf cooking time tends to differ by a few minutes or a few degrees, depending upon the ingredients and procedure of a particular recipe. It is always advisable to check, if the internal temperature of the meat loaf is above 160°F.This temperature ensures that, all the possible germs in the meat are eliminated and the meat is properly cooked. It is also better to trust your judgment, instead of the timer. Take out the meatloaf after its outer surface starts turning golden-brown.

Method

1. Heat oven to 350°F. Spray a 9x5-inch loaf pan with non-stick cooking spray.

2. In a small bowl, blend tomato sauce (reserving 1/3-cup tomato sauce) and Worcestershire sauce.

3. In a medium bowl, combine lean ground turkey, breadcrumbs, egg white, oregano and tomato sauce mixture and mix well.

4. On a piece of foil, form turkey mixture into 12x8-inch rectangle.

5. In a small skillet add a tablespoon of olive oil and add the chopped onions, ginger, garlic and green pepper. Cook for 2-3 minutes and add the spinach, salt and pepper. Stir-fry for 3-4 minutes and set it aside.

6. Spread spinach mixture on turkey meat rectangle; sprinkle with cheese. Roll up tightly. Starting with short end. Place in pan seam-side-down. Press to seal edges. Bake at 350°F for 55 to 65 minutes or until turkey is browned. Spoon remaining sauce over loaf. Bake 5 minutes more. Let stand 10 minutes.

7. Serve it with mushroom gravy and mashed potatoes.

8. 6 servings.

Turkey Meat Balls

Ingredients

8-10 Slices day-old bread, to
     yield 4 cups of 1-inch cubes
2-Lb Ground turkey preferably
     thigh meat
¼-Lb Prosciutto, cut into small
     pieces
½-Lb Fresh, sweet Italian turkey
     sausage, out of its skin
3-Eggs
¼-Cup Parmigian Reggiano
     cheese
½-Cup Pecorino Cheese
2- Bunches Italian parsley,
     chopped
2-Tbsp of Chopped onion
1-Tbsp Chopped garlic
1/8-tsp Nutmeg
½-Cup Fine olive oil
Salt and pepper
1-Cup Tomato Sauce
½-Cup Dry white wine

A meatball is made from a small amount of ground meat rolled into a small ball, sometimes along with other ingredients, such as breadcrumbs, minced onion, spices, and possibly eggs. Meatballs are usually prepared and rolled by hand, and are cooked by frying, baking, steaming, or braising in sauce. Turkey meatballs are a healthier alternative to traditional meatballs. Pair them with your favorite dip or add into a tomato sauce to make classic Spaghetti and meatballs.

Method

1. Soak the bread in water for 5 minutes, squeeze by hand to wring excess water, and add to ground turkey.

2. Add the prosciutto, sausage, eggs, Parmigianino, - cup pecorino, ½- cup parsley, onions, garlic, nutmeg and 4 tablespoons of olive oil and mix lightly.

3. Season with salt and pepper and form the mixture into 3-inch balls. Place the balls on a sheet tray, cover with parchment and chill for 1 hour in the refrigerator.

4. Preheat the oven to 375° F.

5. In a large, heavy-bottomed skillet heat the remaining 4 tablespoons of oil to almost smoking and brown the meatballs in the oil on all sides.

6. Transfer them to a baking dish and add the tomato sauce and the wine and bake for 30 minutes. Serve with the remaining pecorino and parsley. Serve them as an appetizer or over spaghetti or any other pasta of your choice or rice.

7. Makes -2 dozen and serves 4-6.

Turkey Parmigianino

Ingredients

½-Cup All-purpose flour
2-Eggs, slightly beaten
1-Tb Water
2-tsp Oil
1-Cup Seasoned dry
     breadcrumbs
¾-Cup Parmesan cheese grated
1-Cooked breast of turkey cut
     into 4 to 6 slices
¼-Cup Vegetable oil
2-½-Cups Spaghetti or Marinara
     sauce
1/8-tsp Nutmeg
2-Tbsp Chopped cilantro
¾-Cup Shredded mozzarella
     cheese

It is actually a different version of eggplant Parmigianino A Southern Italian dish (Sicily) made with a shallow-fried sliced eggplants layered with cheese and tomato sauce then baked and served in many different ways. In this preparation turkey slices substitute eggplant. Turkey Parmigianino of America has become very popular in other countries also. The fried bread crumb-coated turkey cutlets layered with parmesan cheese and topped with marinara sauce and mozzarella cheese are baked and they are sometimes served as a sandwich or as a side or on top of cooked pasta. Chopped onions or green bell peppers or sliced carrots, sautéed or raw, are sometimes served on the side. It makes quite a satisfying meal.

Method

1. Combine eggs, water and 2 teaspoons oil and set aside.

2. Combine breadcrumbs and ½-cup Parmesan cheese.

3. Dip turkey slices into flour, egg mixture, then again coat them with breadcrumb mixture.

4. Heat ¼ - cup oil in heavy skillet. Brown turkey slices over medium heat, 2 to 4 minutes per side. Layer turkey in 11 x 7-inch baking pan.

5. Top each turkey slice with mozzarella cheese and remaining Parmesan cheese.

6. Bake in 350°F oven 20 to 25 minutes or until cheese melts. Sprinkle with cilantro and Serve on the side or top of pasta or as a submarine sandwich.

7. Combine spaghetti sauce and nutmeg. Pour the sauce over the slices and serve immediately.

8. Serves 4.

Turkey Bourguignon

Ingredients

3-Lb Turkey cutlets, cut into 2-inch strips

Salt to taste

Freshly ground black pepper

Flour for dredging

2-Tbsp Olive oil

2-Small Yellow onions, diced

1-Tbsp chopped ginger

2-Cloves garlic, minced

1-Green chili chopped hot or medium hot (to taste)

2-Sprigs thyme

1-Bay leaf

2-Cups Red wine (preferably Burgundy)

2-Cups Diced, canned tomatoes, with their juices

4-Cups Chicken broth

½-Cup Chopped mushrooms

4-Large Carrots, peeled and cut into ½-inch pieces

4-Large Parsnips, peeled and cut into ½-inch pieces

2-Large Russet potatoes, diced

2-Tbsp Chopped parsley

Americans love Beef Bourguignon and they have adapted it with few changes to fit the American kitchens. Beef Bourguignon is a French staple. From rustic peasant origins, this rich stew braised in red wine had evolved to win a place among the most widely known traditional dishes of French haute cuisine. Traditionally the meat was cooked slowly simmering in wine to tenderize it since the meat used use to be tough and heavily larded but nowadays sufficiently tender and well-marbled meat is available and therefore this old time-consuming technique is now replaced especially when you are cooking lean turkey meat. The meat is generally flavored with garlic, onions and a bouquet garni while pearl onions and mushrooms are added towards the end of cooking. It is then cooked with Burgundy/Bourgogne wine. When delicate tender turkey pieces combine with fresh vegetables it turns into a healthy moist stew that has a classic taste of a Bourguignon. Pair it with a salad and some warm crusty baguette for the perfect dinner on a cold night. It can be cooked fast and it is a good meal for the family.

Method

1. Season the turkey with salt and pepper. Dredge it in flour and shake off the excess.

2. Heat the olive oil in a Dutch oven over medium-high heat. Fry the slices by adjusting the heat so that the meat browns well, but does not burn. Set it aside.

3. Add the onions, garlic, ginger, green chili, thyme and bay leaf and cook 2 minutes

more. Add the braised turkey and red wine. Stir with a wooden spoon to release any caramelized bits that may be stuck to the bottom of the pan and cook until the wine is almost completely evaporated.

4. Add the tomatoes with their juices and the chicken broth and bring to a boil. Simmer the stew and let it cook until the meat is tender, about ½- hour.

5. Add the mushrooms, carrots, parsnips and potatoes and cook until the vegetables are completely tender, about 20 minutes more until the potatoes fall apart and thicken the sauce.

6. Adjust the seasoning with salt and pepper, remove the bay leaf and serve sprinkled with parsley in a deep tureen with pasta noodles, rice or your favorite bread.

7. Serves 4-6.

Turkey Breast Tenderloins Dijon

Ingredients

2- Turkey tenderloins ¾-1Lb / each

2-Large sweet potatoes

Marinade

¼- Cup Dijon mustard

¼-Cup soy sauce

2- Tbsp Olive oil

1- tsp Ginger, ground

1-tsp Garlic powder

1-tsp Cumin powder

2- Tbsp Melted butter or margarine

Sauce

2- Ripe mangoes, peeled and chopped

½- Cup Fresh mint leaves

¼- Cup Fresh limejuice

1-tsp Minced fresh ginger

½-tsp cayenne pepper

¼- Cup Plain yogurt

Salt and pepper to taste

Grilled turkey tenderloin is a tasty main dish. It is a part of global cuisine nowadays, but it has its likely origin from the American cuisine. Turkey breast tenderloins are soaked in tangy Dijon mustard and after marinating them for a short while they are then grilled to perfection. Mustard and honey give turkey a subtle sweet-tangy taste upon grilling. Great for dinner parties or just weekday meals!

Method

1. Combine marinade ingredients in a large heavy-duty, zip-top bag. Add turkey tenderloins. Seal bag and shake until turkey is well coated.

2. Marinate in refrigerator for a minimum of 30 minutes to up to 4 hours, turning bag occasionally.

3. Wash and wrap the sweet potatoes in foil and transfer them to the oven and bake at 425°F for 25 to 30 minutes or until tender.

4. Once the potatoes are done, coat the grill rack with cooking spray.

5. Remove turkey from marinade and place it on the rack. Grill covered for 5 to 7 minutes on each side or until turkey has reached an internal temperature of 170°F (80°C).

6. Meanwhile, in a blender combine mangoes, mint, lime- juice, cayenne pepper, salt and pepper. Puree until blended. Add yogurt and puree until smooth.

7. Peel and chop the potatoes and serve them with broiled tenderloins. Serve the sauce spooned over top and all of the sweet potatoes.

8. Makes 4 servings.

Turkey Divan

Ingredients

1- Lb Fresh turkey breast
Salt, Black pepper as needed
¼-tsp Cayenne Pepper
1-tsp Ginger powder
1-tsp Garlic powder
3-Tbsp Melted butter
1- Head of broccoli chopped
    up in florets and discard the
    tough shoots
¼-Cup water
½- Lb Button mushrooms
½- Cup Parmesan cheese

White Sauce

2-Tbsp Butter
2-Tbsp Chopped onion
2-Tbsp Flour
Salt and pepper to taste
1-Cup milk
Pinch of Garammasala

Takes its name from the Famous Chicken Divan recipe. Chicken Divan was a signature dish of a 1950's New York restaurant, the Divan Parisienne. It is the word "divan" itself that is of interest. In English, divan came to mean sofa, from the council chamber's benches, while in France it meant a meeting place or great hall. It was this meaning that attracted the attention of the owners of the New York restaurant as they searched for a name that would simply be of continental comfort and elegance. "Divan" word was used to refer to two types of palatial buildings in courts (Divan-I-A am-Court's Hall of Public Audience and Dīwān-e-Khās Court's-Hall of Private Audience) of mughal palaces duing the Mughal dynasty in India. Although the restaurant is gone, this dish continues to please families everywhere in various forms. It is easy-to-make for company and you can serve this delicious creamy chicken or turkey and broccoli over rice. Make the best use of left over turkey and serve over a bed of rice. It will become part of your family traditions.

Method

1. Rub the turkey breast with salt, cayenne pepper, ginger powder, garlic powder and one tablespoon of melted butter. Wrap it in a foil and bake it in the oven at 425°F. Cook till it is done. Slice it thin and set it aside.

2. Cook broccoli in a deep pan in ¼- Cup water in remaining 2 tablespoons butter, a pinch of salt and peppers on medium heat for 5 minutes and set it aside.

3. Prepare the white sauce by frying the onions in 2 tablespoons of butter until golden brown. Wisk in flour salt and pepper. Beat in the milk and bring it to a boil. Cook for 2 minutes and add a sprinkle of garammasala and set it aside.

4. Butter the baking dish and place a layer of broccoli, a layer of turkey (light or dark meat). Layer until you've used up remaining broccoli and turkey.

5. Pour white sauce over the top. Place whole button mushrooms and Parmesan cheese on top.

6. Bake at 350° F for about 35 to 40 minutes and serve it on your favorite staple like rice, noodle or any other pasta.

7. Serves 4-6.

Midwestern Turkey Barbecue

Ingredients

¾-Cup Frozen orange juice
concentrate, thawed
1/3-Cup Light molasses
¼-Cup Ketchup
3-Tbsp prepared mustard
2-Tbsp Soy sauce
½-tsp Garlic powder
¼-tsp Ground red pepper
¼--tsp Cumin powder
1-tsp Onion powder
1-Tb Limejuice
1-Lb Turkey breast
tenderloin steaks

It is a simple yet festive main dish. If you're not up to the task of roasting a turkey for thanksgiving this dish is for you. Serve it with cranberry chutney to give that festive thanksgiving touch. Barbecuing turkey tenderloin without skin is little tricky. Since they are low in fat they dry very quickly. To prevent this coat them with breadcrumbs or marinate them in sweet and savory ingredients before you start to barbecue them. Roast, grill, or sauté whatever method of cooking you use, marinating them makes them a little crispy outside and tender, moist and delicious inside.

This turkey barbecue will definitely melt in your mouth and it has great flavor too.

Method

For Marinade

1. In a small bowl stir together thawed concentrate of orange juice, molasses, ketchup, mustard, soy sauce, garlic powder, red pepper, cumin powder, onion powder and limejuice. Pat dry the breast tenderloin steaks with paper towels and marinade them in the above marinade.

2. Place turkey steaks on the rack of an uncovered grill over medium coals and start grilling, turning once. Brushing them with the left over orange sauce marinade during the last 5 minutes of cooking or until turkey is tender and no longer pink and the internal temperature of the turkey reaches 180 °F.

Or

3. Place steaks on the unheated rack of a broiler pan. Broil 4" to 5" from the heat for 8 to 10 minutes or until turkey is tender and no longer pink, turn once and keep brushing with the reserved orange sauce during the last 5 minutes of broiling.

To serve

4. Heat remaining sauce to a boiling point and serve with turkey. You can cover and chill left over sauce for up to 2 weeks, heat to boiling before using.

Stuffing for the tenderloin

5. While the turkey is on the grill prepare stuffing with package directions.

6. Spoon it into prepared aluminum pan and cover with foil.

7. Add pan with stuffing to grill rack. Cover and grill until stuffing is hot and tender. Cool turkey and stuffing for 10 minutes before serving. Cut tenderloins into 1" pieces and serve with stuffing.

8. Serves -4.

Turkey Pot Pie

Ingredients

1-Box 10-Inch -Refrigerated piecrusts, softened as directed on box

Or

1- package unbaked flaky biscuits like Pillsbury grand

1/3-Cup Butter or margarine

1/3- Cup Chopped onion

1-tsp Chopped Ginger

1-tsp Chopped garlic

1-tsp Chopped Green pepper mildly hot

1/3-Cup All-purpose flour

½- tsp Salt

½- tsp Pepper

½-tsp Cumin powder

½-tsp garammasala

2-Tbsp Cilantro leaves chopped

1-Can (14 Oz) Chicken broth

2 ½- Cups Shredded cooked turkey

2- Cups Frozen mixed vegetables, thawed

½- Cup Milk/Cream

A Pot Pie is a type of pie baked with a bottom and top completely encased by flaky crusts and it is baked inside a pie tin to support its shape. An American pot pie typically has a filling of meat (particularly beef, chicken or turkey) with gravy, and mixed vegetables (potatoes, carrots, green beans and peas). Pot Pie gets its ancestry from the Greeks and Romans cuisine.

The left over cooked turkey provides a perfect opportunity to make a delicious Pot Pie a comfort food suitable during a holiday.

Method

1. Heat oven to 425°F.

2. In 2-quart saucepan, melt butter over medium heat. Add onion, ginger, garlic, and green chilies, cook 2 minutes, stirring frequently, until tender. Stir in turkey and mixed vegetables, cooking and stirring for 2 minutes.

3. Stir in flour, salt, pepper, cumin powder, cilantro leaves and garammasala until well blended. Gradually stir in broth and milk until bubbly and thickened.

4. Remove from heat. Spoon into crust lined pie plate. Top with second crust, seal edges and flute. Cut slits in several places in top crust.

5. Bake 30 to 40 minutes until crust is golden brown. During last 15 to 20 minutes of baking, cover edge of crust with strips of foil to prevent excessive browning. Let stand 5 minutes before serving.

Or

6. Transfer the filling into a 10- inch-baking dish and place the one thawed (30 minutes) Sheet of puffed pastry rolled out into a circle (big enough to go over the filling in the baking dish).

7. Firmly pressing the edges to the sides of the dish. Cut 3 slits on the top and bake till it is brown about 20-25 minutes and serve.

8. Serves4-6.

Note: You can make Individual potpies by using smaller disposable tins or glass bowls with wide mouths and using the same filling.

Chicken

The chicken (Gallus gallus domesticus) is a domesticated fowl, a subspecies of the Red Jungle fowl. There are more chickens in the world than any other species of birds. Humans keep chickens primarily as a source of food, consuming both their meat and their eggs. The chicken's "cultural and culinary dominance" could be considered amazing to some in view of its believed domestic origin and purpose. But they have "inspired contributions to culture, art, cuisine, science and religion from antiquity to the present.

Humans first domesticated chickens of Indian origin for the purpose of cockfighting in Asia, Africa, and Europe. Very little formal attention was given to egg or meat production. Recent genetic studies have pointed to multiple maternal origins in Southeast Asia, but most that are found in the Americas, Europe, the Middle East and Africa originated in the Indian subcontinent. Chickens farmed for meat are called broiler chickens. Chickens will naturally live for 6 or more years and they reach slaughter size in 14 weeks to obtain organic meat. But broiler chickens that are raised commercially take less than 6 weeks to reach slaughter size. The meat of the chicken is also called "chicken".

Because of its relatively low cost, chicken is one of the most used meats in the world. Nearly all parts of the bird can be used for food, and the meat can be cooked in many different ways. Popular chicken dishes include roasted chicken, fried chicken, chicken soup, chicken curry, Buffalo wings, tandoori chicken, chicken Tikka masala, chicken rice or Biryani and many more. Chicken is also a staple of many fast food restaurants.

More than 50 billion chickens are reared annually as a source of food, for both their meat and their eggs. Chicken and turkey both contain a higher amount of protein and less saturated fat than red meat. One ounce of turkey and chicken breast contains 9g of protein. They are a rich source of B vitamins, phosphorus and tryptophan. The high level of proteins makes poultry a better and healthier choice.

Chicken Breast Seville

Ingredients

2-Tbsp Butter or margarine
8-Chicken breast halves (about 6-Oz. each), skinned and boned
1-Cup Diced onion
¼-Cup Celery chopped
1-tsp Dried tarragon leaves
2-tsp Minced ginger
1-Can (16 Oz.) Small potatoes, drained
1-Can (14 Oz.) Artichoke hearts drained
1-Can(8 Oz. each) Whole baby onions, drained
1-Cup Pitted ripe olives
1-Jar (15 Oz.) Roasted sweet red peppers, drained, cut in large pieces
½-Cup Dry vermouth
¼-Cup Tomato sauce
1-Cup Chicken broth
1-Can (10 Oz) Frozen juice
½-tsp Red pepper
Minced parsley

Fresh Fruit Market, Barcelona, Spain

Seville food refers to the food of a city of Seville, the capital city of the Seville province and Andalusia community of Spain, which is considered to be the cultural capital of Southern Spain. The city is famous for its food traditions, and the cuisine is famous for fresh ingredients from surrounding regions. Below is a recipe inspired by the Spanish cuisine.

Method

1. In a Dutch oven, melt butter. Quickly brown chicken on both sides, about 5 minutes.

2. Add onions, celery, ginger, tarragon and cook over medium heat, 5 minutes, stirring occasionally.

3. Add potatoes, artichoke hearts, baby onions, olives, roasted peppers, vermouth, and tomato sauce and stir well. Add chicken broth. Heat to boiling. Reduce heat and cover. Simmer 10 minutes or until chicken is no longer pink in the center.

4. Add orange juice. Stir it into the chicken mixture.

5. Cook over high heat, stirring occasionally, until sauce thickens, 1 to 2 minutes. Add pepper to taste.

6. Arrange chicken and vegetables on large, deep platter. Season with red pepper to taste. Sprinkle with parsley. Serve with rice or pasta.

7. Makes 8 servings.

Ingredients

- 1-Whole chicken (about 4 pounds)
- 1-Cup thick yogurt paste
- 1/ Cup vegetable oil or clarified butter
- 2-Tbsp Onion powder
- 2-Tbsp Ginger powder
- 2 ½- Tbsp Garlic powder
- 1 ½- Tbsp Cumin powder
- 1-tsp Chili powder/Cayenne pepper (if you like it hot)
- 1- tsp-Black pepper
- 1-tsp Salt
- 2-Tbsp Tomato puree
- 2-Tbsp White vinegar
- 2-Tbsp Lemon juice
- Cold water as needed
- 1-tsp Garammasala
- 2-Tbsp Chopped cilantro

Rotisserie chicken (Pollo a la brasa) is to Peruvians what pizza is to Americans. South Florida has a huge concentration of Peruvian immigrants. After making their way into kitchens of the rest of Latin America Rotisserie Chicken now have succeeded to win the hearts and stomachs - of Americans. Thanks to the unique seasoning and delicious sauces that accompany the rotisserie chicken.

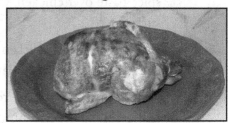

Rotisserie Chicken

Rotisserie is a style of roasting where meat is skewered on a long solid rod while it is being roasted and cooked over a fire. It can be cooked in a fireplace or a camping fire or roasted in an oven at home. This par-

Tandoori Chicken

ticular cooking method is generally used for cooking large piece of meat or entire animals, such as a pig, turkey or a goat. Rotisserie cooking is a great way to extend the versatility of your grill whether you cook on charcoal or gas. The rotation cooks the meat evenly in its own juices and allows easy access for continuous self-basting. Supermarkets commonly mass-produce rotisserie chickens. Tandoori chicken a delicacy of Indian Cuisine and is cooked similarly after it is marinated in yogurt, lemon juice, and spices, then grilled or broiled. It is a great way to cook chicken.

Method

1. Combine yogurt with 2 tablespoons of oil, onion powder, ginger powder, garlic powder, cumin, chili powder, black pepper, vinegar, tomato puree and salt. Mix well to form a paste. Keep the paste thick.

2. Add lemon juice to cold water. Trim chicken of any excess or loose fat. Wash chicken thoroughly with lemon water.

3. Slash chicken meat at places where the meat is thick and apply the mixture or the paste under the skin of chicken and inside the cuts as much as possible. Pour the remaining spice paste over chicken. Coat chicken completely with mixture rubbing into every surface.

4. Seal bag and place chicken in refrigerator for at least 2 hours. The longer it "marinates" in the spice mixture more flavorful it will become. However do not over refrigerate.

5. Preheat grill and prepare rotisserie. Place chicken on rotisserie and baste it sparingly and gently with remaining oil or clarified butter and grill for approximately 1 ½- hours at a temperature around 300 °F. (150° C.) Test chicken for doneness by measuring the temperature in the thickest part of the thigh. Chicken should be done at 165° F. or (89°C).

6. When serving sprinkle garammasala and chopped cilantro and serve with a dipping sauce or mint chutney or ranch dressing.

7. A simple sauce can be is made by combining ½- cup of mayonnaise with 2- tablespoons mustard and 2 tablespoons lime juice.

8. Serves 4-6.

Chicken and Broccoli Au Gratin

Ingredients

2-Tbsp Olive oil
¼-Cup Chopped onion
I-tsp Chopped ginger
I-tsp Minced garlic
I-Tbsp Green chili (mildly hot peppers)
Salt and pepper to taste
2-Pkg Frozen broccoli
1/3-Cup Butter
1/3-Cup Flour
1½- Cups Chicken broth
I-Cup Evaporated milk
I-Cup Sauterne (white wine)
¼-tsp red pepper
Salt and Pepper to taste
Worcestershire Sauce
3-Cups Cooked chicken coarsely diced
I-Cup Grated Parmesan cheese
I-Cup Buttered Bread crumbs
2-Tbsp Chopped parsley

In the culinary arts, the term au gratin refers to a dish that is baked with a topping of seasoned breadcrumbs and cheese. The au gratin topping should be golden brown, which can be achieved by baking or by placing the dish under a broiler. Gratin originated in French Cuisine and term "gratin" has since been borrowed into English. This widely used cooking technique is used in the preparation of numerous dishes including many meats, fish, vegetable and pasta, fennel, leeks crabmeat, celery aubergines (eggplant) and here it is used for chicken and broccoli. A gratin dish refers to the shallow ovenproof container traditionally used to prepare gratins and similar dishes.

Method

1. Cook chopped onion and ginger in 2 tablespoons of olive oil. Add garlic and chopped green chilies and stir to fry.

2. Add the frozen broccoli, reduce the heat cover the pan and wait it is completely thawed and looks bright green. Cook until slightly tender and add few tablespoons of water if needed. Season a little. Transfer them to a greased shallow casserole.

3. Melt butter in a frying pan and stir in flour; add broth, milk and sauterne to make the wine sauce. Cook, stirring constantly, until mixture is thickened and smooth for 2 or 3 minutes. Add red pepper, salt, black pepper and Worcestershire sauce to taste and set it aside.

4. Spread cooked chicken over broccoli in casserole, cover with the wine sauce and sprinkle generously with mixture of grated cheese and buttered breadcrumbs.

5. Bake at 400° F in oven for about 20 minutes or until bubbly. Remove from the oven. Sprinkle parsley and serve.

6. Serves 6.

Holiday Chicken Salad

Ingredients

4 cups diced poached chicken

1 stalk celery, cut into 1/4-inch dice

4 scallions, trimmed and thinly sliced or 1/4 cup sweet onion cut into 1/4-inch dice

½-Cup Chopped green bell pepper

1-Cup Chopped pecans

1-Cup Dried cran berries

1 ½-tsp Finely chopped fresh tarragon or fresh dill

2-Tbsp Finely chopped parsley

1- Cup Prepared or homemade mayonnaise

2-tsp Strained freshly squeezed lemon juice

1-tsp Dijon mustard

2-tsp Kosher salt

Freshly ground black pepper

There's no better use of cold left over meat from a roast or stewed chicken than putting it into a salad. When combined with classic American mayo-and-celery, a vibrant mixture of grapes and nuts, or a sesame-spiked Asian slaw it really makes a mouth watering delicious salad.

We love chicken salad on toasted white bread as a sandwich, with crisp crackers for a snack, simply eaten on its own in a bed of lettuce, or right out of the bowl.

A Chicken salad is any salad that comprises chicken as a main ingredient with common ingredients like mayonnaise, hard-boiled eggs, celery, onion, pepper, pickles and a variety of mustards. Jump to 1863 in U.S. history, and the first American version of chicken salad was served at Town Meat (local restaurant) just down the road in Wakefield, RI. The founder of Town Meets, Liam Gray, mixed his leftover chicken with mayonnaise, tarragon, and grapes. The result? A huge hit so huge and the item became so popular that the meat market was turned into a delicatessen, and the business was still operating up until a couple years ago. Like tuna salad and egg salad, it may be served on top of lettuce, tomato, avocado, or some combination of these. It may also be used for sandwiches. Typically it is made with leftover or canned chicken.

Method

1. In a mixing bowl, toss together the chicken, celery, scallions, bell pepper, pecans, cranberries and herbs. Set aside.

2. In a small bowl, whisk together the mayonnaise, lemon juice, mustard, salt and pepper to taste.

3. Add to the chicken and mix gently until combined. Refrigerate until ready to serve.

4. Serves 4-6.

Note - Everyone likes chicken salad different ways, ground up and fine, large and chunky, chock full of onions, nuts, and any number of other ingredients. Various alterations can be made like in the above recipe the pecans can be substituted by almonds or walnuts and you can leave out celery and add fried bacon bits or add extra spices like onion powder, ginger powder and garlic powder. You also can add some cayenne pepper to give it a little jing or add chopped green tart apple or grapes cut into halves. In reality there is a lot you can do with chicken salad. Add cooked pasta and give it an Asian flavor by adding some soy sauce and sesame seeds chopped fine onion and some ground ginger and a tablespoon of sugar. Serve it on your favorite bread to make a chicken sandwich. Serve some hot soup and some kind of nibblers with it and you have an excellent picnic, lunch or even dinner.

Hearty Chicken Stew

Ingredients

- 2- Lb Chicken breast chopped in 1inch pieces.
- ¼-Cup Butter or margarine
- 1/3-Cup Flour
- 1 ½--tsp Salt
- 1- tsp Pepper
- 1- Medium onion, sliced
- ¼ -Inch Thick celery stalks, sliced,
- 1- tsp Ginger and garlic/ each
- 1- Green pepper chopped hot or mild as desired
- 2- Potatoes peeled and cut into ¾ inch cubes
- 2- Carrots, peeled and sliced ¼ inch thick
- 1 ½- Cup Chicken broth
- ½ -Cup Tomato sauce
- 2-Tbsp Chopped Parsley
- ½-tsp Red pepper
- ½-tsp Garamamasala

Stew is prepared by combining any type of meat (especially tougher cuts of meat that is suitable for slow cooking) and vegetables and slow cooking them in a gravy made by mixing herbs, spices and your choice of liquid. The dish is most suitable meal to make when you are with limited cooking budget. While water, or chicken or beef broth are used as the stew-cooking liquid but wine, stock and beer are also common. The sauce may be thickened by reduction or by coating pieces of meat with flour before searing it or by using a roux (mixture of flour and some kind of fat). Thickeners like cornstarch or arrowroot flour may also be used. Stews are typically cooked at a relatively low temperature (simmered, not boiled), allowing flavors to merge well into the ingredients.

Method

1. Toss chicken nuggets in flour, ½-teaspoon salt and ½-teaspoon pepper.

2. Melt butter in a large skillet. Add chicken (with excess flour), Sauté 3 minutes to brown. Set it aside

3. Add onion and celery, ginger, garlic, and green pepper and cook for 3 minutes.

4. Add potatoes and carrots and sauté 3 minutes longer. Add the chicken broth and the tomato sauce and bring to boil. Cover; simmer ten minutes until vegetables are tender.

5. Add the chicken and simmer till vegetables are tender another ten minutes or so. Season with remaining salt, pepper and red pepper and garammasala.

6. Sprinkle cilantro or chopped parsley and serve with cooked rice, pasta or your bread of your liking.

7. Serves 4.

Chicken Casserole

Ingredients

- 1 ½- Cups Chicken broth
- 1- Cup Nonfat milk
- ½- Cup All-purpose flour
- ½- Cup Plain yogurt
- 1- 14-Oz Can diced tomatoes, drained
- 3-Green chilies chopped /4-Oz can green chilies drained
- 1- Tbsp Chili powder
- 1-tsp Dried oregano
- ½- tsp Ground cumin
- ½- tsp Salt
- Freshly ground black pepper and red pepper to taste
- 2-Tbsp Olive oil
- 1- Large Onion, chopped
- 1- Red or green bell pepper, diced
- 2- Cloves garlic, minced
- 10- Corn tortillas cut in quarters
- 2- Cups Diced cooked skinless chicken
- ½- Cup Shredded cheddar cheese
- ¼- Cup Chopped Fresh cilantro, or parsley

Casseroles are a staple at potlucks and family gatherings. Casseroles usually consist of pieces of meat (such as chicken) or fish (such as tuna), various chopped vegetables, a starchy binder, such as flour, potato or pasta, and often a crunchy or cheesy topping. Liquids are released from the meat and vegetables during cooking, and more liquids are added in the form of stock, wine, beer, gin, cider, and milk or vegetable stocks at the time when the dish is assembled. Casseroles are usually cooked slowly in the oven, often uncovered.

They may be served as a main course or a side dish, and may be served in the same dish in which they were cooked. This serving dish called -A casserole-is derived from the French word for "saucepan". It is a large, deep dish used both for cooking in the oven and as a serving dish. This type of dish is frequently also called a baking dish coinciding with the cooking technique used to cook casseroles. In Minnesota, this type of dish is sometimes called "hot dish." Cooking in earthenware containers has always been common in most nations, but the idea of casserole cooking as a one-dish meal became popular in America in the twentieth century during the 1950s when new forms of lightweight metal and glassware appeared on the market. By the 1970s casseroles took on a very unsophisticated image.

Most of the time casseroles made with creamy canned soups (to save time) and several cups of cheese but this kind of casserole could be very high in fat and sodium. Here is a recipe that has a tangy, creamy sauce made with nonfat milk, nonfat yogurt and chicken broth, plus you can use reduced-fat cheese. Add in lots of chopped fresh vegetables and you can have a casserole with a little Tex-Mex version that you will feel good about eating.

Method

1. Preheat the oven at 375°F.

2. Bring broth to a simmer in a medium saucepan. Whisk milk and flour in a small bowl until smooth. Add to the broth and cook over medium heat, whisking constantly, until thickened and smooth, about 3 minutes.

3. Remove from the heat and stir in yogurt, tomatoes, chilies, 2-tablespoons cilantro (or parsley), chili powder, oregano and cumin. Season with salt, pepper and red pepper. Set aside.

4. Heat the oil in a large nonstick skillet over medium-high heat. Add onion, bell pepper and garlic, cook, stirring occasionally, until tender-crisp, about 3 minutes.

5. Line the bottom of a shallow 3-quart baking dish with half the tortillas. Top with half the chicken and half the onion mixture.

6. Spoon half of the sauce evenly over the top. Repeat layers with remaining tortillas, chicken, onion mixture and sauce. Sprinkle with Cheddar cheese and remaining cilantro.

7. Bake until bubbly, 25 to 30 minutes.

8. Serves 6.

Rolled Chicken Sauté

Ingredients

2-Tbsp Olive oil

½-tsp Cumin seeds

1-Tbsp/ea Chopped ginger, garlic and green chilies

1½-Cups Thawed and chopped frozen mixed vegetables

Salt and red pepper to taste

¼-tsp cayenne pepper (optional)

1-Tbsp Lemon juice

½-Cup Ricotta cheese

6-Thin fancy chicken fillets

1-Egg beaten with Tbsp water

½-Cup plain breadcrumbs

2-Tbsp Olive oil or melted butter

¼ - ½ -tsp Thyme

½- tsp Salt

1-Can (13 ¼ oz.) Chicken broth

¼- tsp Pepper

1½- Cup Cooked rice

It is an American recipe that has borrowed its preparation technique from countries that have roulades, or roll ups of meat, in their cuisine like Germany, France and Italy. In these countries they use veal or chicken wrapped around a stuffing or cheese or another kind of meat or a combination of any of these ingredients. Many of them are then breaded and fried. The names and recipes vary widely, but their connection to the above-mentioned recipe is apparent. This recipe also shares its characteristics with Chicken Cordon Bleu that has become an American classic.

Method

1. Heat the olive oil in a heavy bottom one quart cooking pan and add the cumin seeds and once they stop cracking add the chopped ginger, garlic and green pepper.

2. Stir and cook for few minutes and add 1 cup of the mixed vegetables, salt and peppers to taste and lemon juice.

3. Add ½ cup of drained ricotta cheese. Cook for 2-3 minutes and remove from heat and set it aside.

4. Spreads the chicken fillets one at a time and place one to two tablespoons of chopped vegetables filling in center of each fillet.

5. Roll it up and secure with wooden picks.

6. Sauté rolled chicken in oil in a large frying pan about 10 minutes until lightly browned.

7. Or

8. Secure with toothpicks. Dip in beaten egg, then roll in crumbs; shake off excess. Layer chicken roll ups in a small baking dish, seam side down and drizzle the top with oil or melted butter.

9. Bake 25 to 30 minutes or until golden. Set it aside. Add broth to the remaining vegetables and spices. Bring to a full boil. Stir in rice. Cover and heat it through.

10. Remove from heat. Let it stand 5 minutes, Fluff with fork. Serve the sautéed chicken roll ups or baked roll ups with this rice, and improvise a salad if you wish and serve.

11. Makes 4 servings.

Chicken Cordon Bleu

Ingredients

5-Tbsp Butter, melted
1-Large Garlic clove, minced
1-Tbsp Chopped onion
1-Tbsp Green hot chili
2-Tbsp chopped parsley or
cilantro
¼- Cup chicken broth
½- Cup Dry breadcrumbs
1-Tbsp Grated fresh Parmigiano-
Reggiano cheese
1-tsp Paprika
4-6 Oz Skinless, boneless
chicken breast halves
¼-tsp Salt and Black pepper/ea
¼-tsp red pepper
¼-tsp Dried oregano
4- Thin slices prosciutto (about 2
ounces)
¼- Cup (1Oz) Shredded part-
skim mozzarella cheese
Cooking spray

Chicken Cordon Bleu is a popular dish of boneless chicken breast pounded and rolled around a pork meat (such as ham or prosciutto) and a soft cheese (such as mozzarella, Swiss or bleu cheese) and then either fried or baked. Chicken Cordon Bleu is a relatively recent American creation, drawing upon techniques from Ukrainian dish Chicken Kiev, Swiss dish Veal Gordon bleu and similar Austrian schnitzel dishes. The earliest reference to "Chicken Cordon Bleu" is seen recorded in The New York Times in 1967 and it seems who so ever introduced it substituted veal with chicken because original recipes with veal are not available since 1955. The French term Cordon Bleu is translated as "Blue Ribbon" that refers to an award-winning recipe for culinary excellence. This chicken dish should not be confused with the cooking school of the same name. The recipe has become a mainstay on many American restaurant menus since the latter half of the 20th century.

There are many variations of this recipe, all of which involve a chicken breast, cheese, and pork. A popular way to prepare the dish is to butterfly a chicken breast, place a thin slice of ham or prosciutto inside, along with a thin slice of a soft, easily melted cheese. The chicken breast is then rolled into a roulade, coated in breadcrumbs and then deep-fried. Other variations exist where the chicken is baked rather than fried or omit the breadcrumbs and wrap the chicken around a slice of ham, or in using bacon instead of the ham. You can serve this flavorful chicken dish with rice or baked potatoes for a fabulous meal for Sunday dinner and you cannot go wrong.

Method

1. Preheat oven to 350° F.

2. Heat 5 tablespoons of butter and fry the onion, garlic, green chili and one tablespoon of parsley until slightly brown. Add the chicken broth and stir to mix.

3. Combine breadcrumbs, Parmigiano-Reggiano, and paprika in a small bowl and set it aside.

4. Place each chicken breast half between 2 sheets of heavy-duty plastic wrap, and pound each to ¼-inch thickness using a meat mallet or rolling pin.

5. Sprinkle both sides of chicken with salt, black pepper, oregano, and red pepper.

6. Top each breast half with 1 slice of prosciutto and 1-tablespoon mozzarella.

7. Roll up each breast half jellyroll fashion. And tuck the edges with toothpicks.

8. Roll each chicken roll in wet chicken broth and onion mixture and dredge in breadcrumb mixture.

9. Place rolls, seam side down, in an 8-inch square-baking dish coated with cooking spray. Pour remaining broth mixture over chicken. Bake at 350°F for 25 minutes or until juices run clear and tops are golden. Serve sprinkled with remaining parsley.

10. Serve with cooked rice, pasta bread and some salad and it makes a great meal.

11. Serves 4.

Ingredients

4-Boneless, skinless, chicken breasts (6-8 oz each), butterfly cut

Cheese filling

½- Cup Mozzarella, shredded

2-Tbsp Parmesan, grated

½-Cup Smoked Gouda, chopped

¼-Cup Fontana cheese, shredded

¼-Cup Sun-dried tomatoes, chopped

¼ tsp Black ground pepper

1-Tbsp Green onions, chopped

1-tsp Garlic, minced

2-Tbsp Fresh parsley, chopped

1-Egg

2-Tbsp Heavy cream

Pasta Sauce

1-Lb Pasta (your choice)

2-Tbsp Extra Virgin olive oil

1-Tbsp Garlic chopped

1-Tbsp Onions chopped

2- Medium Red bell pepper cut in 1-inch pieces

½-Cup Kalamata olives

½-Cup Pimiento, chopped

¼-Cup Small capers, rinsed

½-Cup red wine

1-Cup Chopped tomatoes diced

2-(9 Oz) Can Tomato puree

½- tsp Salt and Black pepper/ea

¼- tsp Cayenne pepper

1-Tbsp Sugar

2-Fresh sweet basil sprigs, chopped

Siena is one of the most beautiful heritage cities in Tuscany Italy. Its city centre has been declared a UNESCO World Heritage Site. This recipe has its origins from the famous Sienese Cuisine. Sienese cuisine has ancient origins, first Etruscan, who introduced the simplicity of herbs, and then Roman influence, spices, a valuable commodity of the past, give distinct flavor to Siena's typical cuisine. Dolci (Italian dessert) such as pan forte and Cavallucci, Sienese meats, (Chianina breed of cattle and Cintas- Sienese pigs), vegetables and herbs are of excellent quality, and most recipes call for the use of olive oil (which in this region is among the highest quality).

Sienna's cuisine is appreciated in the world for its fine natural and flavorful ingredients. It is a typical expression of the Mediterranean diet, considered among others, the most wholesome and tasty like olive oil, pasta, fish and first choice meat. Chianti was the first Seines wine to be appreciated in America; Italian immigrants exported this wine to the U.S. in the straw-covered flasks that now symbolizes the finest wine all over the world.

Method

Cheese filling

1. Mix all cheese filling ingredients in a mixing bowl until well blended.

2. Divide into 4 portions; refrigerate until ready to use.

Pasta Sauce

1. Cook the pasta and set it aside

2. Heat olive oil in a small a saucepan, add onions and garlic and sauté for one minute. Add bell peppers and sauté until al dente. Add olives, pimiento and capers and stir.

3. Add red wine and bring to a boil. Add remaining ingredients chopped tomatoes, and tomato puree, except basil and pasta.

4. Bring to a boil, add salt, black pepper, cayenne pepper and sugar, reduce to low heat and simmer for approximately 30 minutes. Add basil to the sauce and stir well and remove Siena sauce from heat and set it aside.

Chicken Breasts

1. Place chicken breast on a cutting board and split to open. Spread cheese filling evenly on both sides.

2. Fold one side over to the other and repeat with other breasts.

3. Place chicken breasts in baking pan coated with cooking spray. Bake at 450°F for 20 minutes or until juices run clear.

4. Place one chicken breast and cooked pasta on each plate. Evenly distribute Siena sauce over chicken and pasta. Garnish with chopped basil and Serve.

5. Serves 4-6.

Sea Food

Uncooked Lobster

America enjoys the best seafood on earth available from the Pacific Ocean, Atlantic Ocean the gulf coast, and all the great lakes and the rivers running across the country. Humans consider any form of sea life as Seafood. Actually in America term "seafood" is extended to any fresh water organisms, so in other words all edible aquatic life may be referred to as seafood. The harvesting, processing, and consuming of sea foods are ancient practices that date back to at least about 40,000 years ago. As the population of world increased the demand for fish has also increased. It is not only the best source of protein but it is also low in fat and cooks very fast. Fish like salmon and tuna are somewhat higher in fat, but since they are a great source of heart healthy omega 3 fatty acids, they are very much favored all over the country and the entire world.

Seafood is also a great alternative to red meat. Proteins found in it help build lean muscle tissue and regulate red blood cells. Omega-3 helps reduce your chances of heart disease and high blood pressure. Eating fish at least three times a week is also great for losing weight.

Shrimp Fry

Ingredients

1-Lb Deveined and cleaned
  shrimp or frozen and thawed
  shrimp
1-Egg, separated
½- tsp. Salt
¼-Cup Cornstarch
¼-Cup Flour
¼-Cup Flat beer
¼-tsp Onion powder
¼- tsp Garlic powder
½-tsp Red pepper
Paprika, for sprinkling
Lemon wedges

Americans do love their decapods crustaceans; they may be grilled, scampied, or slathered (especially when served in cocktail sauce) they are enjoyed either way. Shrimp is, in fact, the most-consumed seafood in the United States. How did shrimp surpass canned tuna, the longtime seafood champ, and become the nation's favorite marine nibble? The only answer is that we have a shrimp farming revolution in United States and besides that shrimp is also very fast and easy to cook. It picks up the flavor of spices and herbs beautifully and provides 100% pure protein and it is delicious any way you cook it.

Method

1. Beat egg yolk and salt and set it aside.

2. Mix flour and cornstarch with half of the beer and make a smooth paste. Mix in egg yolk and remaining beer. Stir in onion powder and garlic powder and red pepper.

3. Beat egg white stiff and fold into mixture. Batter is enough for about 1 pound of shrimp.

4. Dip shrimp in the batter and deep fry in peanut oil and brown it slowly. As soon as the shrimp starts to turn brown remove them from the oil using a slotted spoon and drain on paper towels.

5. Sprinkle lightly with paprika, if desired, to add color. Serve with lemon wedges. Sprinkle with salt and pepper.

6. Season immediately with tarter sauce, French fries or onion rings.

7. Serves 2-4.

Shrimp Creole

Ingredients

- 2-Tbsp Olive oil
- ½- Cup Chopped green bell peppers
- ½- Cup Diced onions
- ½- Cup Diced celery
- 1-Tbsp Chopped ginger, garlic and green chilies/ea
- 1-tsp Chili powder
- 1- (14-Oz) Can tomatoes
- 1- (8-Oz) Can tomato sauce
- 1-Tbsp Hot sauce
- 1-Tbsp Worcestershire sauce
- 1-tsp White sugar
- Salt and pepper
- 1 ½-lbs Peeled and deveined shrimp
- Green onions, for garnish

Shrimp Creole originated in the state of Louisiana. It evolved as a result of intermixing of the 3 different local cultures, French, African and Spanish with their 3 different culinary techniques and it definitely has a style of cooking that is all its own. Shrimp is cooked in a mixture of whole or diced tomatoes, onion, celery and bell pepper, with Tabasco sauce or an other hot pepper sauce and/or cayenne-based seasoning and served over steamed or boiled white rice. Apart from the foundation ingredients of onion, celery and bell pepper Creole dishes -have many variations because the basic recipe is often altered to include whatever ingredients the cook has available. The shrimp may be cooked in the mixture or cooked separately, and then added at the end. These dishes may be made by substituting or by using some other type of meat or seafood for the shrimp, or omitting the meat entirely. Creole-type dishes combine the qualities of a gumbo and a jambalaya. They are typically made with a thicker sauce and are spicier than a gumbo, and the rice is prepared separately and used as a bed for the Creole mixture, rather than cooked in the same pot as with a jambalaya. Creole dishes also do not contain broth or white sauce instead their sauce is their own sauce and they are simmered in to its desired degree of thickness by cooking a little longer. Shrimp are as delicate as eggs in regards cooking time. When they are overcooked, they have a tough and rubbery texture. Creole cuisine uses a rich array of European ingredients and has its origins in recipes like French bouillabaisse, Spanish paella and German sausage. It differs from Cajun cuisine because it is traditionally composed of one-pot meals enriched with the pungent flavors of fresh seafood and game. According to some it is of Caribbean origin, whatever the origin is, it is one of the favorite dishes throughout South of America.

Method

1. In a Crockpot, heat olive oil. Add peppers, onions and celery. Add ginger, garlic and green chilies. Cook until softened. Add chili powder and sauté until onion is caramelized.

2. Add tomatoes, tomato sauce, hot sauce, Worcestershire sauce, white sugar, salt and pepper. Cook for 30 minutes. Add shrimp and cook for about 3 minutes. Serve over cooked rice. Top with chopped green onions.

3. Serves 4-6

Lobster Delight

Ingredients

1-Medium lobster

Or

1 ½-Lbs of Lobster meat

½-tsp Salt and black pepper/ea

2-Tbsp Ginger-garlic and onion
  paste

1-Egg beaten

2-tsp-Lime juice

1-tsp Red chili powder

½--tsp Turmeric powder

½--tsp cumin powder

1-Tbsp brown sugar

½-tsp coriander powder

2-Tbsp Oil, or clarified butter or
  Virgin olive oil

5- Curry leaves chopped

2-Tbsp Chopped cilantro

½-tsp Garammasala

Lemon juice to sprinkle

Lobster preparations were supposedly fit for queens, emperors, and the likes and have a rich history of use.

Lobsters appeared in the art or folklore of many cultures. The Romans portrayed lobsters, along with other edible sea creatures, on mosaic floors that formed part of domestic and public decorations. The mosaic dramas even depicted battles to-the -death between lobsters and wily octopuses. Helmets worn by warrior lobsters immortalized the strength of the lobsters. Lobsters were not only valuable food items, but had medicinal value during the Middle Ages and Renaissance times.

While ancient, Middle Age, and Renaissance people were admiring many aspects of the lobsters they were washing up on North American shores in about 2 feet high piles. Since they were so plentiful and easy to harvest, lobsters were a frequent meal on seacoasts of the new land of early European settlers. The disdain for lobster slowly waned over the last few centuries in America. It wasn't until the 19th century that lobsters regained their status as a luxury food item in America mostly as a result of their popularity with royalty in European countries and the poor man's chicken soon became the rich man's prize. It is now considered a delicacy not only in States but also all around the world. The voracious appetite of the public here in states keeps going up and currently its production in America has risen to over 70 million pounds per year. The fact of the matter is that it boasts healthy omega-3 fatty acids, potassium and the vitamins

E, B-12 and B-6. Lobster is also one of the most tasty and famous of seafood's. Therefore it is considered a delicacy and is quite expensive. It not only has fewer calories but less total fat and less cholesterol (based on 100 grams of cooked product) than lean beef; whole poached eggs; and even roasted, skinless chicken breast. Lobster is also high in amino acids; potassium and magnesium; vitamins A, B12, B6, B3 (niacin) and B2 (riboflavin); calcium and phosphorus, iron, and zinc. So enjoy this bounty of the sea if you can.

In the United States, June 15 is National Lobster Day, a time for savoring and paying tribute to one of America's most beloved crustaceans.

Lobster delight (Lobster grilled meat in its own shell)

Method

1. Fill half a large pot with water and bring to a boil.

2. Add some salt to it and transfer the lobster making sure it is completely submerged.

3. Cook it for 5 minutes for the first kg and 2 extra minutes for every additional kg.

4. If the antenna pulls out easily, then it is cooked.

5. Properly cooked lobster meat is creamy white and the shells are bright red. Allow the lobster to cool and remove its meat from the shell keeping the shells intact.

6. Cut the tail in half lengthwise. Carefully remove the meat from it and chop it into 1 ½-inch pieces. Clean and wash the shell and set it aside.

7. Mix the masala powders, salt, pepper, onion, ginger-garlic paste, egg and limejuice in a bowl. Add red pepper powder, turmeric, cumin powder, brown sugar, and coriander powder and mix well. Add the lobster pieces to it and mix. Marinate for 30 minutes.

8. Heat oil or clarified butter in a pan. Add curry leaves and marinated lobster pieces. Shallow fry on both sides for few minutes until it is cooked.

9. Dip the tail shell into the marinade and broil them in the oven until they turn red.

10. Now stuff the fried meat into the fried tail shell and garnish with fresh cilantro and sprinkle garammasala and lemon juice. Serve with rice or Rotis (Indian griddle bread).

11. Serves 2-4.

> **Note: Here is an easy and very traditional way to cook lobster: Crack and split open the tail to expose the meat. Season with liberal amounts of butter, salt, pepper and paprika and broil or grill right in the shell for 5-10 minutes until the shell is lightly brown and the meat turns opaque. Serve with lemon wedges and melted butter. Serve the meat as a main dish or as an appetizer.**

Lobster Wrap

Ingredients

1-(8 Oz) Container chopped
    lobster meat
1-Cup Finely chopped tomato
¼-Cup Onion chopped
1-Tbsp Chopped green chili
1-Avocado, peeled and diced
½-Cup Ranch dressing
Pinch salt and pepper
½-Lemon, juiced
Whole chives
2-(12-inch) Flour tortillas
Freshly chopped lettuce

Lobsters are probably the most sophisticated shellfish. A lobster recipe is a dish that stands out on any dinner table. You can prepare lobster using different cooking methods, from the simplest -by boiling them or grilling them to baking them or making a roll or bisque (Soup) with them. Lobsters are delicious and very nutritious any way you cook them. They contain less cholesterol, less calories, and less saturated fats than even lean beef, pork, and chicken. Just enjoy this delicious and sophisticated recipe of lobster and appreciate this seafood.

Method

1. In a medium bowl, combine lobster meat, tomato, onion, green chili, avocado and Ranch dressing. Mix together, adding salt, pepper, and lemon juice. Set aside.

2. Blanch several whole chives by dropping in boiling water for 10 seconds. Slice a large tortilla into 4 quarters with knife. Roll each tortilla quarter into a cone shape.

3. Secure by tying blanched chive like a string around cone. Scoop lobster mixture generously into each cone, filling up to the top.

4. Adorn opening of each cone with freshly chopped lettuce and serve as an appetizer or a snack or as a hors d'oeuvre.

5. Makes 8 pieces of appetizers.

Pan Seared Fish with Elegant Orzo Spinach Salad

Ingredients

2-Lbs Fresh or frozen thawed fish fillets (Halibut, White fish, haddock)

2-Tbsp Steak sauce

1 ¼- tsp Salt and pepper

¼- Cup Cooking oil

(16.Oz) Package uncooked orzo

½- Cup Olive oil

2-Tbsp Butter

½-tsp Minced garlic

½-tsp Dried Basil

½- tsp Crushed red pepper flakes

1-Cup Pine nuts

1- (10 Oz.) Bag baby spinach

½- Cup Arugula leaves

1- Fresh tomato Chopped

Salt and pepper to taste

2- Tbsp Balsamic vinegar

There is nothing quite so wonderful as a perfectly seared piece of fish: Crispy crust on one side, just-barely-done meat in the center. It is also one of the great tastes of the world, and it is my go-to method for cooking most any fish. It is one of the easiest ways to cook mouthwatering fillets that your family will love and takes very little time to do so. This method of cooking the fish can be applied to any white Fish, Halibut, Haddock or Mahi Mahi. Searing (or pan searing) is a technique used in grilling baking and roasting, sautéing any meat, poultry or fish at high temperature so a caramelized crust forms. This technique is also a healthy alternative to deep fried fish and when cooked to perfection, the outside of your fish will be beautifully golden brown and crisp, while the inside will be moist, juicy, and tender.

Pan Seared fish with elegant Orzo

Method

1. Rub fish fillets all over with salt, pepper, and the steak sauce.

2. Heat oil as needed in skillet until very hot, about 370°. Brown fillets for about 2 minutes on each side.

3. Reduce heat to low. Cover and cook for about 4 to 6 minutes longer, depending on thickness of fish. Fish should flake easily with a fork and should be well seared. Set it aside.

4. Bring a large pot of lightly salted water to a boil. Add pasta and cook for 8 to 10 minutes). Drain, transfer to a mixing bowl, and set aside.

5. Heat olive oil and butter in a large skillet over medium high heat, stirring to blend. Stir in garlic, basil, and red pepper flakes, and reduce heat to medium. Stir in pine nuts and cook until lightly browned. Add spinach, cover, and cook on low heat for 5 minutes, or until spinach is wilted.

6. Toss spinach mixture with orzo pasta and Arugula leaves. Portion onto serving plates with a drizzle of balsamic vinegar and chopped tomatoes. Allow guests to adjust seasoning with salt and pepper as needed. Serve the seared fish on top of the salad

7. Serves 4.

> **Note:** There are many alternate ways to serve seared fish. You can also serve it with pan fried Shitake mushrooms in butter sauce. In a small skillet melt butter. Add onions and cook for 1-2 minutes. Add white wine and mushrooms and let it simmer for an additional 3 minutes. Remove from heat, let cool slightly and serve over the seared fish. Or serve the seared fish on top of pasta tossed with dressed arugula salad and chopped tomatoes.

Seared Fish with Vegetables and Couscous

Ingredients

2-Tbsp Olive oil
1- Cinnamon stick
1-Pod Green cardamom
½- tsp Cumin seeds
½- Cup Sliced almonds, toasted
½- Cup Sliced dried apricots
½ -tsp Onion powder
½-tsp Ginger minced
½-tsp Garlic minced
1- Cup Couscous
2- Cups water
2-Tbsp Orange juice
3-tsp Salt
4-Tbsp extra-virgin olive oil
2- Tbsp Butter
1- Red onion, sliced thinly
1-tsp minced green chili (mildly hot)
2- Zucchini, julienned
2- Yellow squash, julienned
2-Red peppers, julienned
2 yellow peppers, julienned
1 ½ -tsp Black pepper
½-tsp red pepper
½-Tsp Garammasala
¼- Cup Chopped Cilantro and
    thyme
4 to 6 (6-Oz Pacific Halibut
    fillets or Cod

The cuisine in different parts of our country developed independently. Each regional style of cooking was influenced by the nationality of the colonists that settled in that area and by the types of ingredients locally available. Each state has sampling of the special dishes popular in each region. Southern cooking is famous for barbecuing. Blackened fish or steaks are grilled with coatings of pepper and hot spices and usually are served with vegetables. New England states are renowned for their hearty dishes imported by British colonists and for their cold-water seafood harvested by the local fishing fleet. In California with a very high population of ethnic groups fish can be lightly grilled in salsa and served with Chinese vegetables and Native American fry bread. Almost any combination of ethnic food styles can be found in California cooking. This is the home of avant-garde, experimental cuisine. I would consider this recipe to be one of California style cooking. Hope you enjoy it.

Method

1. In a two- quart saucepan, heat 2 tablespoons of oil add the cinnamon stick, cardamom and cumin seeds. When the seeds stop popping add some chopped apricots and sliced almonds. Stir to mix.

2. Add the mined ginger, minced garlic and couscous. Stir well to roast for a 1 minute and add the water and orange juice Mix and bring it to a to a boil. And add one teaspoon of salt and ½-tsp of black pepper. Cover and lower the heat.

3. In a 12-inch skillet, heat 2- tablespoons of the olive oil and two-tablespoon butter. When the pan is hot add the red onion and the green chili, sauté for 3 minutes until tender; add the rest of the vegetables.

4. Cook over high heat, tossing frequently, until the vegetables are crisp-tender, 5 to 7 minutes. Add the one-teaspoon of the salt, ½- teaspoon black pepper, red pepper and garammasala and toss to combine and then set aside. Keep it warm while you cook the fish.

5. Season the halibut fillets on both sides with the remaining salt and pepper.

6. In a 12-inch skillet, heat the remaining olive oil over medium-high heat.

7. When the pan is hot, add the halibut fillets and cook until golden brown and fish flakes easily, about 3 minutes on each side.

8. Divide the couscous onto serving plates and serve the fillets over the couscous and spread the vegetables around the plate. Serve immediately.

9. Makes 4 servings.

Note: Discard the whole spices from couscous during serving.

Ginger Sweet Mahi Mahi

Ingredients

2- Cups Uncooked jasmine rice/
    Bansmati rice

2- Cups Water

1- Cube Chicken bouillon

2-Tbsp Butter (optional)

¾- (14.Oz) Can coconut milk

3- Tbsp Brown sugar/Honey

3-Tbsp Soy sauce

3-Tbsp Balsamic vinegar

2-tsp Grated fresh ginger root

2- Cloves garlic, crushed

2-tsp Olive oil

Salt to taste

½ tsp Red pepper

½-tsp Ground cumin

24- Oz Raw mahi mahi fillets/
    Salmon Fillets/Red snapper/
    tuna steaks

Salt and lemon pepper to taste

A perfect balance of "sweet" and "savory" fish fillets that are loaded with heart-healthy omega-3 fatty acids, especially delicious when brushed with honey, soy, ginger and garammasala and cooked until browned.

Method

1. Bring the rice, water, chicken bouillon, and 2-tablespoon butter to a boil in a saucepan over high heat. Reduce heat to medium-low, cover, and simmer until the liquid has been absorbed, about 20 minutes.

2. Pour in the coconut milk. Stir, and simmer uncovered until the rice has absorbed most of the coconut milk. While the rice is cooking preheat the broiler.

3. In a shallow glass dish, stir together the brown sugar, soy sauce, balsamic vinegar, ginger, garlic and olive oil.

4. Season fish fillets lightly with salt and red pepper, cumin powder, and place them into the dish. Cover, and refrigerate to marinate.

5. Preheat broiler. Remove fish from the dish, and reserve marinade.

6. Place fish on a baking tray and broil 4 to 6 minutes on each side, turning only once, until fish flakes easily with a fork.

7. Remove fillets to a serving platter and sprinkle ¼- teaspoon garammasala.

8. Keep warm. Pour reserved marinade into the skillet, and reduce until the mixture reduces to a glaze.

9. Serve by placing a Mahi Mahi fillet over a scoop of hot rice. Spoon glaze over fish, and serve immediately.

10. Servings: 4

Barbecuing or Grilling Fish Fillets

Ingredients

- 4-Tbsp butter, melted
- 2-Tbsp Lemon juice
- 1/4-tsp Dried dill weed
- 2- Small Green chili chopped
- 2-tsp Chopped ginger
- 2-tsp Chopped garlic
- 4- Frozen sole or flounder fillets
- 8- Slices onion (¼ inch thick)
- 2-Medium potato, pared and cut
  lengthwise into ¼-inch strips
- 2- Medium carrot, cut into 1/8-
  inch slices
- 1-Cup Frozen Italian green beans
- 2- Green apple cut lengthwise
- Green chilies medium hot
- Salt to taste
- Black pepper, red pepper and
  garammasala
- 2-Tbsp Fresh chopped cilantro

Barbecue is a method and apparatus for cooking meat, poultry, and occasionally fish using heat or hot smoke of a fire, smoking wood, compressed wood pellets, or hot charcoal. This method is used chiefly in the United States, Canada, the United Kingdom, New Zealand and Australia.

The idea of cooking and grilling fish in aluminum foil seems to have originated here in America. The foil prevents the meat from direct burn and cooks it in its own juices and makes the piece of meat or fish more tender and delicious. It is a very clean way of cooking the fish and it also helps seal in the fish's flavor. Closing everything up in a packet steams the fish and vegetables while keeping them moist. For those trying to consume high omega-3 food, foil baked fish fillet is a great option. Grilled fish with irresistible seasonings makes it a hit accompaniment with rice. Bake until fish fillets are flaky and the vegetables are tender. If the fish fillets are large, cut them into equal serving-sized portions or, sear them in a fry pan before you begin grilling or baking. Fish baked in foil also makes an easy weeknight meal. Incorporate side dishes to accompany heart-healthy fish entrees.

Method

1. Preheat oven to 425°. Mix melted butter, lemon juice, dill weed, green chili, garlic, ginger and set it aside.

2. Place each frozen fillet in center of individual piece of heavy-duty aluminum foil 18x 12 inches.

3. Drizzle each fillet with 1- tablespoon of butter mixture and top with 2 slices of onion. Arrange potatoes, carrot and beans on sides of fillets, top with chopped apple and green chilies. Season with salt, black pepper, red pepper and sprinkle with garammasala and fresh cilantro.

4. Seal foil tightly, place on ungreased cookie sheet. Bake until fillets flake easily with fork and vegetables are tender, 30 to 35 minutes. Serve with your favorite pasta and sauce.

5. 4 servings.

Parmesan Fish Fillet Kabobs

Ingredients

8-Large cherry tomatoes

Frozen cod or Haddock fillets

8-Medium mushrooms

8- Large pitted ripe olives

8-(I-inch) Pieces green bell
  pepper

8-Slices (I-inch thick) medium
  zucchini

I/2-Cup Italian dressing or as
  needed

Grated Parmesan cheese

Note: Any combination of vegetables can be substituted; cut into sizes recommended above.

Here is a recipe of broiling fish fillets with vegetable Kabobs. A wide variety of meat and vegetable are pieces marinated in spicy herbaceous marinade and are cooked on open fire. Kabobs have their origin in the in the middle east and are popular worldwide. The vegetables get cooked right along with the meat and you have a complete meal cooked in few minutes. Make sure you make the marinade ahead of time. The American Heart association recommends that you should have 2 servings of fish a week. In this recipe the Italian dressing is substituted for the marinade and it really adds a lot of flavor to the kabobs.

Method

1. Alternate vegetables on each of two 9-inch metal skewers.

2. Place frozen fillets on greased rack of broiler pan; brush with dressing. Broil 4 to 5 inches from heat 4 minutes. Brush with dressing again and carefully turn over. Set aside.

3. Place vegetable kabobs skewers on rack. Brush kabobs with dressing. Broil 3 minutes.

4. Brush both fillets and kabobs again with dressing and place both under broil. Broil fillets until they flake easily with fork, 2 to 3 minutes longer but cook vegetables a longer until slightly brown. To serve, brush fillets with dressing and sprinkle with cheese.

5. Makes 4- Servings.

Fish and Chips

Ingredients

1-Lb Cod fillets
1-Egg
1 ½- Cups Beer
1-Cup All-purpose flour
1-tsp Garlic powder
½-tsp Salt
½-tsp Ground black pepper
2-Cups Crushed cornflake
    crumbs or fine panko crumbs
1-tsp Cajun seasoning
1-Qt Oil for frying

The first restaurant of Fish and Chips was opened in 1965 in Sausalito California by an English couple named Haddon and Grace Salt (Refer to Wikipedia). Winston Churchill called Fish and Chips "the good companions". John Lennon smothered his in tomato ketchup. Michael Jackson liked them with mushy peas. They sustained morale through two world wars and helped fuel Britain's industrial prime. Fish and Chips are a popular take out food in the United Kingdom, Ireland, Australia, New Zealand, Canada and South Africa. It consists of battered fish that is deep-fried and served with French fries.

For generations, fish and chips fed millions of Americans and they have memories of eating them with greasy fingers on a seaside holiday, a payday treat at the end of the working week or a late-night supper on the way home from the work but that was in mid sixties and seventies. They still are a great choice at a restaurant though the fast food joints carrying their names (Fish And Chips) are gone but they still are very much a part of a menu of almost any restaurant all over the world.

Few can resist the mouth-watering combination - moist white fish in crisp golden batter, served with a generous portion of hot, fluffy chips with tarter sauce. They still make a great meal.

Fried Fish with Vegetables

Method

1. In a medium bowl, beat together egg, beer, flour, garlic powder, salt, and pepper. Place cod fillets in this batter in the bowl, and thoroughly coat with the mixture.

2. In a separate medium bowl, mix the cornflake crumbs and Cajun seasoning.

3. Dip the cod in the batter and then in the crumb mixture and thoroughly coat all sides.

4. In a large, heavy skillet or deep fryer, heat the oil to 365° F (185° C). Fry the fish until golden brown or until flesh is easily flaked with a fork.

5. Serve with golden French fries or fried potato chips with tartar sauce. Makes a delicious meal.

6. Makes 2-servings.

Salmon Wellington

Ingredients

4-(4-6 Oz) Fresh wild Alaskan king salmon, skin removed
1- Cup Mushroom duxelle (Sauce)
1- 10" x 16" Sheet puff pastry
Garlic Salt as needed
½-tsp - Roasted cumin powder
½ - tsp Black pepper
2- Tbsp Lemon Juice
Mushroom sauce as needed

It gets its name from the famous dish Beef Wellington (Refer to the recipe for more info).

Salmon was abundant on both the East and West coasts of America. The waters of the Northwest are particularly abundant with salmon, where it is known as "Alaskan turkey." In Hawaii, it is lomi-lomi, a food that is highly prized.

Many Native American tribes depended heavily upon salmon in their diet and looked upon salmon with great reverence and have special rituals and legends for the yearly salmon run. They look upon salmon as life, because salmon has nourished them physically and spiritually since the days when people first came to this region. The life cycle of the salmon is an interesting one. Spawned in freshwater streams, the young salmon travels to sea early. Here they live and grow for three or four years. In the spring after they reach maturity, the adult salmon return to their native streams to spawn. As salmon begin their journey home, they will stop eating and live mainly on the oils stored in their bodies. The distances they travel and their astounding return to the exact point on earth where they emerged from their egg sacs is amazing. They will leap over any dams and waterfalls, hurling itself many feet out of the water until it surmounts the obstacle or sometimes dies of exhaustion in the attempt but there is no turning back. Once reaching the fresh water stream where they hatched from their eggs, the female lays her eggs in a gravel depression and male salmon lays their sperm on top of these eggs. The female covers (after the external fertilization eggs become Gametes) the depression now with more gravel. 5 % to 10% of the fertilized eggs survive to hatch into fish and they again start the same life cycle. For some unknown reason, the male and female salmon always die after spawning. Only 5 to 10 % may survive to spawn depending on the species.

Early European settlers got tired of salmon rich diet very early and their servants had a clause in their contract not to cook salmon meals more than once a week.

Salmon provides you with much needed Beta Carotene and Omega 3 Fatty acids. Elegant yet easy to prepare, salmon wellington makes a lovely entrée for a dinner party or an evening dinner. Cooking them, as a puffed pastry parcel is easy and can be prepared and refrigerated for up to two hours before they are baked. New England first began canning salmon in 1840, shipping it all the way across the country to California. By 1864, the tables were turned because when the waters of the East became fished out, California started supplying the east with canned salmon. Today all Atlantic salmon comes from Canada or Europe. Salmon gets its pinkish red color from the krill and shrimp they live on in the ocean.

Method

1. Cut puff pastry into four approximately equal 5" x 8" (13cm x 20cm) sheets.

2. Spread ¼- cup mushroom duxelle (mushroom sauce) (Recipe below) evenly onto each sheet of puff pastry, leaving a ½ -Inch margin at the edges. Place a salmon fillet in the center of each prepared pastry that already been seasoned with a sprinkle of garlic salt, roasted cumin powder, black pepper and lemon juice.

3. Fold up edges lengthwise and press puff pastry together to seal a seam across the center of the salmon fillet. Flip pastry over so that seam is hidden and gently press the sides together to close.

4. Bake salmon wellington at 400° F (205°C) for 15 minutes. Lower heat to 325° F (165° C) and bake for an additional 15-20 minutes until puff pastry is flaky and golden brown. Serve with Mushrooms sauce.

5. Makes 4 servings.

> **Note: If using previously frozen salmon, allow fillets to completely thaw before assembling the salmon puff pastry.**

Cremini Duxelles or Mushroom sauce

Mushroom Duxelles is a recipe from very classic French cuisine. It's a paste-like reduction of finely minced mushrooms that have been slowly cooked with shallots and butter until all the liquid is gone, resulting in an ingredient that adds rich mushroom flavor to other dishes.

Ingredients

2-Cups Fresh cremini mushrooms
1-Green Serrano or milder green pepper chopped
2-Tbsp Unsalted butter
¼-Cup Shallots, finely diced
1-tsp Chopped garlic
2- Tbsp White wine
¼- tsp Thyme
½-- tsp Salt
½-tsp black pepper
¼-tsp Red pepper
¼- Cup Whipping cream

Method

1. Rinse and thoroughly pat dry cremini mushrooms and green chili pepper before using a food processor or sharp knife to finely mince.

2. Melt butter in a sauté pan over medium heat. Add shallots and sauté until soft. Stir in minced cremini mushrooms and simmer for 7-10 minutes, stirring occasionally, allowing the mushrooms to cook down while their moisture evaporates. Add garlic, stir to fry a minute longer.

3. Add white wine, thyme, black pepper, red pepper and salt. Simmer for an additional 5-7 minutes.

4. Remove from heat and stir in whipping cream. Use immediately or cover and refrigerate.

5. Makes 1 cup. Serve it with salmon pastry.

6. Serves 4.

Crab Cakes

Ingredients

2-Tbsp Olive oil
6- Green Onions, chopped
1- tsp Chopped garlic
1-tsp Chopped ginger
1-tsp Chopped green chilies
1-16Oz-Can crabmeat drained
1- Egg
1-Tbsp Mayonnaise
1-tsp Dry mustard
1-Cup Cracker crumbs
½-tsp Ground Cayenne pepper
1-tsp Old bay seasoning mix
Or
½- tsp Garammasala
Salt to taste
Ground black pepper to taste
1-Cup Panko (Japanese bread
    crumbs) or regular dry bread
    crumbs
½-Cup Olive oil

A crab cake is a dish of American origin made by combining crab-meat and various other ingredients, such as breadcrumbs, milk, mayonnaise, eggs, yellow onions, and seasonings. Occasionally other ingredients such as red or green peppers or pink radishes are added, at which point the cake is then fried, baked or grilled and then served. Crab cakes are traditionally associated with the area surrounding the Chesapeake Bay in particular the State of Maryland and the City of Baltimore. The two most common styles of Maryland crab cakes are known as Boardwalk and Restaurant. Boardwalk crab cakes are typically breaded and deep-fried, and are often filled with stuffing of various sorts and served on a hamburger bun. Restaurant crab cakes, which are sometimes called gourmet crab cakes, are often prepared with no filler, and are composed of all-lump crab -meat served on a platter with a side dish or as open-faced sandwich. Blue crab meat is traditional and is considered the best tasting. They are both served with different kinds of sauces like remoulade, tartar, mustard or ketchup.

Maryland Crab Cakes are the national food of The Preakness race, a horse race that is run on the third Saturday of May each year in Baltimore.

Method

1. Heat 2 tablespoons oil in a skillet over high heat. Sauté green onions, ginger, garlic and chilies briefly until tender, cool slightly.

2. Combine crabmeat with sautéed green onions mixture, egg, mayonnaise, dry mustard, crushed crackers, cayenne pepper, Old Bay seasoning or garammasala, salt and pepper. Form into ½-inch thick patties. Coat the patties with breadcrumbs.

3. Heat ½-cup oil in a skillet over medium high heat. Cook cakes until golden brown on each side. Drain briefly on paper towels and serve hot with tartar sauce or remoulde, with a side dish or as an open sandwich with trimmings.

4. Serves 2-4.

Baked Fish Tilapia with Coconut Sauce

Ingredients
4- Tilapia fillets
3-Tbsp Fresh lemon juice
1-Tbsp Butter, melted
1-Clove Garlic, finely chopped
½-tsp roasted cumin powder
1-tsp Dried parsley flakes
Pepper to taste

Coconut curry sauce
2-tsp Dark sesame oil
2-tsp Minced fresh ginger
2- Garlic cloves, minced
1-Cup Finely chopped red bell
   pepper
1-Cup Chopped green onions
1-tsp Curry powder
2-tsp Red curry paste/ 1-tsp Hot
   sauce
½-tsp Ground cumin powder
4-tsp Soy sauce
1-Tbsp Brown sugar
½-tsp Salt
1- (14-Oz) Can Light coconut
   milk
2-Tbsp Chopped fresh cilantro

Budget-friendly and versatile, Tilapia has rapidly become one of America's best-selling fish. Quick cooking and easy to prepare its mild flavor serves as a base for varieties of wonderful recipes. Tilapia is a fresh water fish native to Africa and the Middle East. They are low in mercury levels and have lean fillets with very low fat contents. Tilapia according to the National Marine Fisheries Service ranks fifth most consumed seafood. Tilapia is considered sustainable, thanks to its herbivore eating habits, feeding mainly on plankton, filamentous algae, aquatic macrophytes and other vegetable matter. As a result, wild tilapia does not accumulate pollutants and other toxins in their bodies. On fish farms Tilapia are fed mostly on grain and are also prone to be toxin-free. Known in the food business as "aquatic chicken" (because it breeds easily and tastes bland) tilapia is the perfect factory fish; it happily eats pellets made largely of corn and soy and gains weight rapidly, easily converting a diet that resembles cheap chicken feed into low-cost seafood. It is rapidly becoming one of the most popular seafood in the United States.

Method

Tilapia
1. Preheat oven to 375° F (190°C). Spray a baking dish with non-stick cooking spray.

2. Rinse Tilapia fillets under cool water, and pat dry with paper towels.

3. Place fillets in baking dish. Pour lemon juice over fillets then drizzle butter on top. Sprinkle with garlic, cumin powder, parsley, and pepper

4. Bake in preheated oven until the fish is white and flakes when pulled apart with a fork (about 10-15 minutes). Serve with a side dish of a vegetable or gently place it in a pan of coconut curry sauce (recipe below) or sauce of your choice and a vegetable as a side dish.

5. Serves 2.

Coconut curry sauce

1. Heat 1- teaspoon sesame oil in a large nonstick skillet over medium heat. Add ginger and garlic and cook 1 minute.

2. Add bell pepper and onions. Cook 1 minute. Stir in curry powder, curry paste/hot sauce and cumin powder and cook 1 minute.

3. Add soy sauce, brown sugar, ½- teaspoon salt, and coconut milk; bring to a simmer (do not boil). Remove from heat; stir in cilantro.

4. Pour sauce over the fish and serve with rice, and lime wedges.

5. Makes 1 ½-Cup sauce.

Ingredients

- 1-Lb Peeled and deveined medium shrimp
- 1-Lb Bay scallops /16 Oz. packaged crabmeat, cut into 1-inch pieces
- 1-Bunch cilantro leaves, chopped
- 3- Roma (plum) tomatoes, diced
- 2-Avocados peeled and diced
- 2-Stalks celery, diced/1- English cucumber peeled and cut into pieces
- 5-Green onions, sliced
- 6-Limes, juiced
- 2-Small Serrano peppers, seeded and minced
- Salt and White pepper to taste
- ½-tsp Garammasala

Note: if you want spicier ceviche add 1-tablespoon pepper sauce and 1-table-spoon of Worcestershire sauce to ceviche mix. Sometimes American Ceviches are served in a cocktail of clam juice and tomato juice in a tall beer glass or tall ice cream sundae glass.

It is a popular international dish prepared in a variety of ways. It is well liked throughout America. Ceviche a seafood dish arrived in America in 1980's. It is popular not only in the coastal regions of the America and the Philippines but it is quite popular in present-day Peru where it likely had its origin. Other coastal societies such as the Polynesian islands of the south pacific are also attributed to the invention of this dish. The greatest variety of ceviches are found in Peru, Ecuador and Chile but other distinctly unique styles can also be found in coastal El Salvador, Guatemala, Mexico, Argentina, Panama, the Caribbean and several other nations.

It is typically made from fresh raw fish marinated in citrus juices such as lemon or lime and spiced with chili peppers. Additional seasonings such as onion, salt, cilantro and pepper may also be added. As the dish is not cooked with heat, it must be prepared fresh to minimize the risk of food poisoning.

Ceviche is usually accompanied by side dishes that complement its flavors such as sweet potato, lettuce, corn or Avocado.

Method

1. Combine the shrimp, scallops, cilantro, tomatoes, avocados, celery, green onions, cucumbers, lime juice and Serrano peppers in a bowl.

2. Season with salt, white pepper, garammasala and stir. Pour into a glass or plastic container.

3. Cover, and refrigerate 3 hours to overnight. Serve the seafood with its own lime -juice marinade. Serve with tortilla chips.

4. Serves 4-6.

Baked Scallops

Ingredients

1 ½- Lb Bay scallops, rinsed and drained
4-Tbsp Butter, melted
½-Cup Orange juice
1-tsp Onion powder
1-tsp Garlic powder
½-tsp Paprika
½-tsp Dried parsley
3-Cloves garlic, minced
½-Cup Seasoned dry breadcrumbs
¼-Cup Grated Parmesan cheese
Dill sauce (see recipe page 115).

Scallops take well to all kinds of cooking methods. Whether grilled, fried, or bacon-wrapped, scallops are ready in a flash. Clean and sweet tasting seafood of the ocean, many people consider scallops a seafood delicacy. Rich in Omega-3 fatty acids and relatively low in calories, they are an incredibly healthy source of protein. You even add them to soups, stews and risottos.

It is very important not to overcook scallops as they can go from succulent to rubber ball pretty quickly. Don't take your eyes off them when cooking to make sure that you remove them from the heat when they are still moist, juicy and plump. There are 3 types of scallops. Sea scallops-are relatively large and usually are served beautifully seared in groups of two or three. Bay scallops- are much smaller therefore are not ideal for searing but are wonderful in stir-fries and even cooked as scampi to be served in a light pasta sauce. Calico scallops- are harvested off of the US Gulf and Southern Atlantic coasts and are less sweet than their Northern cousins and are cooked the same way as bay scallops.

Give them Cajun-flavored crust by grilling them with Paprika and add a zesty flavor to them by serving them with delicious dill sauce.

Garlic grilled scallop are undeniably delicious and a well loved American food. Now they have become one of the most popular side dish around the world. Scallops so easy to make so savory in taste and are a part of a low carb diet. They are invariably served as an appetizer too.

Method

1. Preheat oven to 400° F (200° C).

2. Distribute scallops evenly inside a 2-quart oval casserole dish.

3. Combine the melted butter, orange juice, onion powder, garlic-powder, paprika, parsley and minced garlic in a small saucepan. Bring to a boil until reduced to a sauce consistency.

4. Coat the scallops in this mixture and then roll them in a mixture of breadcrumbs and Parmesan cheese.

5. Bake in pre-heated oven until scallops are firm, about 20 minutes.

6. Serve them with delicious dill sauce (recipe page 115). Serve them as a starter on a bed of lettuce or as a main entrée with rice and a simple vegetable.

7. Serves-4-6.

Pan Seared or Grilled Scallops

Ingredients

1-Lb Fresh or frozen sea scallops
2-Tbsp All-purpose flour
1 -2-tsp Cajun seasoning
3-Tbsp Butter, melted
¼-tsp Black pepper
1/8-tsp Paprika
2/3-Cup Mayonnaise
1-Tbsp Finely chopped onion
2-tsp Lemon juice
1 ½- tsp Snipped fresh dill-
    weed or ½- teaspoon dried
    dill-weed
Lemon Wedges (optional)

Dill Sauce

1 ½-Tbsp Shallots, chopped
1 ½-Tbsp Butter
2-Tbsp Flour
1-Cup Heavy cream
1 ¼- Cup Half and half
6- Drops Tabasco sauce
2 ½-Tbsp Freshly chopped dill
1/3-tsp Salt
¼-tsp Fresh ground white
    pepper

Method

1. Thaw scallops, if frozen. Rinse and pat dry with paper towels. Cut them in half any large scallops.

2. Mix flour with Cajun seasoning and toss the scallops in the mix.

3. Add 3- tablespoons of butter into the pan and cook them in the pan for 5-6 minutes until light brown and serve.

Or

4. Broil them by threading scallops onto four 8 to 10-inch skewers, leaving a ¼-inch space between pieces. Preheat broiler.

5. In a small bowl stir together butter, pepper, and paprika. Brush half of the mixture over the skewered scallops. Place skewers on the greased unheated rack of a broiler pan.

6. Broil about 4 inches from the heat for 8 to 10 minutes or until scallops are opaque, turning and brushing with the remaining melted butter mixture halfway through broiling.

7. Mix the mayonnaise with chopped onion, lemon juice and dried dill weed. Beat it smooth and serve with seared scallops. Serve as an appetizer on a bed of lettuce and serve the dill sauce with them.

8. Serves 4-6.

Dill Sauce

1. Sauté Shallots in 1 ½-tablespoon of butter in a medium size sauce- pan until transparent.

2. Move the onions to one side and add the flour and stir to cook till the flour is slightly brown.

3. Mix half and half and cream in a saucepan and simmer to just about boiling point.

4. Mix it into the cooked flour (roux). Stir the mixture and cook till slightly thickened.

5. Add the Tabasco sauce, dill, salt and black pepper and serve with the scallops.

Italian Specialties

Collosseum, Rome, Italy

Italian American specialties are the creation of Italian American immigrants and their descendents. As immigrants from different regions of Italy settled in different regions of the United States and became "Italian Americans," whatever diverse traditions of foods and recipes that they brought with them identifying them with their regional origins in Italy they eventually infused them with the characteristics of their new home locale in America. Many of these foods and recipes developed into new favorites for town peoples and then later for Americans nationwide, as, for example, the muffuletta sandwich from New Orleans or the "toasted ravioli" (actually breaded and deep-fried) from St Louis, Missouri. A measure of the widespread popularity of Italian American cuisine in the United States is in the Twin Cities Metropolitan Area of Minnesota.

Italian dishes are characterized by their extreme simplicity, with many dishes having only four to eight ingredients. Italian American cooks rely chiefly on the quality of the ingredients rather than on elaborate preparation. Dishes and recipes are often the creation of grandmothers rather than of chefs, which makes many recipes ideally suited for home cooking. As cooking magazines in America popularized Italian recipes targeted at the home cook, (that were once regional) these recipes proliferated with variations throughout the country eventually.

Italian cuisine is noted for its regional diversity, abundance of difference in taste, and is known to be one of the most popular in America and around the world. Cheese and wine are a major part of this cuisine, with many variations.

Dried Tomato Fettuccine

Ingredients

- 8-OZ. Dried fettuccine
- ½- Cup Dried tomatoes, chopped
- 4-Tbsp Butter
- 1-Tbsp Olive oil
- 2-Tbsp Chopped Onions
- 4- Oz Fresh asparagus spears, trimmed
- 4-Oz Fresh Brussels sprouts, quartered
- 1½- Cups Fresh broccoli florets
- 8- Fresh mushrooms, sliced
- 1-tsp Chopped garlic
- 1-tsp Chopped jalapeno or to taste
- 2-Tbsp All-Purpose flour
- 1 ¼- Cups Milk
- ½-Cup Finely shredded Parmesan cheese
- 2 tsp. Finely shredded lemon peel
- ¼--tsp Black pepper and Cayenne pepper /ea

Tomato Fettuccine is a ribbon shaped Pasta popular in Roman cuisine tossed with ragu (meat sauce) has a long history both in Italy and abroad. A popular fettuccine dish in North America is fettuccine alfredo. It was popularized amongst US tourists in Rome by restaurateur Alfredo di Lelio who served fettuccine pasta with a Parmesan cheese and butter with his own name attached as Fettuccine Alfredo. It got associated in every tourist's mind with Rome, possibly because the original Alfredo succeeded in serving it at a spectacle reminiscent of grand opera. Once it was adopted in US cuisine it is now being served with several other ingredients such as broccoli, parsley, cream, tomato, garlic, chicken and shrimp.

Whole-wheat fettuccine is a healthy and hearty pasta choice for a delicious dinner.

Method

1. Cook pasta according to directions adding half of the dried tomatoes in last 2 minutes of cooking. Drain and return to saucepan; keep warm.

2. In a large skillet heat 1 tablespoon of butter and olive oil over medium heat.

3. Add onions, asparagus, Brussels sprouts, broccoli, and mushrooms.

4. Cook over medium heat for 8 minutes or until vegetables are tender. Add the chopped garlic, green pepper or jalapeno and stir to mix.

5. Remove vegetables from skillet and set them aside.

6. In same skillet melt remaining butter over medium heat. Stir in flour. Cook and stir 1 minute. Stir in the milk. Cook and stir until thickened and bubbly.

7. Stir in Parmesan cheese. Gently stir in pasta and vegetables. Stir in additional milk to reach desired consistency.

8. Sprinkle with lemon peel and additional shredded Parmesan cheese and black pepper and Cayenne pepper, remaining chopped dried tomatoes and chopped parsley. Stir to mix and serve.

9. Makes 4 servings.

Classic Lasagna

Ingredients
- 1-Lb. Ground chuck
- 2-Tbsp Salad oil
- 1-Medium onion, finely minced
- 2-3 Cloves garlic, minced
- 1-(3 or 4 Oz.) Can sliced mushrooms with liquid
- 1-(16 Oz) Can tomato sauce
- 1-(6 Oz) Can tomato paste
- 1-Cup Water
- 2-tsp Salt
- ½-tsp red pepper
- 1-tsp Sugar
- 1-tsp Oregano
- 2 Eggs
- 1- (10 oz.) Package frozen chopped spinach thawed and drained
- 1-8 Oz package cottage cheese
- 1-Cup Grated Parmesan cheese
- 1- (8 Oz.) Mozzarella cheese shredded
- 1-8 Oz Package of lasagna noodles

St.Peters Basilica, Venice, Italy

Lasagna, one of the most celebrated of the Italian food staples, has a long and luxurious history. The term "lasagna" comes from the Greek word, "lasagnum," meaning dish or bowl. The ancient Greeks used baking dishes of that name, which they eventually transferred to the Romans. The Romans, who ended up using the same style of dish, also developed a type of food for which they used the term "lasagnum", and it was served in the said dish, with layers of a pasta-like food with different fillings in-between. With the expansion of the Roman Empire, this new "lasagnum" dish spread all across Europe, eventually reaching Britain, where it was published in the very first cookbook available.

The early Italians who migrated to America changed the name from "lasagnum," to "lasagna," which is the current form. Over the years, the word "lasagna" began to change definitions; the word previously referred to the serving dish it was baked in, but began to simply mean the delicious pasta meal in the dish itself. In modern cooking terms, it now means layers of long, flat, broad noodles that are ideally used as layering in a baking dish to make a sort of noodle pie with a layering of assortment of ingredients in between them like meats, cheeses, and tomato sauce. Most markets carry lasagna noodles, often in an assortment of flavors including spinach, whole wheat and plain, and making the baked noodle dish that has these noodles with meat, cheese, and tomato sauce squeezed in between. Lasagna sure has come a long way and has delightfully become a household "One meal Dish" of choice.

Method

1. Cook ground chuck in a frying pan until slightly brown and drain the fat. Set it aside. Add a tablespoon of oil in the same pan and fry the onion and garlic, blend in mushrooms, tomato sauce, tomato paste, water, one teaspoon salt, red pepper1-teaspoon sugar and 1-teaspoon oregano and the cooked meat. Simmer 15 minutes. Meat sauce is ready.

2. Meanwhile mix 1 egg with spinach, and half of the cottage cheese and ½ of the Parmesan and Mozzarella in remaining 1-tablespoon oil and 1-teaspoon salt. Now mix the remaining cheeses and set them aside.

3. Cook the lasagna noodles according to directions. Beat second egg slightly and toss with cooked noodles.

4. Spread I cup of meat sauce at the bottom of the pan and cover the sauce with the noodles, add the meat sauce and then the spinach-cheese mixture over meat sauce.

5. Add another layer of noodles, meat sauce and ½ of the remaining cheeses mixture and again top with lasagna noodles meat sauce and remaining cheese mixture.

6. Bake 45 minutes in 350° F oven until the cheeses melt and sauce is bubbly. Remove from the oven and serve.

7. Makes 8 Servings.

Vegetarian Lasagna

Ingredients
1-Egg
1-10 Oz Package of frozen and
    thawed Spinach
1-tsp Salt
½- tsp Pepper
2-Tbsp Vegetable oil
½-Cup Chopped onions
1-Tbsp Chopped green chilies
1-tsp minced garlic and ginger/ea
1-tsp Salt
½-tsp red pepper
½-Pkg 8 oz lasagna
4 to 5 Cups Spaghetti sauce
1-Lb Ricotta cheese
8-OZ Mozzarella cheese,
    shredded or thinly sliced
1-Cup Grated Parmesan cheese

Method
1. Beat the egg and mix with the thawed spinach, salt and pepper.

2. Heat 2- tablespoons of oil in a pan and add the onions and chili peppers ginger and garlic. Cook for 3-4 minutes and add the spinach mixture. Add salt and pepper. Stir and cook on medium low heat for 15 minutes and set aside.

3. In 13x9x2" baking pan, spread about 1 cup spaghetti sauce.

4. Mix the 3 cheeses together and set them aside.

5. Arrange a layer of uncooked lasagna; top with one cup of spaghetti sauce, 1/3- of spinach mixture, 1/3-mixture (ricotta, mozzarella, parmesan) cheeses and sauce again. Repeat, gently pressing lasagna pieces into cheese mixture. End with a final layer of lasagna.

6. Pour remaining sauce over the top layer of lasagna, making sure all lasagna pieces are covered with sauce; top with remaining mozzarella and parmesan. Bake at 350°F for 45 to 55 minutes until lightly browned and bubbling.

7. Allow it to stand 15 minutes; cut in squares to serve.

8. Makes 6 to 8 servings.

Tortellini Bolognese

Ingredients

4- Tbsp Olive oil
2-Onions, finely chopped
4-Garlic cloves, finely chopped
2-Carrots, finely chopped
2-Celery stalks, finely chopped
1-Lb Ground beef
12- Oz Italian sausage, skinned
2-Cups Red wine
36-Oz Can Crushed tomatoes,
    chopped
1- Dried Bay leaf
2- tsp Fresh rosemary, chopped/
    (½ tsp dry)
2- tsp Fresh sage, chopped /
    (½ tsp dry)
Salt to taste
Pepper to taste
1-Cup Heavy cream
4-Lb Tortellini cooked and
    drained
Parmesan cheese, freshly grated

This pasta is originally from the Italian region of Emilia in Italy (in particular Bologna and Modena). Tortellini is now popular all around America and the world. Packed, refrigerated or frozen, tortellini and tortellino (similar but larger and with vegetable stuffing) appear in many locations around the world, especially where there are large Italian communities.

Tortellini is a ring-shaped pasta, sometimes described as "navel shaped" with their alternative name as "belly button". The"tortellino" is quite rightly the symbol of Bologna's cuisine, because it combines the inimitable flagrance of rolled pasta with the flavor of a rich filling: all the specialties of Bologna's cuisine are captured in a single mouthful. They are typically stuffed with a mix of meat (pork loin, prosciutto) or ricotta, Parmesan and spinach. They are usually served in broth, either of beef, chicken, or both. The origin of Tortellini is connected with a legend from medieval Italy and it tells how Venus and Jupiter arrived at a tavern on the outskirt of Bologna one night, weary from their involvement in a battle between Modena and Bologna. After much food and drink, they shared a room. The innkeeper, captivated by the two, followed them and peeked through the keyhole. All he could see was Venus's navel he rushed to the kitchen and created tortellini in its image.

Method

1. Heat oil in a large pan. Add, onion, garlic and cook about 5 minutes.

2. Add celery and carrots. Cook for 2 more minutes stirring well. Set it aside in a bowl.

3. Lower the heat and transfer the ground meat, sausage and cook 10 minutes over medium heat, stirring occasionally. Drain the fat. Add the sautéed vegetables.

4. Deglaze pan with wine and let it reduce. Add tomatoes , the bay leaf and the remaining ingredients- fresh rosemary, sage, salt and pepper and stir. Simmer for about 1 hour. Add the cream and mix it well.

5. Toss hot, drained tortellini pasta in sauce. Top with Parmesan cheese. Serve immediately.

6. Serves 6-8

> **Note:** Tortellini pasta is delicious as a salad or as a main dish with vegetables called tortellini primavera.

Tortellini Alla Panna

Ingredients

4 -Tbsp unsalted butter

1½ -Cups Heavy cream

¼-Cup Tomato sauce

1-Lb Meat filled tortellini

2-Tbsp Olive oil

2-Cloves garlic grated

2-Freshly chopped green
   medium hot chili peppers

Salt and pepper to taste

¾- Cup Freshly grated
   Parmagiano-Reggiano cheese

You would be hard-pressed to find a more perfect pairing than meat-filled tortellini in a rich cream sauce. This dish is a specialty of the Emilia-Romagna region of Italy.

Method

1. Melt the butter in a large sauté pan, turn the heat on to medium and add the cream, tomato sauce, salt and pepper. Bring to a simmer and cook until slightly thickened, about 1 minute. Take off the heat and set it aside.

2. Bring a large pot of salted water to a boil and add the tortellini. Cook until the tortellini is slightly underdone, 3-5 minutes. Drain well.

3. Heat 2 Tablespoon of olive oil and add the grated garlic, green chilies, salt and pepper and toss the pasta into it.

4. Place the saucepan with butter, tomato sauce and cream back over medium heat. Add the tossed tortellini and Parmagiano-Reggiano cheese and stir gently until cheese is melted and tortellini are well coated with the sauce.

5. Transfer to warm pasta bowls and serve with your favorite vegetable and bread of your choice.

6. Serves 2-4.

Gnocchi

Ingredients

Potato Gnocchi

- 3- Large Russet potatoes
- 2-Cups All-purpose flour
- ½- Cup vegetable oil
- 1- Egg, extra large
- 1-Pinch Salt

Cheese Gnocchi

- 18 Oz. Container Ricotta cheese
- 2- Eggs
- ½- Cup Freshly grated Parmesan cheese
- 1-Salt
- 1-tsp Pepper
- 1-tsp Garlic powder
- 1-Cup All-purpose flour, or as needed

Sauce

- 4- Tbsp Olive oil/ ¼- Cup butter
- 1-Medium Onion chopped
- 2-Garlic cloves, peeled and chopped
- 1-Carrot Chopped
- 2- 15-Oz Cans tomato sauce
- 1-tsp Oregano powder
- 1-tsp Dry basil
- Salt
- 1-tsp Sugar
- ½-tsp Red pepper flakes
- ½- Cup Red wine
- 2-Oz Goat cheese

Gnocchi are soft dumplings. They may be made from semolina, ordinary wheat flour, eggs and cheese, potato, breadcrumbs, or similar ingredients. Gnocchi's are eaten as a first course (primi piatti), alternatives to soups (minestre) or pasta. They are generally homemade in Italian households. They may also be bought fresh from specialty stores and supermarkets. Industrially produced packaged gnocchi are widely available as refrigerated, dried, or frozen.

Common accompaniments of gnocchi include tomato sauces, pesto, and melted butter (sometimes fried butter) with cheese.

The word gnocchi is derived from the Italian word nocchio, meaning a knot in wood, or from nocca (meaning knuckle). It has been a traditional type of Italian pasta of Middle Eastern origin since Roman times. It was introduced by the Roman legions during the enormous expansion of the empire into the countries of the European continent and then to America. In the past 2,000 years, each country developed its own specific type of small dumplings, with the ancient gnocchi as their common ancestor. In Roman times, gnocchi were made from semolina and porridge-like dough mixed with eggs, and are still found in similar forms today, particularly the oven-baked "gnocchi alla romana" and "Sardinia's malloreddus"(although these do not contain eggs) are their true representations. The use of potato is a relatively recent innovation, occurring after the introduction of the potato to Europe in the 16th century.

Trevi Fountains, Rome, Italy

Method

Potato Gnocchi

1. Bring a large pot of salted water to a boil. Peel potatoes and add to the pot. Cook until tender but still firm, about 15 minutes. Drain, cool and mash with a fork or potato masher.

2. Combine 1 cup mashed potato, flour, oil salt and egg in a large bowl. Knead (gently and do not make the dough very dense but keep it fluffy) until dough forms a ball. Shape small portions of the dough into long "snakes". On a floured surface cut snakes into half-inch pieces. Refrigerate until ready to use.

Ricotta Cheese Gnocchi

1. Stir together the ricotta cheese, eggs, Parmesan cheese, salt, pepper, and garlic powder in a large bowl until evenly combined. Mix in 1 cup of flour. Add additional flour if needed to form a soft dough.

2. Divide the dough into 3 or 4 pieces, and roll each piece into ½-inch-thick ropes on a floured surface. Cut each rope into 1-inch pieces, and place on a lightly floured baking sheet. Place in the refrigerator until ready to use.

Sauce

1. Heat oil in a saucepan on medium heat. Add the onions and cook until transparent and the add garlic cloves, chopped carrots and cook for 2 minutes. Add the tomato sauce, oregano, basil, salt, sugar and pepper flakes and wine.

2. As soon as the mixture boils reduce the heat to low and let it simmer, uncovered for 25 to 30 minutes until the carrots are soft.

3. Once the sauce reduces to a medium thick consistency, add the goat cheese, stirring until it is well blended. Add more salt to taste. Sauce is ready.

4. Just before serving boil salted water and drop in Gnocchi and cook 3-5 minutes or until they rise to the top of water. Drain and serve with tomato sauce or meat sauce and extra grated Parmesan cheese

5. Serves 4-6.

Note: For meat sauce -as soon as the carrots are soft and the sauce is ready add the lightly browned meats (½ lb ground turkey and ½ lb ground pork) along with a cup of red wine and 1 cup of chicken broth and let it simmer and cook for another 45 minutes. Serve either kind of Gnocchi with plain tomato sauce or the meat sauce.

Gorgonzola Pasta Primavera

Ingredients

- ¼-Cup Olive oil
- 1-Onion, thinly sliced
- 1-Lb Broccoli cut into florets
- 3- Carrots, peeled and cut into thin strips
- 2- Medium zucchini, cut into thin strips
- 2- Red bell pepper sliced in ¼ -inch cubes
- ¼- Lb Cremini mushrooms thinly sliced
- 1-Bell pepper (any color) cut into thin strips
- Kosher salt and freshly ground black pepper and red pepper to taste
- ½-tsp Roasted cumin powder (optional)
- Several Cloves of garlic
- 1-Tbsp Dried Italian herbs
- 1-Lb Penne pasta
- ¼-Cup Tomato sauce
- ½-Cup Heavy cream
- 15-Cherry Tomatoes, halved
- 3-Oz Gorgonzola cheese
- ½- Cup Grated Parmesan
- 2-Tbsp Basil leaves chopped for Garnish.
- ½-tsp Garammasala

Pasta primavera is an Italian American dish that consists of pasta and fresh vegetables. Meat such as chicken, sausage or shrimp is sometimes added, but the focus of primavera is the vegetables themselves. The dish may contain almost any kind of vegetable, but cooks tend to stick to firm, crisp vegetables, such as broccoli, carrots, peas, onions and green bell peppers with tomatoes. Pasta primavera is usually highlighted by light flavors, aromatic herbs and bright colors ('primavera' meaning the season of spring). Classic primavera sauce is based on a soffritto (to brown or fry) of garlic and olive oil, and finished with Parmesan cheese. However other versions with a heavier cream or Alfredo sauce are also common. There are recipes for cold pasta primavera but they are best classified as antipasti, or appetizers. Pastas served with this dish are typically smaller shapes, such as penne, farfalle, rigatoni and fuslli. If using longer types of pasta, such as spaghetti or fettuccine, the vegetables are normally sliced in thin strips to match the shape of the noodles.

Since primavera means spring, the vegetable choices should be the crisp new vegetables of spring.

Method

1. In a large heavy bottom saucepan heat the oil and add the onions and fry till it is transparent. Toss all of the vegetables, salt, pepper, roasted cumin powder, cloves of garlic and dried herbs. Stir well and cook for about 10 minutes on medium high heat while stirring until slightly brown but still firm. Set the vegetables aside.

2. Meanwhile, cook the pasta according to the directions and keep one cup of pasta water.

3. Toss the pasta with the vegetable mixtures in a large bowl to combine. Toss with the tomato sauce, heavy cream and cherry tomatoes.

4. Add all but 1-tablespoon of Gorgonzola and Parmesan and mix.

5. Season the pasta with more salt and peppers and cumin powder. Add some pasta water if the sauce is too thick.

6. Sprinkle with the remaining Gorgonzola, Parmesan, garammasala and basil leaves and serve immediately.

7. Serves 4-6.

Spinach Carbonara

Ingredients

- ½- Lb Slab pancetta or Guanciale, cut into ½-inch chunks
- 2-Tbsp Butter
- 1-Small Onion chopped
- 1-Tbsp Chopped garlic
- 2-Tbsp Dry white wine
- 1-14 Oz. Can Tomatoes chopped
- 2-Cups Baby spinach leaves
- ¼-tsp Red pepper
- 1-Lb Fresh or Dried spinach fettuccine Pasta
- 1- Large egg plus 2 Large egg yolks, at room temperature
- 1-Cup Grated Parmigiano-Reggiano, plus more for garnish
- 2-tsp Freshly cracked black pepper
- 2-Tbsp Freshly chopped parsley

As the name is derived from carbonaro (the Italian word for charcoal burner), some believe the dish was first made as a hearty meal for Italian charcoal workers.

Carbonara is an Italian pasta (mostly spaghetti, but also fettuccini, rigatoni) dish based on eggs; cheese (Romano or Parmigianino Reggiano) mostly guanciale (un smoked bacon) and black pepper. The pork is fried in fat (olive oil) then hot pasta is dropped into the pan to finish cooking for a few seconds. A mixture of raw eggs, cheese, and a fat (butter, olive oil, or cream) is then combined with the hot pasta away from additional direct heat to avoid coagulating the egg, which must remain a liquid component of the sauce as it cooks. Guanciale is the most commonly used meat. American versions use other cured meats, such as pancetta and local bacon and also add cream sometimes. The dish was created in the middle of the 20th century. Other variations on carbonara outside Italy may include peas, broccoli, mushrooms, or other vegetables. It is possible that carbonara was invented after WW 11 as a result of an influx of eggs and bacon from (American) allied soldiers supporting Italy.

Method

1. Put the bacon in a large high-sided skillet and cook over medium-high heat until crisp, about 10 minutes. Remove from the heat and drain the bacon fat and remove the bacon from the skillet and set it aside.

2. Add 2-tablespoons of butter to the same pan and add chopped onion and garlic and fry

till transparent. Add the wine and cook till the liquid is almost gone. Add the tomatoes, spinach, and red pepper and cook till the tomatoes soften up.

3. Bring a large pot of water with salt to a boil over medium heat. Cook the pasta according to package directions.

4. Drain the pasta but reserve the pasta water. Add the pasta to the skillet. Add also the reserved bacon.

5. Meanwhile, whisk the egg and yolks, 1-cup cheese and pepper together in a small bowl. Using a ladle, slowly whisk about ½- cup of pasta cooking water into the egg and cheese mixture until loosened. Save the additional pasta water.

6. While tossing continually, slowly drizzle the egg mixture over the pasta until it is completely coated. Add more cooking water if pasta seems dry.

7. Transfer the Carbonara to a serving bowl and serve immediately with more cheese sprinkled over the top. Sprinkle the freshly chopped parsley and serve.

8. Serves -6

Note: The key to perfect carbonara is keep cooking the pasta sauce while everything is piping hot; this assures the egg will cook and produce a silky, creamy sauce that sticks to the pasta and does not coagulate.

Broccoli and Chick Peas Rigatoni

Ingredients

- 1- 19-Oz Can chickpeas, drained and rinsed
- 1/3-Cup Fresh lemon juice
- ¾- Cup Extra-virgin olive oil
- Kosher salt and freshly ground pepper
- 1 ½-Lbs Broccoli, cut into florets
- 1-Lb Rigatoni
- ¼- Cup Chopped onions
- 1-Tbsp Chopped garlic
- 1-Tbsp Chopped green chilies
- 1-Cup Chopped tomatoes/ 1-Cup tomato sauce
- ½- tsp Red pepper
- 1-Cup Freshly grated Parmesan cheese
- ½- tsp Garammasla

Rigatoni is a form of tube-shaped pasta of varying lengths and diameters and is used in dishes with lots of sauce and vegetables. It is larger than Penne and Ziti and sometimes slightly curved. The word Rigatoni comes from the Italian word rigati, which means "ridged" and the tube's end are square-cut like Ziti, not diagonal like Penne and it is also commonly used to make baked pasta dishes such as Ziti and pasta salad. Besides "spaghetti alla carbonara" Rigatoni alla gricia, is a dish you will always find in Roman restaurants. It is also a forefather of the more famous recipe "Amatriciana" and is made with guanciale, pecorino Romano cheese and black pepper. The Rigatoni pasta is associated with the cuisine of southern and central Italy. Rigatoni alla Norma is the epitome of Sicilian cooking for many. The interesting mix of flavors, and, of course, the eggplant makes this dish from Catania, an eastern city in Sicily, a favorite dish for locals, visitors, and of course vegetarians. There are many versions of Rigatoni pasta dishes. Here is an American version of Rigatoni with chickpeas, broccoli, tomatoes and onions.

Method

1. In a medium bowl, toss the chickpeas with the lemon juice and ½- cup of the olive oil. Season with salt and pepper as if marinating the chickpeas.

2. In a large pot of boiling salted water, cook the broccoli until crisp-tender, about 4 minutes. Using a slotted spoon, transfer the broccoli to a colander and rinse under cold water until cool. Add the rigatoni to the boiling water and cook until al- dente.

3. Meanwhile, in a large deep skillet, heat the remaining ¼- cup of olive oil. Add the onions, green chilies, and garlic and cook over moderate heat, about 3 minutes and add the chopped tomatoes and red pepper. Add the broccoli and cook until tender, about 5 minutes. Add the marinated chickpea and cook until warmed through, about 2 minute.

4. Drain the Rigatoni, reserving ¼- cup of the cooking water. Add the pasta to the broccoli and chickpeas along with the reserved cooking water and season with salt and pepper.

5. Cook over moderate heat, stirring until the rigatoni is coated with sauce. Remove from the heat and stir in ½- cup of the Parmesan cheese.

6. Transfer the pasta to a bowl, sprinkle with the remaining Parmesan and serve.

7. Serves 6-8.

Ciceri e Tria

Ingredients

For the Chickpeas

1-Lb Tagliatelle pasta/Fresh semolina pasta

1¼-Cup Extra virgin olive oil

1-Lb Can Cooked chickpeas, washed and drained or uncooked chickpeas

1-Medium-sized white onion, peeled chopped

1-Tbsp Chopped ginger

1-Tbsp Jalapeno pepper chopped

Couple Bay leaves

4-Cloves garlic

1-Small celery chopped

1-Small carrot chopped

1-Leek green part only

8-OZ. Can Chopped tomatoes/2 medium size fresh tomatoes chopped

1-tsp Cumin powder

Salt to taste

Cayenne pepper to taste

½-tsp Dry rosemary

½-Cup White wine

Cold water enough to cook the Chick peas

Black pepper/Garammasala to sprinkle

¼- Cup Chopped cilantro or parsley

Ciceri means chickpeas. Tria (means tagliatelle a traditional pasta) is pasta in the dialect of Puglia (southern region of Italy). Combined it means chickpeas and pasta –a distinctive dish and most beloved dish of Salento Italy. It's a brothy pasta dish, with the addition of chickpeas. A third of the pasta used is fried, the rest boiled directly into the broth. Its brothiness varies and sometimes you'll be given a spoon with it, sometimes you won't. Cheese is always absent. The addition of the fried pasta was meant to mimic the texture of meat, back when it was scarce. It is classic and emblematic dish of Salentine cuisine. It's a country dish, infused with ancient flavors, and it represents a classically balanced Mediterranean marriage of proteins and carbohydrates. The spark of genius in this dish is that part of the pasta is fried so that you get a lovely crunchiness alongside the smooth textured chickpeas and the chewy durum wheat pasta. Ciceri e Tria gave those eating it the impression of biting into delicious pieces of fried bacon mixed in with the pasta and chickpeas. It was served in the center of the table and everybody would often gather around this single bowl of pasta. The dish also announces its presence with an inebriating aroma, which becomes an integral part of the entree itself. This recipe has a striking resemblance to an East Indian dish "Chick pea curry" but it is served usually as a side dish with either rice or bread.

Method

1. Cook ½ the pasta according to the package direction but give 2 minutes less for cooking. Drain and set it aside.

2. In a frying pan, heat a cup of extra-virgin olive oil together with one clove of garlic. Break half of the cooked pasta in pieces in the garlic-infused olive oil and fry until slightly brown and crisp and transfer to a plate covered with a paper towel to drain the excess oil, and reserve.

3. Rinse the chickpeas and place them in a bowl. If using uncooked chickpeas then soak in a tablespoon of baking soda overnight, wash the next morning and cook with one teaspoon of salt until tender. On a regular heat it may take 1-2 hrs of pressure-cooking for soaked uncooked chickpeas.

4. Heat ¼ cup of remaining oil in an earthenware cooking pot and add the onions, ginger, green chili and bay leaf and fry till the onion is transparent. Add the remaining garlic, celery, carrots, leek, tomatoes, cumin powder, salt, red pepper and dried rosemary and stir to cook on medium heat for few minutes. Add the canned, drained and washed or cooked chickpeas. Add the wine and stir till it is fully absorbed. Add cold water to cover generously. Cook over medium heat until the chickpeas become very tender. Add more water if needed.

5. Add the cooked half of the pasta to the chickpeas and cook until al dente.

6. Serve hot, drizzled generously with olive oil and sprinkled with black pepper, garammasala and cilantro or parsley. Top it with the reserved fried pasta. Place it in the center of the table and let everyone help them selves.

7. Serves 4.

Risotto

Ingredients

1-Qt Chicken stock
Pinch of saffron
1- Tbsp Olive oil
3- Tbsp Unsalted butter
½- Small onion, chopped
1-Tbsp Chopped green chili
    (optional)
2-Cloves garlic minced
1½- Cups Arborio rice
½- Cup White wine
¼- Cup Grated Parmesan
    cheese
1-Tbsp Chopped Italian parsley
Kosher salt, black pepper or
    red pepper to taste

A classic Italian rice dish, Risotto is traditionally prepared with a variety of starchy, short-grained rice called arborio rice. Such a variety of rice has the ability to absorb liquids and to release starch therefore they are stickier than the long grain varieties. The simple risotto recipe is made with butter and Parmesan cheese. The broth may be meat- fish-or vegetable-based. It is one of the most common ways of cooking rice in Italy. Risotto can be made using many kinds of vegetables, meat, fish, seafood and legumes, and different types of wine and cheese. "Risotto alla Milanese" made with beef stock, beef bone marrow, lard (instead of butter) and cheese, flavored and colored with saffron is an outstanding dish. Black risotto (risotto al nero di seppia) made with cuttlefish cooked with their ink sacs intact, is a specialty of the Veneto region. There are many more varieties. There is a typical Italian strawberry risotto that is quite famous. Outside Italy, dishes made in a similar way are true to risotto but with different grains or cereals and are called"farro (A variety of wheat) risotto", "barley risotto", etc. The procedure for making Risotto involves stirring hot stock into the uncooked rice a ladleful at a time and cooking slowly as the stock is absorbed. This technique, known as the risotto method, releases the Arborio's starches, making it a creamy, velvety dish. Risotto is normally a primo (first course), served on its own before the main course.

Method

1. Heat the stock with a pinch of saffron to a simmer in a medium saucepan and let it simmer on low heat to keep it warm.

2. In a large, heavy-bottomed saucepan, heat the oil and 1-tablespoon butter over medium heat. Add the chopped shallot or onion, chili and minced garlic. Sauté until it is slightly translucent.

3. Add the rice to the pot and stir it briskly with a wooden spoon, until there is a slightly nutty aroma. But don't let the rice turn brown.

4. Add the wine and cook while stirring, until the liquid is fully absorbed.

5. Add a ladle of hot chicken stock to the rice and stir until the liquid is fully absorbed. Keep repeating the process.
   Note: It's important to stir constantly, Continue adding ladles of hot stock and stirring the rice while the liquid is absorbed. As it cooks, you'll see that the rice will take on a creamy consistency as it begins to release its natural starches.

6. Continue adding stock, a ladle at a time, for 20-30 minutes or until the grains are tender but still firm to the bite, without being crunchy. If you run out of stock and the risotto still isn't done, you can finish the cooking using hot water. Just add the water as you did with the stock, a ladle at a time, stirring while it's absorbed.

7. Stir in the remaining 2-tablespoon butter, the Parmesan cheese and the parsley, and season to taste with kosher salt, black pepper or red pepper.

8. Risotto turns glutinous if held for too long and should be served right away. A properly cooked risotto should form a soft, creamy mound on a dinner plate. It shouldn't run across the plate, nor should it be stiff or gluey. Serve it with butter and cheese or with a hearty salad and some vegetable side dish. Usually it is served on its own if it has seafood or any other meat in it.

9. Makes 6-8 servings

> **Note: There are many variations: Fold in oven roasted pieces of pumpkin and asparagus in last 10 minutes of cooking. You can also add chopped mushrooms frozen peas, and fry them with onions in step 2 and then add the rice. Any grilled meat or vegetables like sliced egg plants can be folded into the risotto before serving and top the risotto with crumbled up Feta cheese.**

Pizza Margherita

Ingredients

- ¼- Cup Olive oil
- 1-Tbsp Minced garlic
- ½-tsp Sea salt
- 8- Roma tomatoes, sliced
- 8-Slices onion (optional)
- 2- (12 inch) Pre-baked pizza crusts
- 8-OZ Shredded mozzarella cheese
- 4-Oz Shredded fontina cheese
- 10- Fresh basil leaves, washed, dried
- ½- Cup Freshly grated Parmesan cheese
- ½- Cup Crumbled feta cheese

Twenty eight years after the unification of Italy, when Queen Margherita of Savoy, wife of King Umberto I, visited Naples, chef Raffaele Esposito of Pizzeria Brandi and his wife created a pizza resembling the colors of the Italian flag, red (tomato), white (mozzarella) and green (basil). The queen liked the pizza so much that the chef named the Pizza after her- Pizza Margherita. This pizza set such a standard from which today's pizza has evolved. It also firmly established Naples as the pizza capitol of the world. Since then this pizza not only became favorite in Italy but in America and everywhere else. Pizza Margherita is made with tomato, sliced mozzarella, basil and extra-virgin olive oil.

Pizza Margherita

Method

1. Stir together olive oil, garlic, and salt and set it aside. This is the marinade.

2. Toss the tomatoes and onion in it and set them aside.

3. Preheat oven to 400° F (200° C). Brush each pizza crust with some of the marinade.

4. Sprinkle the pizzas evenly with Mozzarella and Fontina cheeses.

5. Arrange tomatoes over top and then sprinkle with shredded basil, Parmesan, and then feta cheese.

6. Bake in preheated oven until the cheese is bubbly and golden brown, about 10 minutes and Serve.

7. Serves 4-6

Cioppino: Sea Food Salad

Ingredients

- ¾- Cup Butter
- 2- Onions, chopped
- 1-Small fennel bulb, thinly sliced
- 2-Cloves garlic, minced
- 2- (14.5 Oz) Cans Stewed tomatoes
- 2- (14.5 Oz) Cans Chicken broth/Fish broth
- 2- Bay leaves
- 1-Tbsp Dried basil
- ½- tsp Dried thyme
- ½ tsp Red pepper
- ½-tsp Dried oregano
- 1- Cup Water
- 1 ½- Cups White wine
- 1 ½-Lb Large shrimp - peeled and deveined
- 1 ½-Lbs Bay scallops, washed and cleaned
- 18- Small clams, scrubbed
- 18- Mussels, cleaned and debearded
- 1 ½- Cups Crabmeat
- 1 ½- Lb Cod fillets cut into 2 inch pieces
- 1- Bunch Fresh parsley, chopped
- Lemon juice and salt and black pepper and red pepper to garnish

Cioppino is a fish stew that originated in San Francisco in the mid 1800's. Supposedly developed by the Portuguese and Italian fishermen and it is related to various regional fish soups and stews of Italian cuisine. There are two versions of where the name "Ciopinno" came from. Most believe it's based on an Italian soup called "ciuppin." The 2nd version is a an apocryphal story in which it is suggested that the name derived from the heavily Italian-accented cry of the wharf cooks to all the fishermen on the beaches of San Francisco to "chip in" some of their catch to the collective soup pot.

Dungeness crab, clams, shrimp, scallops, mussels and fish are combined together to create cioppiano. This mixture is then combined with fresh tomatoes in a wine sauce, and served with toasted bread, either sourdough or baguette. The trick is using the highest quality seafood like very fresh fish and shellfish. Since it is typically served with the shellfish still in their shells, serving this soup sometimes is a messy affair and requires special utensils, typically a crab fork and cracker and lots of napkins.

Method

1. Over medium-low heat melt butter in a large Stockpot; add onions, fennel and parsley. Cook slowly, stirring occasionally until onions are soft.

2. Add the garlic. Add tomatoes to the pot (break them into chunks as you add them). Add chicken broth, bay leaves, basil, thyme, red pepper, oregano, water and wine.

3. Mix well. Cover and simmer 30 minutes. Stir in the shrimp, scallops, clams, mussels and crabmeat. Stir in fish, if desired. Bring to a boil.

4. Lower heat, cover and simmer 5 to 7 minutes until clams open. Sprinkle with chopped up parsley and some lemon juice. Ladle soup into bowls and serve.

5. Season with salt, black pepper and red pepper if you wish and serve with warm crusty baguette bread or any bread of your choice.

6. Serves 10-12.

Chicken and Veal Ptarmigiana

Ingredients

6- Veal cutlets/chicken breast cutlets

3- Eggs, beaten

Salt, Pepper and basil to taste

¾- Cup Breadcrumbs

½- Cup Parmesan cheese, grated

Olive oil as needed

1-Cup (or more) Spaghetti sauce

Mozzarella cheese as needed

Veal Ptarmigiana or chicken Ptarmigiana is prepared by dipping veal cutlets or chicken breast pieces in a mixture of beaten eggs. They are then breaded and shallow-fried and topped with a marinara sauce (red Sicilian tomato sauce) and mozzarella. It is then usually baked until the cheese is bubbly and brown. The veal dish is known in Italian as "Cotolette alla Bolognese". In the United States and Canada, veal ptarmigiana or chicken ptarmigiana is commonly served as a grinder or a submarine sandwich. It is also popular with a side of or on top of pasta. Sautéed or raw Diced onions or green bell peppers are sometimes added to it. Chicken or veal ptarmigiana is a common dish in both countries Australia and Argentina but with a different name and often served with a side dish of french-fries or mashed potatoes and salad. With its liberal use of aubergines and tomatoes, this is most likely an ancient Sicilian dish.

Method

1. Pound the chicken or veal cutlets until thin.
2. Dip them in the beaten egg seasoned with salt, pepper and basil, then in a mixture of the breadcrumbs and half of the Parmesan cheese.
3. Sauté the cutlets in hot olive oil until they are golden brown. Place in a shallow baking pan.
4. Pour the spaghetti sauce over it and top with thin slices of Mozzarella cheese and sprinkle with remaining Parmesan cheese mixture.
5. Bake in a moderate oven for about 15 minutes or until the cheese melts and just begins to brown.
6. Serve them in a sandwich bun with French fries or mashed potatoes or with pasta, topped with marinara sauce. Makes a great meal.
7. Serves 4-6.

Italian American Wedding Soup

Ingredients

Meatballs
- ¾- Lb Ground turkey
- ½- lb Ground chicken
- 2/3-Cup Fresh white bread crumbs
- 2- tsp Minced garlic
- ¼- Cup Chopped fresh Italian parsley
- ½- Cup Freshly grated Parmesan cheese
- 3- Tbsp Milk
- 1-Large Egg, lightly beaten
- 1-tsp Salt
- ½- tsp Red pepper
- 2- Tbsp Finely chopped onions
- ¼- tsp Oregano

Soup
- 2- Tbsp Olive oil
- 1-Cup Minced yellow onion
- 1-Cup Diced carrots (about 3 medium)
- 1-Cup Diced celery (about 2 large stalks)
- 8- Cups Chicken broth
- ½- Cup Dry white wine
- 1-Cup Orzo pasta
- ¼- Cup Minced fresh dill
- 8-Oz Fresh baby spinach chopped
- Lemon juice to taste
- Parmesan cheese, for serving

Vatican City, Italy

Italian American Soup consists of green vegetables and meat. It is a popular soup in the United States, and is a staple in many Italian restaurants. The modern wedding soup is quite a bit lighter than the Old Spanish version that contained more meats than just the meatballs. The soup has green vegetables like endive and escarole or cabbage, lettuce, kale and /or spinach and meats like meatballs and/or sausage in a clear chicken based broth. This soup sometimes contains cavatelli (small pasta shells like hotdog buns) acini de pepe (pasta shaped like peppercorns) and many different kinds of pasta shells, lentils, or shredded chicken.

Method

1. Preheat oven to 350° F.

Prepare meatballs

2. Place ground meats, bread crumbs, garlic, parsley, Parmesan, milk, egg, one teaspoon salt and ½- teaspoon pepper, onion and oregano in a bowl and combine gently with a fork.

3. With a teaspoon, drop 1-inch meatballs onto a nonstick baking sheet. Bake for 30 minutes, until cooked through and lightly browned. Set aside.

4. Heat olive oil over medium-low heat in a large stockpot. Add onion, carrots, celery and sauté until softened (5 to 6 minutes) stirring occasionally.

5. Add the chicken broth and wine and bring to a boil.

6. Add pasta to the simmering broth and cook an additional 6 to 8 minutes, until the pasta is tender. Add the fresh dill and then the meatballs to the soup and simmer for 1 minute.

7. Taste for salt and pepper. Stir in spinach and cook for few minutes, until spinach is wilted and looks cooked. Ladle into soup bowls and sprinkle each serving with lemon juice to taste and extra grated Parmesan cheese.

8. Serves 6-8.

Linguini with Clam Sauce

Ingredients

1-16 Oz. Package linguine pasta

½- Cup Butter

¼- Cup Olive oil

1-6.5 oz Can Minced Clams

½-Cup Chopped white onions

2-6.5Oz, Cans Chopped clams, drained with juice reserved

1-Tbsp Chopped garlic

1-8 Oz Bottle clam juice

½ Cup White wine

1- Tbsp Cornstarch, or as needed

2-8 Oz Cans Mushroom pieces, drained

2- Zucchini, grated

Cayenne pepper to taste

Salt to taste

½- Bunch parsley/ cilantro chopped

¼- Cup Grated Parmesan cheese

¼-tsp Garammasala (optional)

This is a classic Italian American dish and it is a dish that is very popular in Italy also during the summer. Linguria, where linguine originated, is on the coast of Italy and its pairing with seafood seems very natural. Wider than spaghetti and flat like fettuccine, this pasta is long, narrow, thinner and flatter and cooks a lot faster. It is often served with seafood and cream-based sauces or pesto sauces. One of the most popular and classic linguine dishes is "linguine alle vongole" which is Italian for "linguine with clams." This dish is made with cooked linguine, clams, olive oil, butter, garlic, white wine and fresh Italian parsley. This is a super fast and easy recipe. Fettuccine can also be used. Tastes even better if you use fresh clams and serve it with fresh baked rolls or French bread and a garden salad.

Method

1. Cook the linguine pasta according to package directions but keep the pasta firm. Drain; return to the pot to keep warm.

2. Meanwhile, melt the butter with olive oil in a large skillet over medium heat. Add minced clams, chopped onions and chopped clams and stir the garlic. Cook for 5 minutes. Add 4 oz of the clam juice and wine and cook for a few more minutes.

3. In a separate bowl, whisk the cornstarch with remaining bottled clam juice. Stir the cornstarch mixture into the clam sauce in the skillet. Pour the remaining bottled clam juice into the skillet and mix well.

4. Stir in the mushroom pieces, grated zucchini, cayenne pepper, and salt. Cook over medium heat, stirring occasionally, until zucchini is tender, about 5 minutes. Stir in the parsley; remove from heat. Pour the clam sauce over the drained linguine. Mix and sprinkle the Parmesan cheese and garammasala on the top and serve.

5. Serves 4-6.

Scampi

Ingredients

½- Cup Panko crumbs
¼-tsp Salt
½-tsp Freshly ground black
   pepper
¼-tsp Cayenne pepper
1 ½-Lbs Fresh shrimp, shelled
   and deveined without tails
½- Cup Olive oil
4- Cloves garlic, minced
2-Tbsp Green onions chopped
1- tsp Minced green pepper
½-tsp Dried oregano, crushed
2-Tbsp Lemon juice
2-Tbsp White wine
½ -Cup Shrimp stock
2-Tbsp Butter
2-Tbsp Chopped parsley

Scampi is a culinary name for a kind of small lobster. The name is often used loosely to describe a style of preparation typical for this lobster.

In USA, "scampi" is often the culinary name for the shrimp preparations in the Italian American Cuisine. The term "scampi" is the name of a dish of shrimp that is cooked simply by sautéing it in garlic, butter and olive oil and splashing it with white wine. Let the wine reduce while the shrimp cooks, toss it with fresh parsley and lemon juice and garnish with black pepper.

Shrimp scampi has to be one of the easiest ways to quickly prepare a shrimp dish. It is served either with bread, or over pasta or rice, although sometimes you only serve shrimp. According to some cooks this shrimp is delicate and need to be poached only for a few seconds in court Bouillon (salt, water, white-wine and black pepper). Try to use fresh shrimp because it has sweet flavor.

Method

1. In a small bowl, combine panko crumbs, salt, pepper and cayenne pepper. Mix thoroughly. Dredge shrimp in panko mixture.

2. In a large skillet, sauté dredged shrimp in olive oil for 5 minutes over high heat. Toss shrimp to prevent burning.

3. Transfer it with a slotted spoon to a serving dish. In the same pan, sauté the garlic, green onions, green pepper, oregano, lemon juice, white wine and shrimp stock. Keep cooking until reduced about 5 minutes.

4. Add the butter and mix it well. Spoon the mixture over the shrimp. Return pan to the heat. Sprinkle with parsley and check the seasonings. Serve over rice.

5. Serves 4-6.

Chicken Cacciatore

Ingredients

- 4- Chicken thighs
- 2-Chicken breasts with skin and backbone, halved crosswise
- 2- tsp Salt, plus more to taste
- 1-tsp Freshly ground black pepper, plus more to taste
- ½- Cup All- purpose flour, for dredging
- 3-Tbsp Olive oil
- 1- Large Red bell pepper chopped
- 1- Cup Chopped mushrooms
- 1-Onion chopped
- 3-Garlic cloves, finely chopped
- ¾- Cup Dry white wine
- 1- 28Oz. Can Diced tomatoes with juice
- ¾- Cup Chicken broth
- 3-Tbsp Green chilies finely chopped
- 1 ½-tsp Dried oregano leaves
- ¼-Cup Coarsely chopped fresh basil leaves

Many food names reflect various occupations or trades. 'Cacciatore' literally means 'hunter' in Italian, and this 'hunter style' dish makes good use of mushrooms (easily available to hunters trekking through the forests), onions tomatoes and herbs. If desired, serve over hot spaghetti noodles." This Italian mainstay is best served with pasta. Not only is this main dish satisfying it is easy to fix and it tastes fantastic. The rich flavors of fresh vegetables, herbs, and red wine gives this Italian recipe rich taste with minimum calories. An authentic Chicken Cacciatore recipe doesn't have tomatoes in it.

Traditionally it is a dish that hunters could easily make in the field if they needed to cook a meal? Basically, Italian Chicken Cacciatore is a chicken stew with chicken, garlic, herbs and mushrooms as a base. In southern Italy cacciatore often includes red wine, while northern Italian chefs might use white wine.

Method

1. Sprinkle the chicken pieces with 1 teaspoon of each salt and pepper and dredge them in the flour to coat lightly.

2. In a large heavy frying pan, heat the oil over a medium flame. Add the chicken pieces to the pan and sauté just until brown, about 5 minutes per side.

3. Transfer the chicken to a plate and set aside.

4. Add the bell pepper, mushrooms, onion and garlic to the same pan and sauté over medium heat until the onion is tender, about 5 minutes.

5. Season with salt and pepper. Add the wine and simmer until reduced by half, about 3 minutes.

6. Add the tomatoes with their juice, broth, green chilies and oregano leaves. Return the chicken pieces to the pan gently and turn them to coat in the sauce.

7. Bring the sauce to a simmer. Continue simmering over medium-low heat until the chicken is just cooked through, about 30 minutes for the breast pieces, and 20 minutes for the thighs.

8. Transfer the chicken to a platter; boil the sauce until it thickens and cook for few more minutes. Spoon the sauce over the chicken then sprinkle with chopped basil leaves and serve.

9. Serve with your favorite bread or noodles and may be rice.

10. Serves 2-4

Capri Salad

Ingredients

- 3- Large Fresh Mozzarella balls
- 3- Large Ripe tomatoes
- 2-Cloves garlic chopped
- 1-Tbsp Fresh Basil leaves chopped
- 1- Lemon
- 1-tsp Salt
- 1-tsp Pepper
- 1-tsp Red pepper flakes
- 2-Tbsp Olive oil

This simple salad from the Italian region of Campania (a region in southern Italy) is made of sliced Mozzarella, tomatoes, and basil seasoned with salt, and olive oil. In Italy, unlike most salads, it is usually served as an antipasto (starter) and not a side dish. Some variations include adding chopped garlic, parsley, and various sauces (balsamic vinegar Italian dressing etc). While it's unknown whether the salad actually originated on Capri, but it did become popular after being served to the jet-setting King Farouk of Egypt during the 1950s. He reportedly enjoyed it as a sandwich filling. It is often served when the garden tomatoes get ripe. It is simple and it is perfect for a light lunch or dinner. Serve it with your traditional Italian bread or any other bread of your choice. It has this fresh, deliciousness that makes it also a wonderful beginning to any dinner. A caprese salad is especially delicious with a perfect, juicy steak. It can also be served as a perfect appetizer for get-togethers with friends or family. It is elegant yet casual, and so easy.

Method

1. Slice the fresh Mozzarella Balls into 3 or 4 slices.

2. Core and remove a very thin slice from the bottom of the washed tomatoes and slice into 4 -5 slices.

3. Between 4- salad plates divide the Mozzarella and tomato slices layering the slices alternately.

4. Sprinkle with salt, pepper and red pepper flakes to taste.

5. Sprinkle chopped garlic and basil over the top of salad.

6. Drizzle ½- tablespoon of olive oil over each salad.

7. Serve as an appetizer with lemon wedges or squeeze the lemon on top before serving.

8. Serve as a light lunch. Make a sandwich with this filling and serve with your favorite soup or as an appetizer.

9. Serves 4.

Breaded Fried Calamari

Ingredients

- ½- Cup Semolina flour or cream of wheat uncooked (Indian grocery store or any health food store)
- ½- tsp. Salt
- ¼-- tsp. Dried crushed chili or cayenne pepper
- ¼-- tsp 5-Spice powder or garam masala
- Pinch Ground white or Black pepper
- 2- Large Frozen (or freshly prepared) squid tubes or 3-4 medium tubes.
- 2-Cup Buttermilk
- ½ tsp Crushed garlic
- 1- Cup (or more) Vegetable oil (such as canola) for frying
- Optional bed of lettuce or fresh coriander leaves for serving
- Grated Parmesan as needed
- Thai Sweet Chili sauce for serving (available in most supermarkets)

Calamari is a culinary treat made of squid that is native to Spanish, Italian, and Greek cuisines. Now a-days the most popular appetizer in North America is fried calamari. The dish is relatively simple. It is cut into pieces, creating rings. These are then battered and deep-fried for just a couple of minutes. Fried calamari is often served as a snack or appetizer and forms a part of appetizer platters in North America. It is a staple in Italian, Greek, Turkish and seafood restaurants. When it is served as an appetizer it is garnished with parsley or parmesan cheese and is served with dips like peppercorn mayonnaise, tzatziki, Marinara, Tartar sauce or Cocktail sauce. In Mexico it is served with Tabasco or habanero sauce. Other dips, such as ketchup, aioli and olive oil are also used. In Turkey it is served with tartar sauce. Like many seafood dishes, it may be served with a slice of lemon.

Squid is a popular food in many parts of the world. In many of the languages around the Mediterranean-sea, squid is referred to by a term related to the Latin word "calamarius" which in English has become a culinary name for Mediterranean dishes involving squid, especially fried. Japan consumes the maximum amount of squid in the world. In South Africa and Australia fried calamari is popular at the fish and chip restaurants. Imitation calamari of white fish is also available at some restaurants.

This dish also makes a great appetizer or party food recipe. Serve it with a salad and you have a complete meal. As this recipe will demonstrate below, fried calamari needn't be as difficult as it sounds - simply cut the squid into rings, dip into simple flour and spice mixture, and fry. It is easy and delicious!

Method

1. Place semolina flour in a shallow bowl and stir in the salt and spices. Transfer the flour into a zip lock plastic bag and set it aside.

2. Place squid tubes horizontally in front of you on a cutting board. Using a sharp knife and cutting towards you, simply make slices about ½- inch wide.

3. Transfer them into a medium size bowl that has a cup of buttermilk and crushed garlic and let them marinate in it for at least an hour in the refrigerator.

4. Remove the calamari rings from the buttermilk with a strainer and transfer them into plastic bag with the spiced flour. Shake them well to coat. Transfer them to a mesh strainer and strain the excess flour. Set aside.

5. Pour the oil into a small or medium-sized frying pan. The oil should be about 1 -2 inch deep. You can use a fryer also.

6. Turn heat to medium-high (375°F) until the oil begins to bubble. Place as many rings into the oil as can comfortably fit at one time. Total time should not be more that 2 ½ minutes. Turn heat down to medium to prevent oil from splattering.

7. When rings are done frying (do not overcook) remove from the oil and place on an absorbent towel or paper towel to drain.

8. Serve immediately while still hot. If desired, place calamari on a bed of lettuce or fresh coriander leaves. It can be served sprinkled with Parmesan cheese and garnished with parsley. Serve with chili sauce or a sauce of your choice.

9. Serves 2-4.

> **Note: Serve with the Thai sweet chili sauce or tomato sauce or Marinara sauce or any other sauce of your choice and enjoy. Several coatings are used. Instead of semolina all-purpose flour can also be used.**
>
> **To get a more crispier coating: In step four after coating them in spiced flour or semolina dip them in a mixture of beaten egg and crushed garlic and then finally dip them in breadcrumbs before frying. Strain the excess flour and breadcrumbs before you add them to hot oil.**

Spaghetti with Meatballs

Ingredients

For the meatballs:
- ½-Lb Ground beef
- ½-Lb Ground pork
- ½-Lb Ground veal
- 3-Slices Italian bread soaked in milk or water then squeezed dry and broken into pieces
- ½-Medium Onion, finely chopped
- ½- tsp Chopped ginger fine
- 2-Tbsp Parsley, finely minced
- 1-tsp Garlic powder
- ½ -Cup Grated Pecorino-Romano cheese
- 2-Eggs
- Salt, Black pepper and Cayenne pepper to taste
- 2- Tbsp Heavy cream
- Vegetable oil to pan fry

Sauce
- 2-3-Tbsp Olive oil
- 1-Whole Yellow onion, diced
- 3-Cloves Garlic, minced
- 1- 28-Oz Can Whole tomatoes
- 1- 28Oz Can Crushed tomatoes
- 8- Whole Fresh basil Leaves,
- ½-tsp Oregano dry
- ¼- tsp Salt
- 1- tsp Sugar

(continued)

This is more of an Italian-American dish, because in Italy they do not serve their meatballs on top of pasta as it is done here in U.S. National Pasta Association was the first to publish a recipe for it in the 1920s. Though Spaghetti with meatballs is rare in Italy there is an Italian precursors? Tiny meatballs do get served in Puglia (Sicily). It is noted that meatballs were a sighted addition to feast day pasta sauces in Sicily but because meat was so scarce that meatballs did not get served as often as it is done here in U.S. It is believed that early 20th-century Italian immigrants brought this recipe to New York.

Method
For meat balls

1. Combine all ingredients for the meatballs, except vegetable oil, in a bowl.

2. Gently knead the mixture with your hands without squeezing it.

3. When all the ingredients are evenly combined shape it gently into balls about 1 ½-inches in diameter.

4. In a large sauté pan heat up enough vegetable oil to come ¼ inch up the sides. Add the meatballs fry them on the direct heat by turning them until slightly brown or place the pan in the oven pre-heated to 450°F and brown them on all side

Freshly Ground black pepper
½- Cup White Or Red wine
    (optional)
Water as needed
2-Lbs Spaghetti, cooked
¼- Cup Flat-leaf parsley, minced
Parmesan Cheese grated to
    sprinkle

Sauce

5. Heat olive oil in a heavy pot over medium heat. Add onion and garlic and cook till they are translucent.

6. Add tomatoes, basil, oregano, salt, sugar, pepper, wine and water.

7. Bring to a boil then lower the heat to a simmer. Simmer for 45 minutes then add meatballs. Continue simmering for another ½ hour.

8. While the sauce is cooking cook the spaghetti according to package directions.

9. Drain pasta, put it back in the pot and add some of the sauce to the pot and mix it well.

10. Dish out pasta, spooning meatballs over top and pouring remaining sauce on top.

11. Serve sprinkled with Parmesan cheese and parsley with steamed broccoli, asparagus or baked potato or beans and Italian bread on the side.

12. Serves 4.

Ziti with Steamed Cabbage and Savory Lamb Sauce

Ingredients

1- Cup Fresh chopped mushrooms of your choice

½- Cup Olive oil

1-Lb Onions, diced

10- Medium cloves garlic, minced

1½-Lb Well-trimmed lamb shoulder or leg, cut into 1-inch cubes (substitute lamb with Italian sausages or chicken or ground beef)

Flour, for coating the meat

1-Large Bay leaf

Sprigs Fresh rosemary

1- Cup Chicken broth

1½- Cups Dry white wine

Salt and pepper, Cayenne pepper to taste

¾-Lb Ziti or other tubular pasta (About 6 or 7 cups cooked)

1- Small head cabbage (about 1½ pounds), cored and shredded

4-tsp Rice wine vinegar

1-tsp Salt

3- Tbsp Unsalted butter

It is a classic Italian American comfort food of pasta, cooked with meat sauce of your choice over steamed cabbage. It is an ideal midweek meal.

Method

1. Wash the mushrooms in cold water and set them aside. If using fresh button mushrooms remove the stem and chop them in 4 pieces cross wise and set them aside.

2. In a heavy Dutch oven, sauté the onions in 2 tablespoon of olive oil over high heat until browned. Add the garlic and sauté 1 minute longer. Remove the onions and garlic; set aside.

3. Add the rest of the oil. Toss the lamb cubes in the flour, shaking off excess. Cook the lamb in small batches over high heat until well browned. Return all of the lamb to the pot, along with the cooked onions, garlic and add bay leaf, rosemary, ½ cup broth, wine and salt and peppers to taste.

4. Bring to a boil; reduce heat and simmer covered, for 1 hour stirring occasionally. Remove the lid and simmer until the meat is tender and falling apart. Add the reserved chopped mushrooms for the last half-hour of cooking time and remaining broth.

5. To assemble the dish, cook the pasta according to the package directions.

6. Meanwhile, toss the cabbage with the vinegar and salt in a micro wave-safe dish. Cover with plastic wrap; cut a steam hole in the top.

7. Cook on high power for 5 minutes before removing the plastic and tossing with the butter. Toss hot, drained pasta with the cabbage.

8. Divide among eight warm plates; top with lamb sauce and serve.

9. Serves 4.

Authentic Chicken Marsala

Ingredients

- 1-Cup All-purpose flour
- 4- Skinless boneless chicken breast halves (2 lb total)
- 1- tsp Salt
- 1-tsp Black pepper
- 2-Tbsp Extra-virgin olive oil
- 5-Tbsp Unsalted butter
- 2-Tbsp Finely chopped shallot
- ½-tsp Garlic chopped
- 10- Oz Mushrooms, trimmed and thinly sliced
- 1½-tsp Finely chopped fresh sage
- ¼-tsp Cayenne paper
- ½- Cup+2 Tbsp Dry marsala wine
- 1 ¾ -Cups Chicken broth reduced by boiling
- 2/3-Cup Heavy cream
- 1-tsp Fresh lemon juice
- 1-Tbsp Chopped chives
- Parmesan cheese to sprinkle
- 2-Tbsp chopped parsley
- ¼ -tsp Garam masala

This dish has been a popular one at American Italian restaurants and dinner parties for a long time. Chicken Marsala is a traditional Italian dish that starts with flour coated fried boneless chicken breasts pieces and served in a sauce prepared with rich fortified Italian marsala wine. Some Chicken Marsala recipes also include capers and lemon juice.

It is served with rice pilaf, potatoes or fancy pasta. Quite delicious, easy to make, and elegant enough to serve to company! The dish's name originates from the particular wine, Marsala that is used to create the sauce. Marsala is produced in Sicily, Italy, and is one of the country's most famous wines. The popularity of the dish dates back to the 19th century, when it most likely originated with folks who came from the western Sicily region (Italy) where the Marsala wine is produced.

Chicken Marsala

Method

1. Put flour in a wide shallow bowl. Gently pound chicken to ¼- inch thick between 2 sheets of plastic wrap using the flat side of a meat pounder or a rolling pin.

2. Pat chicken dry and season with ½ teaspoon each of salt and pepper, then dredge in flour, shaking off any excess flour. Transfer to sheets of wax paper, arranging chicken in 1 layer.

3. Heat 2 tablespoon each of oil and butter in an l0-inch heavy skillet over moderately high heat and sauté pounded chicken pieces turning over once, until golden and just cooked through, about 4 minutes total and set it aside.

4. Cook shallot in 3 tablespoons butter in an 8- to l0-inch heavy skillet over moderate heat, stirring, until shallot begins to turn golden, about 1 minute add the garlic. Add mushrooms, 1-teaspoon sage, remaining salt, and peppers and cayenne pepper and cook, stirring occasionally, until liquid is evaporated and mushrooms begin to brown, 6 to 8 minutes. Remove from heat.

5. Add ½- cup wine to skillet and boil over high heat, stirring and scraping up brown bits, about 30 seconds. Add reduced broth, cream, and mushrooms then simmer, stirring occasionally, until sauce is slightly thickened, 6 to 8 minutes.

6. Add the chicken and continue cooking until it cooks through about 5-6 minutes. Add lemon juice and remaining 2 tablespoons wine and ½ teaspoon sage. Sprinkle with chives and parmesan cheese and serve sprinkled with parsley and garammasala.

7. Serves -4

> **Note: Serve with simple pasta dish such as fettuccine with butter and topped with Parmesan cheese.**

Ravioli

Ingredients

2-Tbsp Butter

3-Cups Baby spinach (about 7 ounces)

15-Oz Ricotta cheese

1-Large Egg

1-Cup Shredded Italian-blend cheeses

1-Tbsp Chopped green chilies

2-Tbsp Chopped onions

½-Tbsp Dried basil

¼-tsp Nutmeg

Salt and pepper to taste

1-Package Wonton wrappers (about 48 wrappers)

1-Tbsp Extra virgin olive oil

White wine sage sauce

1-Tbsp Olive oil

2- Clove minced garlic

1-Tbsp Dried sage

1- Cup White wine

Optional

Truffle oil

Panko breadcrumbs

Parmesan cheese (grated or shaved)

Ravioli has become an amazing staple in our society. There is an argument that Ravioli came from Italy but our Russian friends think that they were the originators of this gourmet little mini puff of pasta (with filling) delight. Most of their fillings were meat based. Russian version of ravioli is rapidly decreasing. They are expanding their choice of fillings by choosing other popular American fillings. These fillings always have one two or three of the following cheeses like ricotta cheese, parmigiano-Reggiano cheese, mozzarella cheese and or Parmesan cheese with sautéed vegetables like mushrooms, spinach, pumpkins or squash. Even seafood like lobster and crab-meat with ricotta cheese, chicken marsala, turkey and cranberry fillings are now becoming huge hits in the most posh restaurants of United States. Ravioli is always served with sauces like marinara sauce, white wine sauce, corn lemon sauce, meat sauce, crab meat sauce, mushroom sauce etc.

Because of lack of time Americans are using Chinese wonton wrappers to make Ravioli instead of making the dough and making the wrappers by hand. The ready- made wrappers save a lot of time and cost.

Method

1. Warm one tablespoon of butter in a pan over medium heat; add spinach and sauté until wilted, about 5 minutes. Let cool and then chop coarsely.

2. In a medium bowl, combine ricotta, egg, Italian-blend cheeses, basil and nutmeg. Add onions, green chilies and spinach and mix well. Add salt and pepper to taste, set aside.

3. Line a baking sheet with non-stick parchment paper; you will use this to layout your wontons. Fill a small bowl with cool water. Remove wonton wrappers from package, dip them one at a time in water, and lay flat on parchment.

4. Spoon spinach and cheese mixture onto wrappers. Fold in half and, using a fork, crimp the edges. Seal the edges and then put the tray of ravioli in refrigerator for about 5 minutes to set.

5. Meanwhile, bring a large pot of salted water to a boil. Add a tablespoon of olive oil to the water, to keep ravioli from sticking together.

6. Add ravioli to boiling water; cook for about 8-10 minutes. Remove immediately and drain. Serve with marinara sauce or white wine sage sauce (recipe below) or any other sauce of your choice and grated Parmesan cheese. Serves 4-6.

White wine sage sauce

1. Add the olive oil to a sauté pan. Heat over medium-high heat, and add the garlic and sage.

2. Let it cook for one minute. Add the white wine, and turn the heat down to medium-low. Let simmer for a few minutes until it reduces.

3. Remove from heat and pour over cooked ravioli. Drizzle a little truffle oil and then top the ravioli off with panko and Parmesan cheese.

4. The truffle oil enhances the flavor of the ravioli and the panko adds a bit of a light crunch to the dish. Serve it with bread, vegetables and salad to make a meal.

5. Serves-2-4.

Angel Hair Milano with Lemon Sauce

Ingredients

6-Tbsp Butter or margarine, divided

½ -Chopped onion

1-tsp Crushed garlic

¼-Cup Chicken broth

2-Tbsp Lemon juice

4- Cups (12-Oz)Thinly sliced fresh mushrooms

¼ -Lb Thinly sliced ham or prosciutto (omit if cooking vegetarian)

Or

½- Lb Chopped cooked spinach

1- Pkg (12–Oz) Roasted garlic Angel hair pasta uncooked

1- Cup Frozen peas, thawed

1- Tbsp Chopped green hot pepper (optional)

Salt and Ground black pepper, Cayenne pepper to taste

¼-tsp Garammasala

2-Tbsp Chopped chives

Grated Parmesan cheese

Angel hair pasta is a long and thin noodle with a round shape. It is also known as capellini or capelli d'angelo. This extremely fine pasta is served with light, delicate sauces as well as seasonal fresh vegetables. Several traditional Italian recipes call for angel hair pasta. Angel hair pasta is readily available in most grocery stores. It is usually flavored with additions like pepper and lemon, sun-dried tomato, spinach, asparagus, artichoke hearts, smoked salmon, roasted garlic, or basil in a white sauce and parmesan cheese. Seafood also goes well with angel hair pasta. The noodles are also delicious plain with a little bit of olive oil, salt, pepper, and garlic and can also be served as a side dish or as a base for other dishes. It is also used in Asian recipes that call for fine, thin noodles and act as a base for that dish.

Method

1. In a large skillet over medium heat, melt 4 tablespoons butter. Add onions and garlic and fry till transparent. Add the chicken stock and lemon juice and simmer for 5 minutes. Add mushrooms and ham. Cook, stirring frequently, for 5 minutes or until mushrooms get tender.

2. Meanwhile, cook pasta according to package directions; drain and set aside.

3. Add peas and green pepper to the mushroom mixture and heat through.

4. Add remaining butter; stir until melted and add hot pasta and mix thoroughly. Season to taste with salt and peppers and garammasala. Sprinkle with cheese and chives and serve

5. Serves 6.

Statue of Lord Buddha, Hawaii

Asian Specialties

Asian national cuisines new to the mainstream American pallets are emerging at the heart of the U.S. quick-serve industry lately, acquainting America's biggest non-Asian market with zesty new influences ranging from Filipino to Indonesian to Malaysian and other Asian cuisines. At the same time, fresh concepts are extending the playbook of long-popular ethnic cuisines including Korean, Japanese, Indian, and Chinese.

This trend is being driven in part by increasing commercial and tourist ties between America and Asia. Demographic changes also play a huge role, including an explosion in Asian immigration to the U.S. as well as the broader palate of younger Americans. They appeal to a lot of people because they're perceived to be not as heavy as traditional American food. And they're exotic to some extent, with the types of products as well as some of the flavorings, ranging from peculiar spicy ones to lighter flavorings like Thai basil and lemon grass. They're looking for bolder and spicier flavors, and something different, says Darren Tristano, executive vice president of Technomic, a Chicago-based restaurant-research firm. "And they don't seem to have the stigma that some boomers do." In fact U.S. quick-serve and fast-casual chains are selling about 550 items with Asian names or influences. Most of the new Asian concepts register relatively low on the calorie and fat scale. Any Asian dish employing lemon grass, fresh mint, Thai basil, and cilantro as well as "truly memorable" aromatics, Sushi and sashimi and Dim sum long time favorite of Americans has been a staple of white-table-cloth Chinese restaurants in the U.S. They are now becoming fast food items. Indian food is certainly that next tier of adventure. It's fun because Indonesian, Korean, Chinese, Japanese and Indian are becoming more mainstream.

Sweet and Sour Tofu (Ma Po Tofu)

Ingredients

Sauce

½- Cup Rice vinegar
1-Cup Pineapple juice
2-Tbsp Tamari sauce
2-Tbsp Cornstarch
3-Tbsp Honey
3-Tbsp Tomato paste

Tofu mixture

10-Oz Package Firm tofu, cubed
Vegetable oil as needed
1- Medium onion, sliced
2- Carrots, sliced diagonally
1- Green pepper, sliced
1- Red pepper, sliced
1- Yellow squash, sliced
1½- tsp Grated ginger root
1-tsp Chopped Green medium
    hot chili
8-OZ. Can Unsweetened
    pineapple chunks
Salt and red pepper and soy
    sauce to taste
1-Tbsp Cilantro chopped
¼-tsp Garammasala

Many cultures have a history of playing with contrasting tastes like sweet and sour, sweet and salty, or sweet and bitter in their cooking, using the interplay of flavors to enhance the flavor of their cuisines. Sweet and sour sauce and flavoring are very popular aspects of Chinese food. In fact, this is one of the rare examples of a kind of oriental food that is popular in both American "Chinese food" and the real thing served in China. Sweet and sour Tofu is one of the most influential flavors of Sichuan cuisine, served in every Sichuan restaurant. The name Ma Po Tofu is roughly translated as "pockmarked grandmother bean curd," named for the old woman who supposedly invented the dish. It is very easy to make and so delicious and for all ages even for those who don't have teeth. Tofu because of its high protein, low fat content, is excellent as a diet food. Making it ideal for vegetarians, vegans or meat-eaters. A single serving of tofu provides 9.2 grams of protein, or 18.3% of the daily RDA, and it comes virtually free of saturated fat (less than 1 gram). This dish is a standard on most menus in Chinese restaurants. Simply substitute tofu instead of meat in your favorite sweet and sour recipe and you have a classic vegetarian Tofu dish. Tofu tends to soak up any liquid, which makes it excellent for marinating. Frying can leave its protein full of oil. For this reason, grilling or sautéing with a little oil at a high temperature is best for it, as it does not need to be cooked to eliminate bacteria.

Sweet and Sour Tofu

Method

1. Make sauce by combining vinegar, pineapple juice and tamari. Blend in cornstarch, then honey and tomato paste. Set aside.

2. For tofu mixture, brown tofu cubes in skillet lightly coated with vegetable oil. Remove tofu and set aside.

3. Add 1 or 2 tablespoons oil to skillet to coat bottom. Stir-fry onion, carrots, green and red pepper, squash and ginger root and green chili. Stir to mix.

4. Return tofu to pan and add pineapple chunks with their juice. Stir in sauce. Cook, stirring gently, just until sauce thickens and becomes clear. Serve preferably with brown rice. Sprinkle with chopped cilantro and Garamasala.

5. Serves 3-4.

Pork Schumai

Ingredients

For the filling
- ½- Lb Boneless pork loin, ground
- ¼- Cup Minced raw shrimp
- 1 ½- Oz Bacon slices minced
- 2- Oz. Fresh shiitake or oyster mushrooms, brushed clean and tough stems removed, minced
- 2- Tbsp Minced bamboo shoot
- 1- Tbsp Peeled and finely grated fresh ginger
- 1 ½- Tbsp Cornstarch
- 1- Tbsp Dry sherry
- 2- tsp Asian sesame oil
- 1- tsp Sugar
- ¾- tsp Fine sea salt
- ¼- tsp Freshly ground pepper, to taste
- 30-Round dumpling wrappers
- Napa cabbage leaves for lining steamer

Soy-ginger sauce
- ½- Cup Soy sauce
- ¼- Cup Mirin
- ¼- Cup Rice vinegar
- 2- Green onions, including 2 inches of tender green tops, finely chopped
- 4- tsp Peeled and minced fresh ginger

Shumai are also called pork dumplings and they are a type of traditional Chinese dumplings served as Dim Sum (small Chinese dishes served with tea). In the Qing Dynasty, the fillings varied by season: spring- garlic chives, summer- mutton and pumpkin, autumn- crabmeat, winter- mixed seafood. Many varieties have been created as the shaomai was gradually introduced to all provinces of China where it adapted to the different regional tastes of whole China. However, most people in western countries associate shaomai only with the Cantonese version due to the Cantonese settlement here in U.S. The preparation is simplified with purchased dumpling wrappers (sometimes labeled shumai wrappers). If you have two bamboo steamer baskets (or a two-tiered metal steamer), you can steam all of the dumplings at on

Pork Schumai

Method

To Make the filling

1. In a bowl, combine the pork loin, shrimp, bacon, mushrooms, bamboo shoot and ginger and stir briefly to combine.

2. Add the cornstarch, sherry, sesame oil, sugar, salt and pepper and stir until the mixture has a smooth, even consistency.

3. Working with 1 dumpling wrapper at a time and keeping the others covered with a damp kitchen towel, assemble the shumai: Place a heaping 1-tablespoons of filling in the center of the wrapper.

4. Make the wrapper in a cup shape in your hand and using the index finger and thumb of your other hand pleat the top edge. Squeeze the dumpling gently in the center to indent slightly and tap the bottom to flatten.

5. Using the back of a teaspoon dipped in water, pack the filling gently and smooth the top. Repeat with the remaining filling and wrappers to make 24 dumplings. (The extra dumpling wrappers allow you to lose a few while practicing.)

6. In a wok or large, wide saucepan, pour in water to a depth of 2 inches and bring to a boil over high heat.

7. Line a bamboo steamer basket or a plate with a single layer of cabbage leaves and top with half of the dumplings, spacing them about ½- inch apart.

8. Place the basket in the wok or on top of the pan, or place the plate on a steamer rack in the wok or pan. Make sure the steaming water does not touch the basket or plate.

9. Cover tightly and steam until the wrappers are translucent and the visible filling is opaque, about 6 minutes.

10. Transfer the dumplings to a large, wide, shallow platter and keep warm in a 200°F oven while you steam the remaining dumplings. Serve the dumplings immediately. Pass the soy-ginger sauce (recipe below) at the table or serve it in individual dipping bowls.

11. Serves 4 to 6.

Soy-ginger sauce

1. In a small bowl, whisk together the soy sauce, mirin, vinegar, green onions and ginger. Set it aside until ready to serve.

Egg Fu Young

Ingredients

1-tsp Sesame oil
¼- Cup Chopped green onion
½-tsp Chopped green hot peppers
½-Cup Chopped celery
½-Cup Bean sprouts
¼-tsp Cornstarch
½- Lb Shrimp, peeled, deveined and roughly chopped
2-Tbsp Soy sauce
1-tsp Salt
¼-tsp Black Pepper
8- Eggs, well beaten

Egg Fu Yung is based on an authentic Chinese dish that has been enjoyed in Chinese-American restaurants since the 1950's and 1960's - a deep-fried pancake filled with eggs,

All it takes is a few eggs, crisp vegetables and Asian seasonings to create an elegant dish that is perfect for breakfast, a main entrée or late night snack. Egg Foo Yung is one of the few Chinese dishes where a sauce is prepared separately and served over it.

When choosing fillings, there are no hard and fast rules about what ingredients that go into Egg Fu Yung: Chinese sausage, barbecued pork, shrimp, and even tofu are all popular and vegetables like mushrooms, onion, and green onion are frequently used. Various incarnations of egg "pancakes" filled with meat or vegetables and seasonings have existed since ancient times. Furthermore, the dish ancient Persians feasted upon probably bore more resemblance to Egg Fu Yung (and Italian frittatas for that matter) than the classic French omelets, with its moist interior and modest amount of filling. Ancient Persian omelets were probably similar to modern-day *Kookoo* (a Persian style egg dish) made by mixing up "a generous amount of chopped herbs into beaten eggs, frying it in a round pan until it is firm and then (usually) cutting it into wedges for serving".

Method

1. In a skillet over medium heat, heat sesame oil and lightly fry the onions, green peppers, celery and sprouts.

2. Stir in cornstarch and add shrimp, soy sauce, salt and pepper. Stir until well blended. Remove from heat and transfer to a bowl.

3. Return the pan to the heat, and add the beaten eggs. Fry the eggs while stirring gently.

4. Return the vegetable and shrimp mixture to the pan while the eggs are still liquid. Finish frying until eggs are fully cooked and serve.

5. Serve 4-6.

Peanut Noodles with Mango (Thai)

Ingredients

For the peanut dressing
- ¾- Cup Smooth natural-style peanut butter
- 3-Tbsp Rice vinegar
- ¼- Cup Plus 2-tablespoon soy sauce
- 4-Tbsp Dark sesame oil
- 1-Tbsp Grated ginger
- ¼-tsp Red pepper flakes
- ¼-Cup Brown sugar
- ½--Cup Hot water

Noodle Salad
- Kosher salt
- 1-Lb Thick spaghetti
- 2- Cups Sugar snap peas, strings removed, or snow peas
- 2-Ripe mangos
- Juice of 1 lime
- 2- Scallions, thinly sliced
- ½- Cup Loosely packed cilantro leaves, coarsely chopped
- ¼- Cup Roasted peanuts

These yummy noodles with mango are the perfect things to bring to or serve at a party. They can be made hours, even a day, ahead of time and they won't become gummy. Add Mango (adds juiciness and bright color and Sugar snap peas provide crunch) at the serving time.

Method

1. Make the peanut dressing by combining the peanut butter, vinegar, soy sauce, oil, ginger, red pepper flakes, brown sugar, and ½-cup hot water in a mini food processor. Blend well and set aside. Store in an airtight container in the refrigerator.

2. Cook the spaghetti according to package directions.

3. Meanwhile, bring a small saucepan of water to a boil. Cook the peas until they turn bright green, about 30 seconds. Drain and immediately plunge into a bowl of ice water to stop the cooking. Drain, pat dry and chop them a little and set them aside.

4. Cut and chop the flesh of the mangoes into cubes and set the bowl aside.

5. Squeeze excess juice from the trimmings into the bowl. Squeeze the lime onto the mango cubes and season with a little salt. When the spaghetti is done, drain, rinse with cold water, and drain again. In a large bowl, toss the spaghetti with the peanut dressing until well coated.

6. Add the peas and three quarters of the scallions and toss to combine. Place the noodles on

a large serving platter, sprinkle the mango over the noodles, and garnish with the remaining scallions, the cilantro, and peanuts.

7. Serve immediately. If making in advance reserve about one third of the dressing and toss the noodles with the reserved dressing immediately before serving.

8. Serves 4-6.

Chinese Chicken Salad

Ingredients

3-Tbsp Hoi sin sauce
2-Tbsp Peanut butter
2-Tbsp Brown sugar
¾- tsp Hot Chili paste
1-tsp Grated fresh ginger
4-Tbsp Rice wine vinegar
1-Tbsp Sesame oil
1-Lb Skinless, boneless chicken breast halves cooked and diced
2-Tbsp Vegetable oil
16- (3.5 inch square) Wonton wrappers, shredded
4- Cups Head lettuce- torn, washed and dried
2-Cups Shredded carrots
4- Green onions, chopped
2-Stalks Celery sliced thin
¼- Cup Chopped fresh cilantro
2-Tbsp Sesame seeds
¼--Cup Walnuts chopped

There are many different types of cold chicken salads in China, although most of them seem to originate in Szechwan. Here is a recipe for American Chinese salad that originated in California. Hollywood gave rise to not only the Caesar and Cobb salads but also Chinese chicken salad. This salad was made popular at Madame Wu's in Santa Monica in 1960's. Cary Grant asked her to put it on the menu after eating it at another restaurant. As the name suggests Chinese chicken salad has cooked chicken flavored by Chinese seasonings. Though many variations exist but the common features of this salad popular in America contain lettuce, chicken, ginger and sesame oil in the dressing and crisp pieces of deep-fried noodles. Other recipes may contain a combination of water chestnuts, bamboo shoots, peanuts, almonds and mandarin orange slices.

Method

1. To make the dressing -whisk together the hoi sin sauce, peanut butter, brown sugar, chili paste, ginger, vinegar, and sesame oil.

2. Grill or broil the chicken breasts until cooked, about 10 minutes. An instant-read thermometer inserted into the center should read 165° F. Cool and slice.

3. Preheat oven to 350° F. Spray a large shallow pan with vegetable oil and arrange shredded wontons in a single layer and bake until golden brown, about 20 minutes. Cool.

4. In a large bowl, combine the chicken, wontons, lettuce, carrots, green onions, celery, cilantro, sesame seeds, walnut and toss with dressing and serve.

5. Serves 4-6.

Ginger Steak with Stir-fry Vegetables

Ingredients

3-Tbsp Salad oil/sesame oil

¼- Cup Soy sauce

½- Cup Red Wine

2-Tbsp Honey

1½-Lb Beef flank steak

¼-Cup Chopped onion

3- Garlic cloves, minced

1-Tbsp Grated fresh ginger

1-Tbsp Oyster sauce

½-Cup Chicken stock

1-tsp Cornstarch

1-Medium head broccoli, cut into small pieces

1-tsp Ground Cumin

¼-tsp Red pepper

Salt to taste

¼-tsp Coarsely ground black pepper

1- Green Onion top, thinly slice

A beef stir-fry is a great option for a midweek meal that is high in protein and it is quick, easy and economical to make. Recipes vary in kind of sauce used, quantity of vegetables and spiciness. Steak strips tossed in this Thai Beef & Broccoli Stir-Fry is even more delicious than the Chinese version, with more depth of flavor and slightly more spiciness (this can be adjusted according to your liking). The beef is cut thinly and stir-fried quickly and easily put together with broccoli, red pepper, and a delicious stir-fry sauce. The broccoli really works in this dish, as it fully absorbs the sauce and provides that nice added bit of crunch. Serve with plain steamed jasmine rice for an easy Asian comfort food dish your family will love.

Method

1. Combine 2-tablespoon oil, soy sauce, wine, honey in a plastic bag.

2. Place beef in bag, turning to coat. Close bag securely and marinate in refrigerator 4 hours or overnight, turning occasionally.

3. Remove the steak from the marinade and save the marinade.

4. Turn the broiler on and place steak on rack in broiler pan so surface of meat is 4 inches from element and broil 6-8 minutes (rare to medium). Turn once, basting with reserved marinade. Carve steak diagonally into thin slices.

5. Heat the remaining oil in a wok and add the onions, garlic and ginger and stir-fry for a minute. Add the beef together with the marinade.

6. Add the oyster sauce. Add ½- cup of chicken stock with 1 teaspoon of cornstarch mixed into it. Stir to mix.

7. Cook a little and add the chopped broccoli and cumin, red pepper, salt coarsely ground black pepper and stir to cook it for 4-5 minutes. Sprinkle with green onion and serve over Jasmine rice or noodles or rice of your choice.

8. Serves 6.

Kung Pao Chicken

Ingredients

1-Lb Skinless, boneless chicken breast halves - cut into chunks
2-Tbsp White wine
2-Tbsp Soy sauce
1-Tbsp Sesame oil
½- Egg
1-Tbsp Cornstarch, dissolved in 2-Tablespoon of water

To make Sauce

1-Tbsp Wine
1-Tbsp Soy sauce
1-Tbsp Sesame oil
1-Tbsp Cornstarch, dissolved in 2-tablespoons water
1-Oz, Chile paste, hot
1-tsp White vinegar
2-tsp Brown sugar
2-Tbsp Peanut oil
2-3 Sichuan Peppercorns (optional)
4-Oz Chopped dry Peanuts
4- Green onions, chopped
1-Tbsp Chopped Garlic
1-Tbsp Chopped ginger
1 (8Oz.) Can Water chestnuts/ Precut stir fry vegetables
Chopped green onions to garnish

Kung Pao Chicken

The dish is popular both in China and in the American Chinese cuisine of North America. Kung Pao chicken also translated, as Gong Bao chicken is a spicy stir-fry dish made with chicken, peanuts, vegetables and chili peppers. The original Sichuan version uses diced chicken as its primary ingredient that is typically mixed with a prepared marinade. The wok is seasoned and then chili peppers and Sichuan peppercorns are flash fried to add fragrance to the oil. The Use of hot and numbing Sichuan peppercorns and Sichuan style chili peppers and their flavor is a typical element of Sichuan cooking.

The cooking of the dish starts with the frying of fresh and moist peanuts in this hot oil. The dish is believed to be named after Ding Bautzen, a late Qing dynasty official and a onetime governor of Sichuan. His title was Gong Bao. The name "Kung Pao" chicken is derived from this title.

Method

To Make Marinade

1. Mix together 1- tablespoon wine, 1-tablespoon soy sauce, 1- tablespoon oil, egg and 1 tablespoon cornstarch/water mixture. Place chicken pieces in a bowl and add marinade. Toss to coat. Cover the dish and place it in the refrigerator for sometime.

To Make Sauce

1. In a small bowl combine remaining marinade ingredients: 1- tablespoon wine, 1- tablespoon soy sauce, 1-Sesame oil 1- tablespoon cornstarch/water mixture and chili paste, vinegar and sugar. Set aside.

2. Heat 1 tablespoons peanut oil in a wok or large skillet over medium-high heat and add Sichuan peppercorns and add the peanuts. Stir fry them light brown. Set them aside.

3. Add the marinated chicken and stir-fry until it turns white. Transfer to a plate.

4. In the same skillet add remaining peanut oil and add onions, ginger, garlic and fry for a minute.

5. Add the water chestnuts/stir-fry vegetables. Stir to mix and cook for 5 minutes. Add the cooked chicken, the peanuts and cook until chicken looks cooked about 3 minutes.

6. Add the above sauce and cook till sauce is aromatic and it thickens. Serve it topped with chopped green onion on top of cooked rice of your choice, Chinese white rice or brown rice or regular rice.

7. Serves 2-4.

Chicken Satay with Peanut Sauce (Thai)

Ingredients

8-12 Skinless Chicken thighs/ chicken breasts/ cut into thin strips

1- Package wooden skewers

Satay Marinade

¼- Cup Minced lemongrass, fresh or frozen

2- Shallots or 1 Small onion, sliced

3- Cloves garlic

1-2- tsp Cayenne pepper or to taste

1- Thumb-size piece galangal or ginger, thinly sliced

½- tsp Turmeric powder

2- Tbsp Ground coriander

2- tsp Cumin

3- Tbsp Dark soy sauce

4- Tbsp Fish sauce (optional because it has a strong smell)

5-6- Tbsp. Brown sugar

2- Tbsp Vegetable oil

Peanut sauce for dipping

1/3-Cup Peanut butter

1/3- Cup Milk

2- Green onions, chopped

1- Small jalapeno pepper, seeded and finely chopped

2 to 3 Tbsp Lime juice

2 Tbsp Soy sauce

1- Garlic clove, minced

1- tsp Sugar

1-tsp Minced fresh cilantro

1-tsp Minced fresh gingerroot

1/8-tsp Coconut extract

It is one of the most delicious Thai dishes that America loves. Strips of chicken (or beef) are marinated in a special Thai paste, then skewered and grilled on the BBQ or broiled in the oven. It is then served with homemade peanut sauce for the ultimate taste sensation. Even your kids will love it.

Chicken Satay also makes a great party food! Satay originated in Java, Indonesia. Satay is available almost anywhere in Indonesia, where it has become a national dish. It is also popular in many other Southeast Asian countries such as: Malaysia, Singapore, Brunei, Thailand as well as in the Netherlands as Indonesia is a former Dutch colony. Indonesia's diverse ethnic group's culinary arts have produced a wide variety of satays. In Indonesia, satay can be obtained from a travelling satay vendor, from a street-side tent-restaurant, in an upper-class restaurant, or during traditional celebration feasts. In Malaysia, satay is a popular dish—especially during celebrations—and can be found throughout the country.

Close analogues are Yakitori from Japan, Shish Kabob from Turkey and India, Shashlik from Caucasus, Chunar from China, and Sosatie from South Africa. It is listed at number 14 on World's 50 most delicious foods.

Method

1. Soak the skewers in water while you cut chicken into thin strips and place them in a bowl.

2. Process all marinade ingredients in a food processor or chopper. Test for it being salty, sweet and tangy.

3. Pour the marinade over the chicken pieces and stir well to combine. Marinade at least 1 hour or overnight.

4. When ready to cook, thread meat onto the skewers. Cover only ¾- of the skewer, leaving the lower half clear so that there is a "handle" to hold and to easily turn the satay during cooking.

5. Grill the satay on your barbecue or your indoor grill, basting it with the left over marinade while it is grilled.

6. You can broil them in the oven or on a broiling pan or on a baking sheet with the oven set to "broil" Place satay close beneath the heating element and turn the meat every 5 minutes until cooked depending on how thin your meat is, the satay should cook in 10 to 20 minutes.

7. Serve them with jasmine rice, or brown rice or regular rice with peanut sauce(recipe below) for dipping.

8. Serves 6-8

Peanut sauce for dipping

1. In a small bowl, whisk the sauce ingredients until blended. Cover and refrigerate until serving.

Pad Thai (Thai)

Ingredients

- 1/3- Cup Fish sauce
- ½- Cup Palm sugar
- ½- Cup Tamarind juice concentrate or 1-Tbsp tamarind paste dissolved in ½- cup of hot water
- 4- Oz Dried rice stick noodles
- 6- Tbsp Vegetable oil, divided
- 1 ½- Cups Thinly sliced chicken, beef, pork, shrimp, or tofu
- 4- Cloves garlic, minced
- 1-Cup Red onion, thinly sliced
- 2- Eggs beaten
- 1- Cup Carrots cut as match- sticks
- 1-Cup Green onion cut diagonal in ½ inch pieces
- 1- Cup Mung bean sprouts
- 1-Cup Cilantro leaves chopped
- 1-Cup Toasted peanuts chopped
- Lime wedges

This is another Thai specialty of worldwide appeal.

It is a dish of stir-fried rice noodles with eggs, fish sauce, tamarind juice, red chili pepper plus any combination of bean sprouts, shrimp, chicken or tofu garnished with crushed peanuts, coriander and lime, the juice of which can be added along with Thai condiments (crushed peanuts, garlic, chives, pickled turnip, cilantro, lime, spicy chili oil, chili powder, vinegar, fish sauce, sugar). It is usually served with green onions and pieces of raw banana flower. It is listed at number 5 on World's 50 most delicious foods.

Method

1. Heat fish sauce, palm sugar, tamarind concentrate and 2 cloves of garlic in a medium size pan on medium low heat. Cook sauce until palm sugar has completely dissolved. At this point, you will want to taste the sauce. To make it more spicy add a little Thai chili powder. Remove from heat and allow it to cool 10 minutes before storing it in a jar or plastic container.

2. Boil noodles for 4-5 minutes and drain immediately rinsing with cold water for a few seconds. Noodles should be slightly firmer than Al dente. They will continue to soften and cook later when stir-frying. Using kitchen shears cut the noodle clump in half.

3. Heat 3 tablespoons of oil in a wok or frying pan on high and cook raw chicken, pork, beef, tofu or shrimp for 3-4 minutes. Remove it into a small bowl. Next add the remaining oil,

heat it and then add the remaining garlic and red onions to the hot pan and stir-fry for 1 minute. Add noodles and stir for 1 minute.

4. Add 3-4 tablespoons Pad Thai sauce continually stirring noodle mixture until well coated with sauce.

5. Add cooked meat/tofu/seafood and fry for 2-3 minutes. Move the noodle and meat mixture to one side of the pan and add the beaten eggs on the other side. Scramble the egg with a wooden spoon and cook for 30 seconds.

6. Add carrots, green onions, and sprouts and cook for one more minute frying everything together. Test the firmness of the noodle. Fry for an additional minute. If your noodles need more flavors add another tablespoon of sauce and fry another half minute. Remove from heat and serve.

7. Garnish with cilantro, toasted peanuts, and a wedges of lime.

8. Serves 2-4.

Grilled pork sticks with Turmeric (Moo Sa-Te) (Thai)

Ingredients

1 ½-Lbs. Pork tenderloin cut into 1 inch cubes
½-tsp Roasted coriander seeds powder
½-tsp Roasted cumin seeds powder
¼-tsp Turmeric powder
½-tsp Curry powder
¼ -tsp Cayenne pepper
3-Slices Galangal/ginger
½-Tbsp Finely chopped lemon grass
5-Garlic cloves
2-Tbsp Chopped green onions
½-Cup Soy sauce
½-Cup Roasted peanuts
1-Cup Coconut milk
2-Tbsp Sugar/Honey
2-Tbsp Melted butter
2-Tbsp Lemon juice
Small wooden skewers

Moo Sa Te (Grilled Pork Sticks with Turmeric). This tantalizing sweet-flavored grilled pork sticks are refined with rich, juicy sauce made of turmeric and curry powder. Moo Sa Te makes a savory hors d'oeuvres that will appease any taste buds. These juicy grilled pork sticks are usually served with two saucy dips – one is a mildly spicy thick sauce with ground peanuts, coconut milk and curry powder and another one is a sweet and sour vinegar sauce with chopped shallots, pepper and cucumber to mitigate its oiliness. Pork Satay and Beef Satays are one of Thailand's most popular appetizers. Satay is also a popular delicacy in Malaysia, Singapore and Indonesia.

Method

1. Slice the pork with the width of about 1½- Inches.

2. Process together the roasted coriander seeds powder, roasted cumin seeds powder, turmeric powder, curry powder, cayenne pepper, galangal, lemon grass, garlic cloves, green onions, soy sauce, peanuts and coconut milk in a food processor.

3. Add the sugar, melted butter and lemon juice and blend it into a marinade.

4. Soak the meat in the newly mixed marinade for 2 hours.

5. Take the slices of meat out and thread them onto the skewers while heating the marinade until boiling. Set it aside.

6. Roast the meat on the skewers on the grill until lightly brown (10-15 Minutes) and apply the marinade to it during roasting. Save the rest of the marinade and serve as a satay sauce.

7. When the meat is thoroughly cooked, serve it with satay sauce or cucumber sauce or peanut sauce and rice if you are making a meal out of it. Otherwise they make excellent appetizer too.

8. Serves 4-6

Panang Curry with Chicken (Thai)

Ingredients

5-Tbsp Panang curry paste
   (recipe below)
Or
2- Tbsp Red curry paste
4-Cups Coconut milk
6- Kaffir lime leaves, torn
1-Cup Sliced onion
¼- Cup Fresh Thai basil leaves
1 ¼-Lb Skinless, boneless
   chicken breast chopped
1-Large bell pepper cut into 2-
   inch strips
2-tsp Tamarind paste
2-Tbsp Fish sauce, or to taste
2-Tbsp Palm sugar
½-Cup Bamboo shoots drained
   from a can
2- Fresh Red Chile peppers, sliced
4- Tbsp Roasted ground peanuts
   (optional)
Steamed rice

Panang Curry Paste
Chili peppers (5 large dried
   red chili peppers, seeded
   and soaked (no need for
   authentic chili)
1-tsp Galangal
1- tsp Thinly sliced Lemongrass
1- tsp Coriander powder
1- tsp Chopped Cilantro
1- tsp Ground Cumin
1- Clove garlic
5- Chopped Shallots
¼- Cup Peanuts (optional)
12- Kaffir Lime leaves,
1- Tbsp Shrimp paste (optional,
1- tsp Sea Salt
2- tsp Pepper (white or black)

Panang curry with chicken represents the diversity of Thailand's southern region. Panang refers to the island of Penang in Northern Malaysia bordering southern Thailand. Panang curry takes it name from the city island off the West coast of peninsular Malaysia, Penang, or Pulau Pinang in Malay. This type of curry is richer, sweeter, and creamier than the more herbal Thai red curry or green curry making it very popular with westerners. This curry carries with it flavors and aromas of spices of distant places – like Malaysia, India, and Burma. With its homemade combination of spices and fresh herbs, this Panang Curry with chicken is a super delicious curry and can easily be made from scratch.

Method

1. Fry the curry paste in the oil in a large skillet or wok over medium heat until fragrant. Stir the coconut milk and kaffir lime leaves into the curry paste and bring to a boil. Stir in the onions and basil leaves and let it come to a boil.

2. Add the chicken, cook and stir until the chicken is nearly cooked through, 10 to 15 minutes.

3. Stir in the bell pepper, tamarind paste, fish sauce, palm sugar, bamboo shoots and simmer together for 5 minutes. Taste and adjust the saltiness by adding more fish sauce if necessary.

4. Garnish with peanuts and sliced red Chile peppers and serve with rice or quinoa.

5. Serves 4

Panang Curry Paste

1. Process all the ingredients together in a chopper or a blender and use it as in the recipe above.

> **Note: Serve over spaghetti instead of jasmine rice for a fusion dish. For a very Thai taste, serve with boiled salted eggs. For a festive occasion serve in crispy golden cups, called Krathong Thong, topping with kaffir lime leaf shreds and red chilies.**

Green Curry Chicken with Peas and Basil

Ingredients

2-tsp Olive oil
1-Cup Chopped onion
1-tsp Minced green chili pepper (hot if you like)
1-lb Boneless chicken, cut into stripes
1-Cup Un sweetened coconut milk
½-Cup Chicken broth
1-Tbsp Thai green curry paste (use recipe for Thai red curry paste on page 207 except use Thai green chili or jalapeno)
4-Tbsp Thinly sliced fresh basil
2-tsp Minced fresh ginger
1-Tbsp Chopped fresh cilantro
1½-Cups Snow peas, stringed
¼-Cup Thinly sliced green onions.

Salt and pepper to season

Green Curry tends to be one of the milder curries of Thai cuisine. The name "Gaeng Kiaw Wan" literally means 'sweet green curry' but if you prefer a spicy curry, simply increase the amount of fresh green Serrano peppers. Serve over steamed jasmine rice, accompanied by crispy fried fish Delicacy of Thai land) a cooling clear soup (gaeng joot) with fresh steamed or raw seasonal vegetables. This recipe features chunks of tender chicken simmered in a homemade green curry sauce along with healthy vegetables. The result is a gourmet-style Thai green curry that is very aromatic and beautiful to serve (great for entertaining!). Use only smaller pieces or cuts of chicken, allowing for faster cooking and the freshest possible taste.

Method

1. Heat oil in a large skillet over medium high heat. Add onion, green hot chili pepper and sauté until fragrant (1 minute). Add chicken, sauté until golden brown (about 3 minutes). Using slotted spoon, transfer mixture to a bowl.

2. Add coconut milk, broth and curry paste to the skillet. Stir until smooth. Add 2 tablespoons basil, cilantro and one teaspoon ginger and cilantro. Bring to a boil. Reduce heat; simmer until sauce thickens (5- 7 minutes).

3. Return chicken mixture to skillet. Add snow peas and green onions; simmer until chicken is cooked through (about 5 minutes). Season with salt and pepper. Sprinkle with remaining basil and chopped cilantro.

4. Serve with jasmine rice or regular rice if you like. Makes a great meal.

5. Serves 4.

Beef Broccoli

Ingredients

2-Tbsp Chopped onions
2-Tbsp Minced garlic
4-tsp Grated ginger
2-tsp Finely Chopped green chilies to taste
4-tsp Chinese black vinegar
2-Tbsp Soy sauce
3-tsp Hoi sin sauce
4-Tbsp Peanut oil divided
2-Lbs Beef flap steak, thinly sliced
4-Tbsp Cornstarch
2-Large head Broccoli, cut into florets and blanched
1 ½- tsp Red pepper
Salt and Pepper to taste
3-tsp Honey
Steamed white rice

Beef and broccoli stir-fry is a standard item on Chinese restaurant menus in America. It's not even a Chinese dish but rather, it's a Chinese American invention. That's because broccoli is an Italian vegetable. You can switch the protein (Beef) to chicken, pork, tofu or shrimp. Broccoli beef is most likely an American contrived recipe that didn't appear until sometime after the 1920's when Italians immigrant introduced the vegetable to the U.S. There are several types of broccoli used in China but none resembles the one (Italian) that we use here in U.S. This dish was undoubtedly there in Asia but was usually paired up with proteins other then beef. Cattle were much too valuable as beasts of burden to use for food especially Chinese food. It had to be adapted to American taste because Chinese food as is, is blander, thicker and sweeter for the American public.

Beef with Chinese Broccoli

Method

1. Combine the chopped onions, garlic, ginger, green chilies, vinegar, soy sauce, hoi sin sauce and honey. Mix well and set -aside until ready to use.

2. Preheat a wok or a large skillet. Once it has reached a medium heat, add the peanut oil.

3. Dredge the beef in the cornstarch, lightly shake off any excess cornstarch and add the beef to the pan. Cook for 2 to 3 minutes. Add the broccoli to the pan and shake frequently.

4. Add the sauce and stir to evenly coat the beef and broccoli. Garnish with red pepper, salt and pepper and honey and cook until the sauce thickens about 5 minutes. Serve immediately with steamed white rice or Jasmine rice.

5. Serves 6-8.

Ingredients
4-Oz Frozen Uncooked
shrimp, unshelled or small
cooked chicken breast
cubes or beef cubes

Marinade
1-Tbsp Oyster sauce, or to taste
1-Tbsp Soy sauce, or to taste
1-tsp Salt, or to taste
Pepper to taste
1-tsp Cornstarch mixed
with 1½- tsp water

Other ingredients
2- Eggs (more if desired)
5-Tbsp Sesame oil
1-Medium onion Chopped
2- Green onions chopped
1-Tbsp Chopped ginger
1-tsp Chopped garlic
1-tsp Chopped green chili to
taste
½- Cup Peas
4-Oz Cooked ham chopped
4- Cups Cold Cooked rice
2-Tbsp Sesame seeds
Soy sauce and Oyster sauce as
needed
Chopped cilantro

Chicken Fried Rice

Fried rice is a popular component of Asian cuisine, especially in Southeast Asia, where it is a staple as Southeast Asian foods. It is made from steamed rice stir fried in a wok often with other ingredients, such as eggs, vegetables and meat. It is sometimes served as the penultimate dish in Chinese banquets. Fried rice is also a common staple of American Chinese cuisine especially in the form sold as fast food. The dish is not only a staple of Chinese restaurants all over the world but is very popular in the West African nations of Nigeria, Ghana and Togo both as restaurant and as street food. As a home-cooked dish, fried rice typically is made with leftover ingredients from other dishes, leading to countless variations.

Shrimp fried rice is a great recipe for nights when you're looking for a quick way to use up leftovers. Feel free to experiment it by replacing garnishes like fresh mushrooms or other vegetables in place of the peas, and to double up on the ham, cooked chicken, pork or beef if you don't have frozen shrimp.

Method

1. Run the frozen shrimp under warm running water, pat dry with paper towels, shell and devein. Chop into small pieces. Mix the marinade ingredients and marinate the shrimp for 15 minutes.

2. Beat the eggs lightly, add a dash of salt, and couple drops of sesame oil, mix. Set aside.

3. Heat the wok and then add 1-tablespoon oil. When oil is ready, pour ½- of the egg mixture into the wok and cook over medium heat, turning over once. Remove and set aside and cook the other half the same way. Cut the egg into thin strips, and save for later.

4. Add 2-tablespoons oil, or as needed. Stir fry the onion, ginger, garlic, green chili, and cook for 2 minutes and then add marinated shrimp on high heat for a few moments, remove and set aside. Do the same for the green peas, and then the diced ham.

5. Add 1 - 2 tablespoons oil, turn the heat down to medium and stir-fry the rice. Add a bit of soy sauce and oyster sauce if desired. Add shrimp, green peas and diced ham and combine thoroughly.

6. Serve the fried rice with the strips of egg on top and the green onion as garnish. You can also add a bit of oyster sauce if desired. Sprinkle with sesame seeds, cilantro and serve.

7. Serves 4.

Note – You can use small cooked chicken cubes or lean beef cubes instead of shrimp to make Chicken fried rice or Beef fried rice similarly.

Chicken Curry (Indian)

Ingredients

Marinade
- ½ -Cup Yogurt
- 1- tsp Salt
- 1-tsp/Each- Chopped ginger, garlic, green chilies (optional)
- ½-tsp Red pepper
- 2-Tbsp Lemon juice
- 1- Tbsp Oil

For the curry
- 2-Lbs Boneless skinless chicken breast halves, cut into 2-inch pieces (You Can use skinned chicken legs or thighs
- 3-4 Tbsp Ghee (clarified butter) or Olive oil
- 1-Large onion, chopped
- 3- tsp Minced peeled fresh ginger
- 6-8 - Garlic cloves, minced
- 3- Tbsp Minced green chilies (select the chili (mild, medium hot or hot) according to your taste
- 1- 1 Inch Stick of cinnamon,
- ½-tsp Each Whole peppercorns, Cloves, Cardamoms
- 1- tsp Cumin seeds
- 2- Tomatoes, chopped
- ½- Cup Tomato sauce
- 1-tsp Turmeric powder

(continued)

Chicken Curry with Pea Pulav (rice with peas)

Chicken curry has become an all time favorite here in America.

Chicken Curry (also referred to as Curry Chicken) is a common delicacy all over Asia as well as in the Caribbean. The main ingredients in this dish are chicken and curry. The curry powder along with an array of other spices including, garam masala, onions, ginger, tomato sauce, turmeric, cumin, coriander powder, cilantro and so on are mixed to form a sauce to blend in with the chicken. There are endless variations to the chicken curry but this chicken curry is prepared with the same basic ingredients as any normal chicken curry. You can add cashew nut paste (chicken Korma) or coconut milk (south Indian chicken curry) or tamarind paste. The spice that makes the curry hot is due to the level of use of black pepper and cayenne powder. But the blending of cashew nut paste or

2- tsp Coriander powder
1-tsp Red pepper
1- tsp Cumin powder
Salt to taste
1-Tbsp Coconut powder
1- Tbsp Dry fenugreek leaves
1- Cup Chopped red bell pepper or
    chopped mushrooms (optional)
¾- tsp Garammasala
2-Tbsp Chopped fresh coriander
    leaves
Pinch of saffron

coconut milk or tamarind paste with the spices offsets the heat of the curry and gives this dish its unmistakable, not-too-rich, subtly sweet, warm and spicy flavor.

Curry Sauce with an Indian spice container

Method

1. In a bowl transfer yogurt and beat it smooth with a fork. Add 1 teaspoon of salt, 1 teaspoon each of green chilies, ginger, garlic and ½ tsp of red pepper, 2-tablespoon of lemon juice and 1-tablespoon of oil.

2. Add the chicken cubes. Mix well to coat chicken pieces with spices and yogurt. Leave the chicken in the marinade preferably overnight or for at least 1 hour.

3. Heat the oil and fry the onions remaining green chilies and ginger until the onions turn brown and then add the garlic.

4. Add all the whole spices, cloves, peppercorns, cinnamon sticks, cardamoms, cumin seeds, and wait till the cumin seeds start to pop.

5. Add the tomato sauce, chopped tomatoes and all the ground spices like turmeric powder, coriander powder, red pepper, cumin powder, salt, desiccated coconut and dried fenugreek leaves.

6. Stir well to mix for few minutes or until the oil separates from the sauce.

7. Add the marinated chicken along with the marinade and stir and cook for 5 minutes on medium, low heat. Cover the pan with a lid.

8. Simmer over medium heat till the chicken is tender (about 20–25 minutes).

9. Fry the mushrooms and bell peppers in a one- tablespoon of oil on high heat for 2-3 minutes and set them aside.

10. Now at this point you can add the fried chopped bell pepper or chopped mushrooms if you wish and stir well. Cook not more than for 5–10 minutes. Do not overcook them and leave them crunchy.

11. Add the cream, coriander leaves and garammasala and mix. Cook for another 2 minutes and bring it to boil.

12. Serve in a serving dish sprinkled with few chopped coriander leaves and garammasala and saffron and enjoy with pea pulav or white rice.

13. Serves 4-8.

Cold Sesame Noodles with Shrimp and Crispy Vegetables

Ingredients

For noodles

8-Oz Large Shrimp, peeled and deveined

1- Cup Snow peas

1- Red Bell pepper, cut into 1/8-inch-thick strips

4- Scallions thinly sliced

Half Seedless cucumber, thinly sliced

1-Cup Firm or extra-firm tofu, ½- inch cubes

¾- Lbs Dried soba noodles/ dried linguine/ spaghetti/Lo Mein/Chinese egg noodles

For peanut dressing

½- Cup Smooth peanut butter

¼- Cup Soy sauce

1/3- Cup Warm water

1-Tbsp Chopped peeled fresh ginger

1-Medium garlic clove, chopped

2-Tbsp Rice vinegar

1 ½- Tbsp Asian toasted sesame oil

1 ½-Tbsp Honey

1-tsp Dried hot red pepper/ Chili sauce

1- Tbsp Sesame seeds, toasted

2-Tbsp toasted crushed peanuts

You could find them all over New York City in the 1970s and '80s, or at Hwa Yuan on East Broadway, at the Empire Szechuan chain uptown, at Tang Tang's near Gramercy Park. Bright with flavor, slippery against the plastic chopsticks, they represented one of the great steps forward for Chinese food in the United States in the post-chop-suey era. Away from bland monotony and toward real complexity of flavor these sesame noodles were soft and luxurious, bathed in an emulsified mixture of sesame paste and peanut butter, rendered vivid and fiery by chili oil and sweetened by sugar, cut by vinegar, made fantastic by technique. After 1965 there was a flow of new immigrants and during this period some good Chinese chefs arrived in New York and set up restaurants that over time began to offer a new kind of Chinese food, one remodeled first to fit and then to mold American tastes. They called it "Szechuan food," this new style of cooking became as much a part of 1970s Manhattan as the drugs, Hippies and disco. And as New York went, so went the nation, a cold and fiery dish meant to combat the lazy, brutal humidity of a Chinese summer became a staple of take-out menus across the United States.

In fact, now traditional Szechuan dishes can be found at nearly every Chinese restaurant across America. And of all the Szechuan dishes to earn a place in Americans' hearts, cold sesame noodles might be the most loved. The dish—thin egg noodles tossed in a spicy sauce of peanut oil and peanut butter, sesame oil, and hot Chile, could not be more simple or palate pleasing.

Method

1. Boil 4-5 cups of water in a saucepan. Add shrimp, cook for 2 minutes. Add snow peas, cook shrimp and snow peas for 1 minute longer. Transfer to a bowl filled with cold water with a slotted spoon and drain the water.

2. In a large serving bowl place shrimp, snow peas and add red bell pepper, scallions and cucumber julienned, tofu and set it aside.

3. Cook pasta according to package directions; rinse under cold water; drain. Add to serving bowl.

4. Meanwhile, in a blender blend all the ingredients of peanut dressing: peanut butter, soy sauce, water, ginger, garlic, rice vinegar, sesame oil and honey.

5. Stir the peanut dressing into pasta and shrimp and vegetable mixture; toss to coat well. Sprinkle with crushed red peppers and sesame seeds. Garnish with sliced cucumber, if desired.

6. Serves 4.

> **Note: If not serving immediately, prepare as above but toss with peanut sauce just before serving.**

Chicken Chow Mein (Fried Noodles)

Ingredients

- 12-Oz Soba noodles or other Chinese noodles
- 1 ¼-Cup Peanut oil or vegetable oil
- 1 ½- Lbs Lean pork or Chicken or Beef thinly sliced
- ¼- Cup cornstarch
- 2-tsp Sugar
- ¼ -Cup Dark soy sauce
- 3- Tbsp Sesame oil
- 2-Tbsp Chopped ginger
- 1-Tbsp Chopped garlic
- 2- Stalks celery diced
- 1-Large onion chopped
- ¼- Cup Oyster sauce
- 1 ½- Cup Chicken broth
- 1-Tbsp Molasses
- 1-8 Oz Can Water chestnuts sliced
- 1-Lb Bean sprouts/15 Oz can of corn
- 1-4 Oz Can Mushrooms, drained
- Salt and pepper
- 1-Bunch green onions
- Blanched almond, lightly toasted
- Red pepper flakes to garnish
- 3- Cups White rice/Jasmine rice

Chinese invented the noodles and changed the way we eat, that's not an overstatement. In American Chinese cuisine, Chow mein is stir fried noodles dish consisting of noodles, chicken, pork, beef or shrimp, onions and celery. It is often served as a specific dish at all westernized Chinese restaurants.

Chow Mein Noodles is one of the most popular Chinese noodles dish in the US. It literally means, fried noodles in Cantonese dialect. Chow mein is also a favorite Chinese take-out item. The dish consists of some shredded vegetables and some protein (either chicken, pork, beef, seafood, or combination) in gravy and it is cheap, filling, and sinfully gratifying. Chow Mein noodles are versatile. There are so many ways to prepare them–stir-fry, pan-fry, boil, blanched, in soup, with gravy, or dry. The pronunciation chow mein comes from the Taishan dialect of Chinese, spoken by immigrants from Taishan to America. There are two main kinds of chow miens' available in the market- Steamed chow mein, and-Crispy chow mein, also known as Hong Kong style chow mein. The steamed chow mein has a softer texture, while the latter is crispier and drier. Crispy chow mein uses fried, flat noodles, while soft chow mein uses long, rounded noodles.

Method

1. Cook the noodles according to package directions, rinse under cold- water and pat them dry with a towel. Heat 1 cup of peanut oil and fry by turning them once until golden brown.

2. Cut meat into thin strips. Combine 2-tablespoon cornstarch with sugar, blend in soy sauce and 3-tablespoon sesame oil and mix to blend. Add the pork strips and marinade them for 20 minutes.

3. In a wok or large sauté pan heat remaining ¼- cup peanut oil and add ginger, garlic and then the marinated meat. Brown on all sides lightly. Add the celery and the onions. Cook few more minutes.

4. Wisk together 3- tablespoon oyster sauce and 1 ½-cup of chicken broth with remaining cornstarch and add it to the meat mixture. Simmer, covered on low heat for few minutes until well blended.

5. Add molasses, water chestnuts, bean sprouts and mushrooms; heat thoroughly.

6. Season with salt and pepper. Garnish with chopped green onions and toasted almonds and red pepper flakes.

7. Transfer the chicken or pork chow mein onto a warm plate and top with fried noodles. Serve over white rice.

8. Serves 6-8.

Crab Rangoon (Thai)

Ingredients

8-OZ Cream cheese

8- Fresh crab meat or canned Crabmeat, drained and flaked

2-Green onion thinly, chopped

1-tsp Minced ginger

1- tsp Worcestershire sauce

1-tsp Soy sauce

Freshly Ground black pepper, to taste

1-tsp Brown sugar/white sugar

1- Large Clove garlic, smashed, peeled, and finely minced

1- Package Won ton wrappers

1- Small bowl Water

Oil for deep-frying, as needed

Crab Rangoon is an appetizer in American Thai cuisine. They are deep fried dumplings stuffed with a combination of cream cheese, lightly flaked crabmeat (more commonly, canned crab meat or imitation crab meat), scallions and/ or garlic. The fillings are wrapped in Chinese wonton wrappers in a triangular or flower shape and then deep fried in vegetable oil. The history of Crab Rangoon seems unclear. Cream cheese, like other cheeses, is essentially nonexistent in Southeast Asian and Thai cuisine, so it is unlikely that the dish is actually of east or Southeast Asian origin. Crab Rangoon has been on the menu of the "Polynesian style" restaurants like Trader Vic's in San Francisco since at least 1956. Although the appetizer is allegedly derived from an authentic Burmese recipe, the dish was probably invented in the U.S.A. Crab Rangoon is served often with soy sauce, plum sauce, duck sauce, sweet and sour sauce or mustard for dipping.

Method

1. Combine the cream cheese and crabmeat. Mix in the remaining 7 filling ingredients one at a time. Set aside.

2. On a flat surface, lay out a won ton wrapper in front of you. Wet the edges of the won ton.

3. Add 1½- teaspoon of filling to the middle, bring up corners and pinch together, along with sides.

4. Keep the completed Crab Rangoon covered with a damp towel or paper towel to keep them from drying out while preparing the remainder.

5. Heat wok and add oil for deep-frying. When oil is ready (the temperature should be between 360 - 375°F) carefully slide in the Crab Rangoon few at a time.

6. Deep-fry until they are golden brown, about 3 minutes, turning once. Remove with a slotted spoon and drain. Serve hot, with sweet and sour Sauce or Chinese hot mustard sauce.

7. Serves 3-4.

Szechuan Chicken

Ingredients
4-Chicken breasts, boneless,
    skinless, about 7 ounces each
2- Egg whites
2-Tbsp Cornstarch

Sauce
2-Tbsp dry sherry /cooking wine
1-tsp Worcestershire sauce
2-tsp Tabasco sauce
2–tsp Sesame oil
1- Soy Sauce
2-Tbsp Brown sugar
¼-tsp Cayenne pepper
½- tsp Crushed dried red chilies,
    or to taste
1-Tbsp Chopped ginger

Other
1-Cup +1-Tbsp Vegetable oil
3-Green Onions, chopped
4- Carrots, cut into thin strips
½- Red Bell pepper, sliced
½- Green Bell pepper, sliced
¼-Cup dry roasted peanuts

Szechuan cuisine originated in Sichuan China. Sichuan is colloquially known as heavenly country due to its abundance of food, natural resources and hot and spicy food but in reality only a small portion of the Szechuan cuisine is spicy. According to at least one Chinese culinary writer, Szechuan cuisine is composed of seven basic flavors: Sour, pungent, hot, sweet, bitter, aromatic, and salty. Sichuan food is divided into five different types: Sumptuous banquet, ordinary banquet, popularized food, home-style food, and food snacks. Szechuan cuisine has changed little over the years and remains a staple of Chinese-American cuisine.

The Great Wall of China

This spicy Szechuan chicken recipe gets its heat from Tabasco sauce, cayenne pepper and crushed chilies. Parboiling or "oil poaching" the chicken in hot oil prior to preparing the dish helps make it extra tender. It consists of breaded chicken bits tossed in a spicy and flavorful sauce. The sauce uses ingredients such as oyster sauce and chicken broth to give it that amazing flavor. This dish reminds me a lot of Kung Pao Chicken. A light coating of cornstarch would be better if you want your chicken bits to be crispy. This dish is great served with rice and vegetables. Enjoy.

Method

1. Cut the chicken breasts into thin strips.

2. Combine the sauce ingredients in a small bowl and set aside.

3. Whisk the cornstarch into the egg whites. Coat the chicken strips in the cornstarch mixture.

4. Heat 1-cup oil in the wok. Cook the chicken strips briefly in the hot oil until they turn white. Remove the chicken and drain on paper towels.

5. Clean out the wok and add remaining 1–tablespoon oil. When the oil is hot add some of the chopped onions, carrots and then add both the peppers. Stir it for few minutes.

6. Add the prepared sauce. Heat and mix the sauce in with the vegetables.

7. Return the chicken to the wok.

8. Stir-fry 1 to 2 more minutes. Sprinkle the remaining green onions and peanuts and serve with rice.

9. Serves 4.

Chicken with Walnuts

Ingredients

- 1½- Tbsp Cornstarch
- ½ -Cup Chicken bouillon or Beef broth
- ¼- Cup molasses/ brown sugar/ corn syrup
- ¼- Cup Soy sauce
- 2- Tbsp Dry sherry / cooking wine
- ¼- tsp -Red pepper to taste
- 4-Tbs Vegetable oil
- 1-Cup Walnut halves/cashews
- 1-Lb. Boneless chicken breast in 1-inch cubes
- 1- Cup Sliced onion1 ½- tsp Fresh ginger, minced
- 1-tsp Chopped garlic
- 1- Green or Red bell pepper, cut into strips

Try this Stir-Fried walnuts and Chicken recipe! It's a gorgeous oriental celebration of colors and tastes - and it's quick and easy to make. Serve this with white rice and serve for quick delicious dinner. Here is the recipe I found very appetizing and that became a favorite of my family.

Method

1. In a small bowl stir together cornstarch, bouillon, corn syrup, soy sauce, and sherry and ground red pepper. Set aside.

2. In large skillet or wok, heat 3-tablespoon oil over medium-high heat.

3. Add walnuts, stir- fry for 2 minutes. Remove walnuts, reserve.

4. Add chicken, Stir-fry for 2 minutes or until chicken turns white. Remove chicken, reserve.

5. Heat remaining one-tablespoon oil. Add onion, ginger, garlic and pepper strips. Stir-fry for 1 minute.

6. Return chicken to skillet. Restir cornstarch mixture, add to the skillet and mix well. Bring to boil over medium heat and boil 1 minute. Stir in the fried walnuts. Serve with white rice. Makes a quick week- day meal.

7. Makes 4 servings.

Szechuan Eggplant

Ingredients

1 ½- Lbs Asian eggplant diced
4-Tbsp Soy sauce
¼- Cup vegetable stock
1-tsp Chili sauce
1-tsp White sugar
½-tsp Ground black pepper
2-Tbsp Oyster sauce
1-Tbsp Cornstarch
4-Tbsp Water
2-Tbsp Vegetable oil
2-Cloves garlic, minced
4-Large green onions, finely
    chopped
1-Tbsp Chopped fresh ginger
    root
1-Tbsp Sesame oil
1-Tbsp Sesame seeds and
    chopped cilantro for garnish
3-Cups Cooked white
    rice/Jasmine rice

Folks who love spicy food will approve of this fantastic vegetarian eggplant dish! Common preparation techniques in Szechuan cuisine include stir-frying, steaming and braising but there are many more distinct techniques to preparing this dish. Szechuan cuisine has changed little over the years and remains a staple of Chinese-American cuisine. Beef is somewhat more common in Szechuan cuisine than it is in a typical Chinese cuisine. Egg -plant is a great substitute to make this vegetarian dish.

Method

1. Cut the Eggplant into 1-inch cubes. In a medium bowl combine the soy sauce, vegetable stock, chili sauce, sugar, ground black pepper and oyster sauce. Stir together well and set it aside.

2. Combine the cornstarch and water, and set aside.

3. Heat 2-tablespoon vegetable oil over high heat and once it is hot sauté the garlic, half of the green onions, ginger stirring constantly, until browned.

4. Transfer the eggplant into the pan and stir all together. Pour the reserved soy sauce mixture over all, cover the pan, reduce heat to medium low and let simmer for 15 minutes, stirring occasionally. Stir in the reserved cornstarch mixture and let it cook until thickened. Finally, stir in the rest of the green onions and the sesame oil. Garnish with sesame seeds and chopped cilantro. Serve with white rice.

5. Serves 4-6.

Cashew Chicken

Ingredients

Marinade for the chicken
- 4-tsp Soy sauce
- 4 tsp Egg white
- 4 tsp Corn Starch
- 1-Tbsp Sesame oil

Other
- 1 ½ Lbs- Breast of chicken cut up into 1-inch pieces
- ¼-Cup peanut oil
- ¼-Cup Cashew nuts
- 2- Tbsp Chopped onions
- 1- Tbsp Ginger chopped
- 1-Medium-sized green bell peppers, seeded and cut into 1 inch squares
- ¼- Lb Fresh mushrooms, washed and quartered
- 1, 4- Oz Water Chestnuts, drained and quartered,

Sauce
- 2- Cups Chicken broth
- 2- Tbsp Hoi sin sauce
- 1-Tbsp White sugar
- 2-Tbsp Soy sauce
- 1-tsp Gound white pepper
- 1-tsp Chopped ginger
- 4-Tbsp Cornstarch
- 1-Tbsp Chopped Cilantro

Tiananmen Square with their Imperial palace in the background, China

It is a simple Chinese-American dish that combines chicken and cashews, and a thick oyster sauce. Chicken cashew is easy to make. You marinade the chicken overnight with a little cornstarch so that the chicken retains its moistness and flavor. A particularly notable version of the dish, using breaded, deep fried chicken rather than stir-fried is closely associated with the city of Springfield, IL. David Leong, a chef, who moved to the United States from China in 1940, struggled to gain acceptance for the foods of his homeland and he began searching for a dish that would appeal to local residents' taste buds. Local's love of fried chicken prompted Leong to come up with an idea of combining fried chicken chunks with Chinese oyster sauce, and a handful of chopped green onions. Some how it hit the pallet of the people and it was an immediate hit with the local crowd. His famous cashew chicken recipe was so popular he soon opened Leong's Tea House in Springfield. The dish became so popular in the Springfield area that it is often cited as the unofficial "dish of the city". Many variations keep coming up and it is hard to say which is the best one. Here is one.

Method

1. Mix the ingredients for marinade and marinade the chicken.

2. Heat 2 tablespoons of oil in a wok or skillet and add the marinated chicken. Fry about three to four minutes until it is no longer red and turns white.

3. Remove the chicken to the paper towels with a slotted spoon. Drain off the oil.

4. Heat another one tablespoon oil and slightly brown the cashew nuts, remove and set them aside

5. Add the remaining 1-tablespoon of oil and add the chopped onions, ginger, green bell peppers, fresh mushrooms, and water chestnuts to the same wok. Fry to cook for 2 minutes. Set them aside.

6. Heat 2 cups of broth to boiling in a medium saucepan. Add hoi sin sauce, sugar, soy sauce and white pepper and ginger, Mix 4 tablespoons cornstarch with a small amount of cold water in a cup. Stir cornstarch mixture slowly into broth mixture to thicken, then simmer for another 5 minutes over medium-low heat.

7. Add this sauce mixture to the wok with all the vegetables. Mix and bring it to a boil.

8. Add the chicken pieces from the paper towels, stirring, until the sauce is thickened and translucent. Add the fried cashews. Sprinkle with cilantro and serve.

9. Transfer the entire mixture to a serving dish or platter, and serve immediately with white rice.

10. Serves 4-6

Tofu Curry

Ingredients

- 1- Tbsp Vegetable oil
- 12-Oz Extra-firm tofu, drained and cubed
- ½- tsp Salt
- 2-3Tbsp Butter or margarine
- 1- Small onion, chopped
- 2- Cloves garlic, minced
- 1-tsp Minced ginger
- 2-3 Bell peppers, cut into nice chunks
- 2- Zucchinis, sliced thick
- ½- tsp Turmeric powder
- 1-tsp Coriander powder
- ½-tsp Cumin powder and Cayenne pepper /ea
- 1-Tbsp Fresh or frozen lemongrass
- 1-tsp Salt
- ½-tsp Black pepper
- 10- Oz Can coconut milk
- ¼- Cup Chopped Fresh coriander

This Thai Tofu Coconut Curry recipe is very delicious plus simple to make. A lot of vegetarian curries tend to be rather bland and tasteless, but not this one! Made with tofu and lots of fresh vegetables, this dish is vegetarian, vegan, and gluten-free but great for anyone who wants to eat something healthy and nutritious without sacrificing taste.

To make a very flavorful Tofu Curry first fry the tofu on low heat until light brown without any oil. Frying leaves your tofu dry and firm, ready to suck up the flavors of a marinade like a sponge. Place the dried tofu pieces in the marinade and stir well, making sure the tofu is submerged. Marinate for at least a half an hour and then use this delicious firm and flavorful tofu in a stir-fry- that leaves even meat-eaters impressed.

Method

1. Heat one tablespoon of oil in a large skillet over medium-high heat. Add tofu cubes, salt and fry until golden on all sides, stirring occasionally. Set aside in a bowl.

2. Melt butter or margarine in the same skillet over medium heat. Add the onion, ginger and garlic cook and stir until translucent. Add bell peppers and zucchini; cook and stir 5 minutes.

3. Add turmeric, coriander powder, cumin powder, Cayenne pepper, lemongrass, salt, pepper and stir for ½ minute and add the coconut milk and fresh coriander and return the tofu to the skillet.

4. Simmer over low-medium heat, stirring occasionally, until the liquid has thickened up.

5. Serve on noodles, Bansmati rice or Jasmine rice.

6. Serves 4-6.

Sweet and Sour Pork

Ingredients

½-Cup Flour

Salt and pepper to season the flour

¼-Cup Corn Starch

½-Cup Soy sauce

¼-Cup Oyster sauce

1-Lb Bone less pork, cut into cubes

Corn oil for frying

1-Cup Orange juice

½- Cup Ketchup

2-Tbsp Sugar

¼ -Cup Red wine vinegar

2-Tbsp Plum sauce

1- Clove garlic, minced

1-Tbsp Minced ginger

2- Tbsp Diced celery

1- Cup Cubed green and sweet red pepper

½- Cup Sliced green onions

1-Cup Orange sections or pineapple chunks

Salt, Black pepper and red pepper to taste

Sprinkle of garammasala

This dish became popular in the United States in the early 20th century after the Chinese migrant gold miners and railroad workers turned to cookery as trades. The original meaning of the American term chop suey (A traditional Jiangsu dish called Pork in sugar and vinegar sauce) refers to sweet and sour pork.

Records show that the origin of sweet and sour pork was in 18th century Canton or earlier by the renowned Long Family in the prosperous neighborhood of Shunde County (is a district of Foshan in the Guangdong province, China) who used sweet and sour pork to test the skills of their family chefs. The recipe below does not use the fried pieces of pork but you can fry the pieces if you like.

Sweet and Sour Pork, the ubiquitous and arguably the most well known Chinese recipe in the world, is a classic Cantonese dish and is called "goo lou yok" in Cantonese dialect. Sweet and sour pork is very pleasing to the palate because of the flavorsome sweet and sour sauce—the sweetness from sugar and tanginess from ketchup and sharp rice vinegar and crispiness from crispy fried pork pieces. The green and red bell peppers and pineapple pieces are just icing on the cake. The secret of an authentic sweet and sour pork dish lies in the perfect balance of the sweet vs. sour taste of the sauce. To master this dish learn to make the sweet and sour sauce because it is the soul of this dish. If you fail the sweet and sour sauce, you fail the dish. To bring extra zing also use and substitute plum sauce, Worcestershire sauce and oyster sauce wherever necessary.

Method

1. Mix the flour with salt and pepper. Mix I/4-cup cornstarch with ¼ cup of seasoned flour, soy sauce and oyster sauce.

2. Marinade the pork pieces and toss them well into this mixture of marinade for one hour to overnight.

3. Dredge the pieces in remaining seasoned flour and fry them in a large frying pan in one inch of corn oil until golden brown. Drain them on paper towel and set them aside.

4. In a separate wok combine orange juice, ketchup, sugar, vinegar, plum sauce, garlic and ginger and wisk to blend. Add celery, peppers and green onions.

5. Stir in the pork fried pieces. Stirring constantly, bring to boil over medium heat and simmer until the pork is tender.

6. Stir in oranges or pineapple chunks and serve with white Chinese rice.

7. Test the sauce and adjust the seasoning according to taste. Garnish with red pepper and garammasala.

8. Serves 4.

Chicken Chop Suey

Ingredients

- ¾- Cup Precooked thin sliced chicken
- ½- Egg White
- 1-Tbsp +1-tsp Cornstarch paste made with a little water
- ¼-Cup Peanut oil or shortening
- 3-4 Green onions chopped
- 1-tsp Finely chopped garlic and ginger each
- 12- Oz Stir-fry vegetables
- 1-tsp Sugar
- ½-tsp Red pepper or to taste
- 2-Tbsp Soy sauce
- 1-Tbsp Rice wine
- ½-Cup Bean sprouts
- ½- Cup Chicken stock
- Few drops Sesame oil and Chopped Cilantro to garnish

It is this Chicken Chop Suey dish that heralded Chinese food to the western world at the end of the nineteenth century. It is rather amazing to think that one of the world's greatest cuisines could have been represented by a dish that did not even originate in China itself, but thousands of miles away in San Francisco, USA. It does have its roots from Taishan (Toisan) a district of Guandong province (Canton), which was the home of many of the early Chinese immigrants to the U.S. Chop suey consists of meat (often chicken, fish, beef, Prawns or pork) and eggs, cooked quickly with vegetables such as bean sprouts, cabbage and celery and bound in a starch-thickened sauce. It is typically served with rice but can become the Chinese-American form of chow mein with the addition of stir-fried noodles. Chop suey has become a prominent part of American Chinese cuisine, Filipino Chinese cuisine, Canadian Chinese cuisine, German Chinese cuisine, Polynesian Chinese cuisine and Indian Chinese cuisine.

Method

1. Coat the chicken slices in a mixture of egg white and one- tablespoon paste of corn flour made with little water and a pinch of salt.

2. Heat 2 tablespoons of peanut oil or shortening until hot. Add the coated chicken and sauté for 2 minutes. Remove it from the skillet and set aside.

3. Add remaining 2 tablespoons of oil. Add the onions, ginger, garlic and sauté for a minute and add the stir-fry vegetables. Stir to mix and add sugar, red pepper, soy sauce, rice wine and the bean sprouts.

4. Add the sautéed chicken and stir-fry for 2 minutes.

5. Mix the remaining one- teaspoon cornstarch paste into the chicken broth and add it to chicken and vegetable mixture. Cook for 3 minutes or until the Sauce reaches the consistency you desire. Season to taste.

6. Sprinkle with drops of sesame oil and cilantro and serve at once with hot cooked rice.

7. Serves 2-4

Note: Substitute beef, pork or shrimp for chicken if you wish.

Orange Chicken

Ingredients

Preparation of Chicken
 1-Egg well beaten
 Salt and pepper to taste
 2-Tbsp Cup flour and 2-Tbsp
  Corn starch mixture
 ½- Lb Chicken breast (cut into
  bite-size cubes)
 2- Tbsp Oil
 1-tsp Garlic (minced)
 1-tsp Ginger (minced)
 5- Dried chilies (cut into 1.5 inch
  length, seeded and soaked in
  warm water)
 1-tsp Minced orange zest
 2-Green onions (white
  part only) chopped into
  threads for garnish

Orange Sauce
 ¼- Cup Freshly-squeezed orange
  juice
 3- Tbsp Canned chicken broth
 1-Tbsp Soy sauce
 2-tsp Chinese rice wine or dry
  sherry
 ½-tsp Sesame oil
 1-tsp Rice vinegar
 5-tsp Sugar
 1/8-tsp White pepper powder
 1-tsp Cornstarch
 Salt to taste

The Chinese-American dish of Orange Chicken is of Hunan origin. The dish originated in the Hunan province of China. Located in the southeast. It has a subtropical climate with mild winters, making it ideal for growing the oranges, tangerines and lemons that are native to Asia. Hunan cuisine is also known for it's liberal usage of chili peppers. This popular dish found in Chinese restaurant in the United States is a variation of General Tso's chicken (dish is named after General Tso Tsung-tang, a Qing Dynasty general and statesman) and real roots of the dish lie in the post 1949 exodus of chefs to the United States. The authentic Orange chicken found in China is deep- fried first then stir fried in soy based sauce that has been flavored with dried chopped orange peels. It is garnished with bok choy and baby carrots. The variety of orange chicken most commonly found at North American fast food restaurants consists of chopped, battered, and fried chicken pieces coated in a sweet orange-flavored chili sauce, which thickens or caramelizes to a glaze. The dish is very popular in the United States and Chinese restaurants in North America serve it in varying levels of spiciness depending on levels of included peppers. It can be prepared either by pan- frying or deep-frying.

Method

1. Mix together egg, salt and pepper and in a bowl and add the chicken pieces into it. Coat them with the mixture of flour and cornstarch and set them aside.

2. Mix the orange sauce ingredients and set aside.

3. In a wok, add 1-tablespoon of cooking oil and quickly stir-fry the chicken pieces until golden brown. Set them aside.

4. Add the remaining 1-Tbsp of oil and add minced garlic and ginger until aromatic. Add in the dried red chilies and cook until aromatic, about one minute. Follow by the minced orange zest and then add the stir-fried chicken pieces.

5. Cook the chicken thoroughly then add the orange sauce mixture. Continue to stir-fry until the sauce thickens. Transfer to a serving bowl, garnish with the scallion threads and serve immediately with steamed rice.

6. Serves 2-4.

Kimchi Fried Rice with Korean Pepper Paste

Ingredients

- 2-Tbsp Soybean oil (can substitute canola), divided use
- 1- Egg
- 2-Tbsp red bell pepper chopped/1-Cup cooked pieces of chicken/ fried pieces of tofu
- 3-Tbsp Fresh corn kernels, removed from stalk (can substitute frozen)
- 1-Cup Kimchi drained and chopped
- 3-Cups Cooked white rice, cooled to room temperature (preferably a day old)
- ½-tsp Salt -and-pepper mix
- 2- Scallions, green part only
- 1-tsp Korean hot-pepper paste (Taeyangcho Gochujang)*

Kim chi Fried rice (bokkeumbap) is a popular dish in South Korea. Its name literally translates as "Kim chi fried rice". Kim chi bokkeumbap is made primarily with Kim chi and rice, along with other available ingredients such as diced vegetables or meats. Pork or spam are the most common, however, beef, chicken, bacon or ham can be used. Instead of meat, canned tuna, shrimp or mushrooms can be used as a replacement. Meat ingredients are chopped into the dish together with vegetables such as onion, carrot or zucchini. However, ingredients depend on personal preferences and occasion. A small amount of minced garlic and sliced green pepper can be used as seasoning. These ingredients are fried in a pan with a little vegetable or sesame oil.

Method

1. Heat wok and add 1- tablespoon soybean oil and swirl around wok.

2. Add egg and scramble until just done, remove from wok and set aside.

3. Add remaining tablespoon soybean oil and swirl around wok. Add bell peppers and corn (Add chicken pieces or tofu pieces or any other vegetables) and stir fry for a minute. Also add chopped Kim Chi and cook for 1 minute.

4. Add rice, spreading and pounding rice to break it up. Stir rice to prevent burning.

5. Add scallions and egg, and stir-fry for 5 seconds.

6. Transfer the rice to a serving bowl. Makes a great snack or use it as a filling for a burger.

7. Dollop 1- teaspoon Korean hot pepper paste (below) in the center of a plate and serve the rice around it.

8. Serves 4-6.

*Note: Gochujang Korean pepper paste is a core to Korean cuisine. It is a savory and pungent fermented Korean condiment made from red chili, glutinous rice, fermented soybeans and salt. This chili paste is essential for any Korean food lover. Traditionally, it has been naturally fermented over years in large earthen pots outdoors, more often on an elevated stone platform, called jangdokdae in the backyards of their homes.

Mexican Specialties

Mexican, Salsa folk dance

Mexican cuisine is known for its varied flavors, colorful decoration and variety of spices and ingredients, most of which are native to the country. The cuisine of Mexico has evolved through thousands of years of blending indigenous cultures with European elements added after the 16th century. In November 2010 UNESCO added Mexican cuisine to its lists of the world's "intangible Cultural Heritage". The staples of Mexican foods are typically corn and beans. Corn is used to make masa dough for Tamales, Tortillas, Gorditas and many other corn-based foods. Mexican cuisine is considered one of the most varied in the world, after Chinese and Indian. The most frequently used herbs and spices in Mexican cuisine are chili powder, oregano, cilantro, epazote, cinnamon and cocoa. Chipotle (smoke-dried jalapeno chili) is also common in Mexican cuisine. Many Mexican dishes also contain garlic and onions.

Before the arrival of Europeans, New Mexico's current borders overlapped the areas of the Navajo, Mescalero and Chiricahua tribes. The Spaniards brought their cuisine that mingled with the indigenous. At the end of the Mexican American war, New Mexico became part of the United States, and was strongly influenced by incoming American tastes.

When Americans speak about Mexican food, they are usually referring to Tex Mex (or Cal-Mex) cooking, an extremely popular cuisine that spans the long border between the New Mexico (United States) and Mexico. The food of the southwestern US state of New Mexico, and the dishes of many of the Native American people of the southwestern US, employ similar dish names to many Tex-Mex and some Mexican dishes, but use different flavorings and cooking techniques. An authentic Mexican restaurant, perhaps an expensive one in a major city, will usually go out of its way in its advertising to distance itself from Tex-Mex cuisine. A more informal restaurant may offer both types of food from the same menu.

Dishes like Chili, Fajitas, Salsa, Tortilla Chips, Corn Chips, Chimichangas, Quesadillas, Burritos, and Nachos may be great food, but they are home grown American inventions. Even dishes that exist in Mexico like Enchiladas, Tacos, and Tamales are cooked and served differently than in the United States. True Mexican dishes are not cooked to be burning hot (with chilies), as are many of their relatives north of the border. Chile sauce is a condiment in Mexico, to be added according to the taste of the diner.

American variants of Mexican cooking also add prodigious quantities of cheese either shredded or melted, to nearly every dish, a practice rare in Mexico itself. The same heavy hand applies to the American use of sauces of all kinds. North of the border portions are larger, plates crammed with dishes that tend to run into one another. In Mexico the soft corn tortilla performs the function that bread on the table performs in the United States, it is a side starch. In the United States, Tortillas, often fried up to a state of crispiness, becomes an ingredient in nearly every dish.

Of all dishes enjoyed on both sides of the border, Guacamole may be the hardest to vary: a simple dip made from avocados, onions, chilies, spices and limejuice. Even here, Americans tend to mash the avocado into too mushy a paste, overdo the chilies, add too much cilantro or otherwise botch this Mexican classic. The Mexican chef will ideally prepare the guacamole using the traditional lava stone mortar and pestle called the Molcajete, first grinding the chilies, onions and cilantro together with salt before gently folding in—not mashing— slices of the avocado, then adding lime juice or possibly a small dollop of diced tomato.

Mexican Tamale

Ingredients

Tamale Filling
- 1 ¼- Lbs Pork loin
- 1- Large Onion, halved
- 4 –Cloves Garlic
- Water as needed to cover pork
- 4- Large Tomatillo
- 1-Large Jalapeno Chile
- 1-Cup Water
- 2- Tbsp Roasted cumin powder
- 1 ½- tsp Salt
- 2- Tbsp Chopped cilantro

Tamale Dough
- 2/3-Cup Shortening
- 1-8 Oz Package dried cornhusks
- 2- Cups Mesa harina
- 1-(10.5Oz) Can Beef broth
- 1-tsp Baking powder
- ½-tsp Salt
- 1- Cup Sour cream

Classic Mexican tamales are a very popular Christmas Mexican food. The tamales are made from mesa harina like corn tortillas, and filled with a variety of fillings. Tamale fillings range from savory vegetarian bean to beef, and pork, chicken and seafood versions to sweet, fruit-filled desserts. Just about anything you can eat can be used to make tamales, even sweet potatoes. Which by the way are absolutely delicious. Making tamales can be very labor intensive; usually families will gather together and divide the process in assembly line fashion making dozens of incredible homemade tamales. While pork is traditional filling but chicken is great substitute, it's tender, it's fresh, and it's full of flavor. As a bonus, you can simply buy a rotisserie chicken and use the meat from it, if you like. It'll make your life a little easier. While beef isn't used in an authentic Mexican tamale recipe, it's a good option if your family doesn't like or doesn't eat pork.

Tamales are typically made with corn masa dough and a filling of beans, meats, corn or chilies and cooked over an open fire. Today, these little packages of perfection are simply steamed in their cornhusk wrapper. The wrappings provide a portable device for the filling and add a little flavor too. Tamales can be considered the Mexican version of a sandwich and are open to many interpretations. Here is a recipe for pork tamale. Chicken and Beef can easily substitute pork. Serve with sides of Spanish rice, Refried beans topped with cheese and frosty margaritas'.

Method

1. Place pork into a Dutch oven with ½- of chopped onion and two cloves of garlic, and add water to cover. Bring to a boil then reduce heat to low and simmer until the meat is cooked through, about 2 hours.

2. Place Tomatillos and chili on a baking sheet and roast until they are soft and charred at 400 °F for 20 minutes. Once they are cool enough remove stems and seeds from the chili and tomatillos.

3. Pulse the roasted tomatillos, chilies, remaining onions and garlic in a food processor until smooth and add 1 cup water, the cumin powder, salt, cilantro and pulse once or twice to combine and set the chili sauce aside.

4. Shred the cooked meat and mix it in to the chili sauce. Heat 2-tablespoons of shortening in saucepan and transfer the chili sauce with pork and cook for 10-15 minutes or until the sauce is thick.

5. Soak the cornhusks in a bowl of warm water in a large bowl.

6. Combine 2 cups mesa harina with enough beef broth to make stiff dough.

7. Beat the remaining shortening, baking powder and salt until it is fluffy.

8. Add half of the masa harina dough and mix it with some of the remaining beef broth. Keep beating to keep it fluffy. Keep adding rest of the broth and the other half of the harina to form spongy dough.

9. Spread a piece of dough out over the cornhusks to ¼- to ½- inch thickness. Place one tablespoon of the meat filling into the center. Fold the sides of the husks in toward the center and place in a steamer. Steam for 1 hour.

10. Remove tamales from husks and drizzle remaining chili sauce over them. Top with sour cream. For a creamy sauce, mix sour cream into the chili sauce and serve tamales with Spanish rice and refried beans, topped with cheese, salsa and a margarita.

11. Serves 6-8

Mexican Style Squash Soup

Ingredients

¼-Cup Butter or margarine
½- Cup Diced fresh onion
3-Cloves Garlic
1-tsp Chopped Green chili
½-Cup Chopped tomatoes
1-Lb. Cut in half zucchini, sliced
1½-Qt Chicken stock
1- tsp. Salt
½- tsp Black pepper
½-tsp Cumin powder
¼- Cayenne pepper
2-Tbsp Flour
2-Egg yolks
½-Cup Heavy cream
¼-Cup Crumbled crackers
Ground nutmeg, chopped
    cilantro and Garammasala to
    garnish

Mexican bean and squash soup is a versatile soup and each time you make it, it will be slightly different from the previous time. Start with hearty beans, broth and nutrient-rich winter squash, then embellish the basic soup with additional vegetables and Mexican-style seasonings to suit your flavor preferences. All winter squashes (are low in calories and) provide a wealth of nutrients, including fiber, beta-carotene and potassium. Season the soup with Mexican-style seasonings such as cumin, chili powder or red pepper flakes and a squeeze of fresh limejuice. Serve the soup with a dollop of reduced-fat sour cream or a sprinkling of skim milk and Monterey jack cheese.

Method

1. In a saucepan, melt 2-tablaspoons of butter. Add onions and cloves of garlic and chili. Fry few minutes and add the tomatoes. Cook until the tomatoes are softened. Gradually add sliced zucchini and 3 cups of chicken stock. Also add salt, pepper, cumin and cayenne.

2. Cover and cook 30 minutes or until squash falls apart. Mash and put through a sieve into large bowl. Add remaining stock and set aside.

3. Heat remaining 2-tablespoon of butter in a large saucepan and add the flour. Fry till it is slightly brown. Add the soup to the saucepan.

4. Cook until soup has slightly thickened, 5 to 7 minutes. Blend egg yolks with cream and crackers and stir into the hot soup.

5. Serve it hot and garnish each serving with dash of nutmeg and chopped cilantro and a dash of garammasala.

6. Serves 6-8.

Tacos Salad

Ingredients

- 1-Tbsp oil
- 1-Small onion diced
- 1-Clove garlic chopped
- ½- Lb Ground beef
- 1-Tbsp Taco seasoning
- ¼- Cup Water
- 2-Ripe tomatoes, diced
- ½-Lb Sharp Cheddar, diced
- 1-Small onion, diced
- 1-Head iceberg lettuce, washed, drained and shredded
- 1-Cup Chili beans
- 1-Tbsp Jalapeno pepper chopped
- 1-Avocado, diced
- 2-Tbsp Sliced black olives
- ¼- Cup Sour cream
- 1- Cup Salsa
- 1-Handful taco flavored chips, crushed
- 1- Cup Salad dressing (Catalina or French)
- Tortilla chips, to serve

The taco salad is a Mexican inspired dish with many variations. It first appeared in America in the 1960s. The salad is often served as a fried flour tortilla shell stuffed with shredded iceberg lettuce and topped with diced tomatoes, shredded cheddar cheese, sour cream, guacamole and salsa. The salad is topped with taco meat (ground beef) or seasoned shredded chicken. The salad may also have a base of refried beans in the shell before the lettuce is added.

Variations include a similar salad served without the tortilla base but with a "bowl" of Spanish rice and refried beans dressed out with similar ingredients.

The taco salad also takes a twist in many American homes. Instead of using a tortilla or a bowl of Spanish rice as a base the meat is tossed with tomatoes, lettuce, onions, black beans, black olives, avocado, and crushed tortilla chips and topped with sour cream and salsa, making the dish very similar to the Mexican dish of nachos and it is then served with tortilla chips.

Method

1. Heat 1-tablespoon oil in a saucepan over medium heat.

2. Add the onions and sauté until tender, about 5-7 minutes. Add the garlic and sauté until fragrant, just a few minutes

3. Add the ground beef and cook draining any grease when done.

4. Mix in the taco seasoning and water and simmer until most of the liquid has evaporated, about 3-5 minutes. Set it aside.

Assemble salad

5. Combine the tomatoes, cheese, onion, lettuce, and add it to the cooked beef in a large bowl. Add the chili beans, Jalapeno, avocado, black olives, sour cream, salsa and mix well.

6. Just before serving, add the taco chips, tossing to combine with other ingredients.

7. Top each serving with dressing. Serve with tortilla chips.

8. Serves 4.

Note: Usually Ranch dressing or Italian dressings works very well with Taco salads.

Hearty Beef and Chicken Chimichangas

Ingredients

1-Tbsp Paprika
1-Tbsp Cayenne pepper
1-Tbsp Garlic powder
1-tsp Cumin powder
1-Tbsp Flour
2- Tbsp Vegetable oil
3-Lbs Beef tenderloin cut into
     1-inch cubes
2- Yellow onions, chopped
3-tsp Seeded and minced jalapenos
2-Tbsp Chopped garlic
2 ¼- Cups Beef or Chicken Broth
¼- Cup Red /White wine
     vinegar
1-15 Oz Can Pinto beans drained
     and washed
1-15 Oz Can, Black beans
     drained and washed
¼- Cup Lime juice
½- Cup Chopped fresh cilantro
     leaves
4 to 6 Cups Corn oil for frying
10 (11-inch) Tortillas slightly
     moistened
2 ½- Cups Shredded pepper jack
     cheese
2-Cups Shredded iceberg lettuce
¾- Cup Salsa
1-Cup Sour cream
½- Cup Seeded and diced
     tomatoes
1- Avocado, diced

Beef and chicken chimichangas are prepared by folding the tortillas over fillings of meat, hot chilies, onions, 2 kinds of cheeses, herbs and spices. Lard is used for frying the ground beef because it is a traditional Mexican ingredient, but feel free to substitute vegetable oil if you prefer. If you have enjoyed a beef and chicken chimichanga in a Mexican restaurant, you will be delighted how easy it is to make the exact same dish yourself at home. Chimichangas are quintessentially Mexican and their crunchy fried exterior complements their soft, juicy filling perfectly. This is a dish of contrasts and you will enjoy the blend of flavors in every bite.

Method

1. In a small bowl, combine paprika, cayenne, cumin powder, garlic powder and flour. Set aside.

2. In a heavy bottomed, large stock-pot, heat vegetable oil over medium-high heat. Add beef cubes and brown on all sides.

3. Add onions and jalapenos and sauté for 4 to 5 minutes. Add I-tablespoon garlic and sauté for 1 minute more. Mix in flour mixture, stirring frequently, for 2 to 3 minutes and add the beef broth, vinegar and stir well to mix.

4. Lower heat to medium-low and simmer for 2 hours, adding additional beef broth, if necessary, when meat is fork tender, add the Pinto beans, black beans and lime-juice and half the cilantro. Cook until mixture is heated through. Remove from heat and allow it to cool.

5. Preheat oven to 350° F. In a large skillet, heat 4 cups corn oil to 325° F. While oil is heating, prepare chimichangas. Fill bottom half of a tortilla with ¾- cup of the beef and bean mixture using a slotted spoon and 2 tablespoons pepper jack cheese.

6. Lift the edge of the tortilla and roll it over the filling to secure it. Fold in both sides and continue rolling until you reach the opposite end. Secure with a 6-inch skewer weaved through the seam side of burrito. Repeat with remaining tortillas. Slowly lower chimichangas into hot oil and cook 2 minutes on each side or until golden brown.

7. You can cook 4 burritos per batch. Remove from oil, drain on paper towels and keep warm in oven until all are cooked.

8. To serve, place a bed of shredded lettuce on each plate, then a spoonful of salsa. Place chimichangas on top and add a dollop of sour cream, sprinkle with diced tomatoes, avocado and remaining cilantro to garnish. Serve immediately.

9. Serves 8-10

> **Note: If tortillas tear while folding, make them more pliable by wrapping tortillas in a damp paper towels, then fully cover with foil. Place it in 250 °F oven to warm it up.**
>
> **If you want to know what to serve, with fried chimichanga then here is the answer- Serve some salad made with lettuce, cucumber and tomatoes, as well as a dollop of sour cream? (It would go so well with the hot chili flavor of the chimichanga.) Also serve some tomato salsa, Spanish rice and guacamole, to complete the meal.**

A Vegetarian Chimichanga with Cheese and Beans Filling

Ingredients

1-Cup Grated monterey Jack cheese

1-Cup Grated cheddar cheese

2-Lb Canned refried beans

2-tsp Ground cumin

1-Cup plus 3-tablespoons mild tomato salsa

8-Flour Tortillas

Oil, for frying

1-Avocado

1-tsp Minced garlic

1-tsp Salt

2-tsp Lime juice

2-Tbsp Fresh cilantro

Sour cream, for garnish

Method

1. Preheat the oven to 475 ° F.

2. Mix the cheeses, beans, cumin and 1 cup of the salsa together.

3. Use this mixture to fill the flour tortillas.

4. Fold them up like envelopes and fold the cover over and seal them by wetting the edges of cover with water. Fry them in the oil until golden brown all over. Make sure that the oil is hot otherwise the chimichangas will get soggy.

5. They can be baked also for 10-15 minutes.

6. While they are baking or frying peel the avocado and mash the pulp with a fork.

7. Add the garlic, salt, lime-juice, and remaining salsa and mix well.

8. Serve the chimichangas with the avocado mixture, as well as some salsa and sour cream on the side.

9. Serves 6-8

Ingredients

4-Medium Zucchini and/ or Yellow summer squash, quartered lengthwise

1-Medium eggplant cut in ½ -inch slices

1-Large red onion cut in ½ -inch slices

Or

4-Small Chicken skinless breasts cut in half

4-Tbsp Olive oil

1-Tbsp limejuice

Taco seasoning to taste

½-tsp sugar

16- 4 to 6-inch Toasted corn tortillas

1- 8-oz. Carton sour cream

1-Cup Crumbled questo fresco or feta cheese

Avocado slices

Fresh Cilantro

For Mole Sauce

2-Tbsp Pumpkin seed

1-tsp Sesame seeds

2-Tbsp Vegetable oil

1-Medium onion,

2-Cloves garlic

2 to 3 tsp Chili powder

½-tsp Ground cumin

¼- tsp Ground cinnamon

1-Cup Barbecue sauce

½-Oz.Bittersweet chocolate, chopped

Hot pepper sauce (optional)

Tostada initially had their origin in the need to avoid waste stale tacos (no longer fresh enough to be rolled into tacos) and they started to use them in the form of Tostadas. These stale tortillas were submersed into boiling oil until they became golden, rigid and crunchy, like traditional slices of bread. Tostadas were and now are quite popular topped with seafood, such as cooked tuna, shrimp, crab, chopped octopus and ceviche or also act as a companion for shrimp stew. Vegetarian tostadas only topped with vegetables, are rare, since vegetables are considered only bed for the main ingredient. A popular way to eat tostadas in Mexico is as a dish of its own. Beans, cheese, sour cream, chopped lettuce, sliced onions and salsa is spread onto the tostadas like an "open faced" rigid taco mostly like a pizza. Then it is finally topped with the main ingredient, usually meat cooked and chopped specially to dress the tostada. The "Tostada de Pata" (chopped pork fingers in conserve) has become an icon of Mexican tostadas, and it is found in almost every place where tostadas are prepared.

Method

For Tostadas

1. Cut vegetables in pieces and brush them (zucchini or squash, eggplant, and onion) with 1-tablespoon olive oil, limejuice and season with taco seasoning and sugar.

2. Cook vegetables directly over medium heat for 5 to 8 minutes or until tender or grill them if you wish. Set them aside.

3. If making chicken tostadas, brush chicken with olive oil and limejuice, sprinkle with taco seasoning and sugar.

4. Place chicken in pan coated with 1-tablespoon olive oil and grill 4 minutes on each side or until chicken is done. Cool slightly. Cut chicken into ¼-inch strips, set aside.

5. Heat the oven at 425 °F. Place tortillas on grill rack or grill pan coated with remaining olive oil and grill 30 seconds on each side or until golden brown.

6. Spread a little mole sauce (recipe below) over the tostadas, top with grilled chicken strips, vegetables, sour cream, cheese, avocado, and cilantro and top again with the mole sauce and pumpkin seeds and serve. If making vegetarian omit the grilled chicken strips.

7. Makes 8 servings.

For Mole Sauce
1. In a large dry skillet over medium heat toast pumpkin seeds and sesame seeds for 2 to 3 minutes or until toasted. Remove from skillet.

2. In the same skillet cook chopped onions and minced cloves of garlic in 2-tablespoons of hot oil for 3 minutes or until tender.

3. Stir in chili powder, ground cumin and cinnamon and cook 1 minute more or until fragrant.

4. Stir in barbecue sauce, bittersweet chocolate and hot pepper sauce (optional). Bring to a boil reduce heat. Simmer until chocolate is melted. Cool slightly.

5. Transfer this inions and chocolate mixture and toasted seeds to blender or food processor. Cover and blend and process until smooth. Thin with water if needed, cool and serve with tostadas.

Albondigas Soup

Ingredients

Soup
2-Tbsp Olive oil
1-Large Onion, chopped
1-tsp Chopped ginger
1-Large Garlic clove, minced
1-Tbsp Chopped mildly hot
    green chilies
3-Qt Chicken stock or beef
    stock or water
½ tsp Cumin powder
1-Cup Tomato sauce
1-Large Carrots, peeled and sliced
1-Small Zucchini or ½-Lb String
    beans chopped
1- Cup Frozen or fresh peas
1-tsp Dried oregano/ fresh
    oregano chopped
Salt and pepper
1-Tbsp Adobo sauce
½- Cup Chopped fresh cilantro

Meatballs
1/3-Cup Raw white rice
½-Lb Ground beef (or ground
    turkey)
½-Lb Ground Pork or uncooked
    chorizo sausage casing removed
¼-Cup Chopped fresh mint leaves
¼-Cup Chopped parsley
    or cilantro

(continued)

Albondigas soup is a traditional Mexican meatball soup ("albondigas" means "meatballs" in Spanish). It is our version of comfort food. What makes the flavor of albondigas soup distinctive is the chopped mint in the meatballs. The deeply flavored broth is spiked with chipotles and adobo sauce. You can even omit the chipotle, but don't skip out on the adobo sauce. It adds a wonderful smoky kick.

Vary the vegetables in the soup depending on what you have on hand like Snow peas instead of regular peas. Add some chopped fresh zucchini or corn if they are available. Feel free to substitute ground turkey for the ground beef. A bowl of this soup with a side of Mexican rice and a couple of warm tortillas makes a hearty meal.

Method

1. Heat oil in large heavy-bottomed pot (5-qt) over medium heat. Add onion and cook until tender, about 5 minutes. Add the ginger, garlic and green chilies and cook a minute more. Add broth, cumin powder and tomato sauce. Bring to boil and reduce heat to simmer. Add carrots and string beans.

2. Prepare the meatballs. Mix rice into ground turkey and pork, adding mint leaves and parsley, salt, black pepper, cumin powder, corn tortilla crumbs and cayenne pepper. Mix in raw egg. Form mixture into 1-inch meatballs.

3. Add the meatballs to the simmering soup, one at a time. Cover and let simmer for half an hour. Add the peas to the soup towards the end

1½-tsp Salt
½-tsp Black pepper
½- tsp Ground cumin
4- Corn Tortilla chips- crumbs
½-tsp Cayenne pepper (or as needed)
1- Egg

Adobo Sauce
10 Good size dried chipotle chilies
3- Cups Hot water
1/3-Cup Minced onion, divided
2- Tbsp Minced garlic, divided
Salt as needed
4-Tbsp Ketchup
½-tsp Dried oregano
½-tsp Dried thyme
1-tsp Sugar
½-tsp Ground cinnamon
1- tsp Ground cumin
1/8-tsp Ground allspice
1- pinch Ground cloves
¼- Cup Cider vinegar

of the half hour. Add a few pinches of oregano and sprinkle with salt, pepper and adobo sauce.

4. Garnish with chopped fresh cilantro and serve.

5. Serves 6-8.

Adobo Sauce

1. Heat a large skillet over medium heat and toast the chilies, turning frequently, until very pliable and soft; do not allow them to burn.

2. Remove from the skillet and transfer to a plate. Remove the stems and seeds and place in a saucepan.

3. Add enough hot water to just cover and bring to a boil.

4. Cover the pan, remove from the heat and allow chilies to soak until very soft and plumped, about 20 minutes.

5. Strain in a fine mesh sieve over a bowl and reserve soaking liquid separately. In a blender, combine the chilies, onion, garlic, salt, ketchup, oregano, thyme, sugar, cinnamon, cumin, allspice, cloves, and vinegar and puree until smooth, adding a little of the Chile soaking liquid (only as much as is needed) to enable the mixture to blend.

6. The consistency should be thick but smooth. Cover and refrigerate or freeze until ready to use.

Enchiladas

Ingredients

- ¼-Cup peanut / Grape seed oil / canola oil
- 2-tsp Cumin seeds
- 1- Onion, chopped
- 4-Cloves garlic, minced
- 1-tsp salt
- ¼-Cup Freshly chopped green chilies (Anaheim)
- 4-Skinless chicken breast cut into pieces/ 1½-Lb ground beef
- 12-Corn tortillas
- 4- Tomatoes cut crosswise
- 3- Tomatillos cut crosswise
- 2-Tsp Olive oil
- 4-Ancho chilies or 2-Jalapeno
- 1-Cup Tomato sauce
- 1-Cup Water
- Salt as needed
- ¼- Cup Cilantro leaves chopped
- ½-Cup Chopped green onions
- ½-Lb Any Mild yellow cheese, grated
- ½--Cup Black olives
- 1-Cup Sour cream
- Half head of iceberg lettuce

An enchilada is a corn tortilla rolled plain or around a filling and covered with a chili pepper sauce. It is a kind of Mexican street food. Enchiladas were simply corn tortillas dipped in chili sauce and sometimes can be eaten without fillings. They now have taken many varieties, which are distinguished primarily by their sauces. Enchiladas can be filled with a variety of ingredients, including meat, cheese, beans, potatoes vegetables, seafood or combinations. Enchiladas originated in Mayan times where the practice of rolling tortillas around other food originated. Even to this day people living in the lake areas of Mexico wrap a tortilla around a fish and serve it.

Method

1. Melt 2 tablespoons peanut oil in a stockpot. Add 1-teaspoon cumin seeds. Wait till they pop. Stir in ½ onion, 2 cloves garlic, one-teaspoon salt and Anaheim peppers and cook and stir until onions are soft, 5 to 8 minutes. Add chicken breast pieces, cover, and simmer until the liquid is practically gone.

2. In a large fry pan add remaining 2-tablespoon of peanut oil. Coat the tortillas one by one in this fry pan by quickly turning them once. Set them aside.

3. Cook tomatoes and tomatillos in a dry skillet on medium-high heat until soft and charred, 3 to 4 minutes per side.

4. Sauté up the remaining chopped onion and garlic, and remaining cumin seeds and 2-tablespoons of olive oil. Add the ancho chilies

and cook till they are soft. Add 1-cup of tomato sauce and a cup of water to pan. Add the roasted tomatoes and tomatillos and add salt and cook till they are soft. Add cilantro leaves. Transfer these to a blender and wisk it twice. This is the chili sauce.

5. Dip each Tortilla into the chili sauce mixture and spread them on a flat surface and place 1/3-cup chicken mixture, chopped green onions, cheese and olives in the center of the tortilla. Roll and place seam side down on the bottom of a large casserole pan that has been coated with a little oil. Continue with remaining tortillas. Pour remaining sauce, cheese, green onions and cilantro over the enchiladas. Bake them in the preheated oven heated to 350°F for 10-15 minutes.

6. Serve with a dollop of sour cream and Iceberg lettuce that has been dressed only with vinegar and salt.

7. Serves 4-6.

> **Note: For cheese enchiladas spread 2/3-cup of cheese on the warm tortilla and roll it seam side down and serve as above with chili sauce, sour cream and cilantro.**

Ingredients

Marinade

- ¼- Cup Lime Juice
- ¼ - Cup Olive oil
- 2- Cloves Garlic, peeled, minced
- 1-Tbsp Onion powder
- 1-tsp Ginger minced
- 1-tsp Ground cumin
- 1- tsp Chili powder/cayenne pepper
- Black pepper and salt to taste
- ½- tsp Fresh Jalapeno pepper, seeded, finely chopped

For the fajitas

- 2-Tbsp Olive oil
- 1 ½-Lb Flank steak or skirt steak

Or

- 1 ½- Lbs Boneless chicken breast halves, cut in thin strips/deveined shrimp
- 1- Large Yellow onion sliced half and sliced into half rings
- 1- Sweet red bell pepper, seeded and cut in strips
- 1- Green bell pepper, seeded/cut in strips
- 1- Zucchini, trimmed, cut in strips
- 1-Large Tomato chopped
- 1-Tbsp Limejuice
- ¼-Cup Chopped fresh cilantro
- Shredded cheddar cheese, Salsa, Iceberg lettuce shredded, Sour cream, Guacamole
- Warm tortillas, Spanish rice and refried beans on the side

According to the study fajitas originated in Texas around 1930's around the Texas ranches by the Mexican cowboys. The ranchers presumably gave away the cheaper cuts of beef like hide, the trimmings and skirt steaks to the cowboys as part of their pay. In Spanish "faja" means belt or girdle. Considering the appearance the meat, (the skirt steak used to make Fajitas) a strip about 18 inches long and about one inch thick and its placement in the beef carcass beneath the heart and lungs, fajita (little belt) is a particularly correct nickname. The term Fajitas is typically used for grilled strips of skirt steak with onions and bell peppers, and served sizzling hot with fresh tortillas, guacamole, sour cream, and salsa.

The range cowboys created the dish when they learned to barbecue the pieces of this beef by marinating them before cooking it over an open fire. The beef was cut into strips and rolled inside tortillas. Fajita is a Spanish term found in both traditional Mexican cuisine and Tex Mex cuisine commonly referring to any grilled meat served with taco of regular flour or corn flour tortilla.

The meat now used is the leanest meat available. This most sophisticated American Mexican dish has ironically very humble origins.

You can make fajitas with steak or chicken, or even make them with plain vegetables. Here's a quick and easy recipe for steak fajitas. Popular condiments are shredded lettuce, sour cream, guacamole, salsa, pico de gallo, cheese and tomato. Fajitas have become popular in Mexico and of course very popular all over America. They are usually brought to the table sizzling loudly (in a very appetizing way) on hot metal skillet or platter surrounded by the vegetables with hot tortillas and other condiments on the side

Method

1. Mix all marinade ingredients. Set the steak and vegetables in the marinade and let it sit at least an hour.

2. Heat to high heat in a large cast iron pan or griddle. Add one teaspoon of olive oil to the pan. Add the steak, frying on each side for 3 minutes, or to desired doneness. Remove from the pan and let it sit for 5 minutes.

3. Reduce heat to medium high. Add a little more oil to the pan if necessary. Add the onions, bell peppers zucchini and tomato. Cook stirring frequently, for 5 minutes, until the onions are slightly translucent.

4. Slice the meat against the grain into thin slices and add it to the pan. Sprinkle the limejuice and fresh cilantro on top of the vegetables and meat while it is sizzling.

5. Serve immediately with shredded cheese, salsa, shredded iceberg lettuce, sour cream, guacamole and warm flour tortillas.

6. Serves 4 or more.

Burritos

Ingredients

- 4- Tbsp Olive oil
- 1-Cup Red bell peppers, sliced
- 1- Cup Sliced onions
- 2- Clove garlic, minced
- ½-tsp Cumin powder
- ½- tsp Dried oregano
- 2-Tbsp Chilies Mild or hot
- ½--tsp Red pepper
- Salt and pepper to taste
- 1½-Cups Canned kidney beans, drained, rinsed and mashed/ a can of refried beans
- 8-Flour tortillas
- 2- Cups Cooked white rice
- Washed and drained black olive (optional)
- Shredded lettuce
- 1-Cup Chopped tomatoes
- 2 Cups Shredded Monterey Jack cheese, grated
- Salsa and or guacamole, sour cream
- Hot Pepper sauce/Dressing of your choice
- Tortilla chips to serve on the side

A Burrito comprises a warm tortilla, wrapped around a filling. In Mexico, burritos are quite small and have the fillings of refried beans or meats. It is a kind of a finger food in Mexico with a long history.

The word burrito means "little donkey" in Spanish, The name burrito as applied to the food item possibly is derived from the appearance of a rolled up wheat tortilla, which vaguely resembles the ear of its namesake animal, or from bedrolls and packs that donkeys carried.

Burritos first appeared on American restaurant menus at the El Cholo Spanish Cafe during the 1930s. American style burritos are larger than Mexican ones, and are stuffed with more ingredients than the primary meat and/or vegetable filled burrito in Mexico. Many Mexican fast foods giants are flourishing in U.S. by just serving different varieties of burritos on their menu. Ingredients like grilled chicken, pork, beef, sweet potato, black beans, refried beans and rice and grated cheese are the staples and the ingredients like chopped fresh green pepper grilled green pepper and onions, tomatoes, stemmed corn, black olive, lettuce topped with sour cream, guacamole and your favorite dressing give the finishing touches. These burritos are usually served with tortilla chips and chili sauce and salsas and side garnishes of chopped onions and cilantro. These variations you can also try even when you want to make your own burrito.

Meat is not essential to make Mexican food even though you might be more used to the typical chicken and beef based fare in Mexican fast food joints. Vegetable recipes and seafood recipes are also very popular in Mexico as well. Here is quick simple version but you can make it as elaborate as you want by using the different ingredients mentioned above.

Method

Burritos

1. Heat the 2 tablespoons of oil in a skillet. Add the bell peppers and the onions cook for about 3 minutes until slightly tender. Add the cumin, oregano, chilies, red pepper, salt and pepper stir well. Add the refried beans and mix the mixture together and set aside

2. Add the remaining oil to the skillet and warm the tortillas over a medium heat and heat through, turning once. Set them aside.

3. Spread the warm tortilla in a plate and spread 2 tablespoons refried beans and couple of tablespoons of rice, olives, lettuce, tomatoes, tablespoon of cheese, salsa, hot pepper sauce (optional) and dressing of your choice over the top. Repeat with the remaining tortillas.

4. Roll the tortilla up seam side down and wrap it up in aluminum foil and keep them warm in the oven in a serving dish, until ready to serve.

Just before serving

5. Take out of the oven. Serve them with extra guacamole, hot pepper sauce, and sour cream, tortilla chips and Salsa.

6. Serves 8.

Note: To make chicken, beef or fish burrito, grill the chopped well-seasoned meat on broil or gas grill and use it as one of the filling ingredient.

Mexican Tortilla Soup

Ingredients

1-tsp Chili powder
1-tsp Ground cumin powder
1-tsp Coriander powder
½-tsp Cayenne pepper
Salt and pepper to taste
2-Tbsp Vegetable oil
1-Medium onion, chopped
2- Tbsp Chopped garlic
½-Cup Chopped red bell pepper
½-Cup Fresh zucchini chopped
1-Cup Diced tomatoes
½-Cup Tomato sauce
1-Chopped Chipotle pepper
   fresh or canned
½-Cup Cooked black beans
1- Cup Frozen corn
2-14-Oz Can Chicken stock
6-Oz Cooked chicken breast
   strips, diced
2-Tbsp Fresh lemon juice
4-Corn tortillas cut into ¼
   inch pieces and deep-fried

Garnish

½- Cup Sour cream
1-Cup Shredded cheddar or
   pepper jack cheese
1 Ripe avocado, diced and
   soaked in the 2 teaspoons of
   lemon juice
2 Tbsp Chopped onions
Chopped Cilantro, to garnish

Tortilla Soup seems to have come on the menu's of Mexican and Tex-Mex restaurants around the late 1970's early 1980's in the area of south central Texas. The origins of tortilla soup may be a mystery, but its intriguing flavor has long made it to be one of California's favorite soups. The soup has become so much a part of American culture that Hollywood made interesting movie named "Tortilla Soup" on the Tex Mex culture too. It is a 2001 American comedy-drama film directed by Maria Ripoll.

"Tortilla Soup" is a fairly recent incarnation. In American Southwest and Texas beef and vegetable soup are also made in a similar fashion as the tortilla soup, topped with Spanish rice and fresh chili sauce. Even chicken soups are made topped with fried tortilla strips, avocado chunks, and limejuice and chili salsa.

This soup is quick to make, flavorful, and filling! Serve with warm corn bread or tortillas. This also freezes well. Garnish with chopped fresh avocado, Monterey Jack cheese, crushed tortilla chips and green onion.

Method

1. Mix together cumin powder, chili powder, coriander powder, cayenne pepper and salt and pepper. This is the spice powder mix.

2. Heat 2 tablespoons oil over a medium heat in a large pan and add the chopped onions. Fry the onion until light brown and add garlic, stir it and add the chopped bell pepper, chopped

zucchini, tomatoes, tomato sauce, chipotle pepper, washed and drained black beans, corn, chicken stock and spice powder mix.

3. Let it simmer on slow heat for 15 minutes. Add the cooked chicken and cook for another 10 minutes. Add 2-tablespoons fresh lemon juice and stir to mix.

4. Cut tortillas into strips or cut them into pieces and deep-fry them. Drain the oil on a paper towel.

5. Add tortilla strips to serving bowl and add the soup on the top of them. Let it sit for 2-3 minutes.

6. Top it with a dollop of sour cream, grated cheese, chopped avocado, chopped onions, couple more chips and serve sprinkled with cilantro.

Tortilla Soup

7. Serve lime wedges on the side. Delicious.

8. Serves 4-6.

Tacos

Ingredients

2-Tbsp Olive oil

1 ½- Cups Onion, finely
    chopped

3-Tbsp Minced garlic

1- Tbsp Chopped ginger

1 Tbsp Chopped green chilies
    (select to taste)

1- Tbsp Ground cumin

2-Lbs Ground beef or turkey

½-tsp Cayenne pepper (or to
    taste)

¾- tsp Garammasala (optional)

1 ½- tsp Kosher salt

½ - Cup Water or Turkey or
    Beef broth or as needed

1-Cup Tomato sauce

12 to 16 Taco shells or
    soft tortillas warmed
    a little in the oven.

For Garnish

Grated Monterey Jack or
    Cheddar grated

Diced tomatoes

Minced jalapenos

Sour cream

Shredded Ice burg lettuce

Guacamole

Salsa,

Chopped Green onion

Freshly chopped cilantro

When the traditional taco is served, it is flat, not pinched up into the hard shells that many Americans consider the essential base. Hard shells that are in a semi-circle form are largely an American invention.

It is a traditional Mexican dish composed of a corn or wheat tortilla folded or rolled around a filling. A taco can be made with a variety of fillings, including beef, chicken, seafood, vegetables and cheese allowing for great versatility and variety. It is generally eaten as a finger food and is often accompanied by garnishes such as salsa, avocado or guacamole, cilantro, tomatoes, onions and lettuce. Beginning from the early part of the twentieth century, various styles of tacos have become popular in the United States and Canada. Restaurants like "Taco Bell" serve a variety of Tex Mex cuisine foods including tacos, burritos, quesadillas, nachos and other specialty items, and a variety of "Menu" items. There are many variations in tacos like soft shell tacos, puffy tacos, Indian tacos and the traditional tacos like fish tacos and shrimp tacos and many more. Most common in U.S.A. and Canada are these hard-shell, U-shaped version of tacos sold by restaurants and by fast food chains and even by non-Mexican oriented fast food restaurants. They are a great fast food favorite of America, especially among the younger population. These crisp-fried corn tortillas filled with seasoned ground beef, cheese, lettuce, and sometimes tomato, green onion, salsa, sour cream, and avocado or guacamole have won the hearts of young and old alike.

Feel free to use ready made taco seasoning mix to season the ground beef ground turkey or chopped cooked chicken and follow directions on the package to prepare taco filling if you wish. In this recipe below seasoning is made using the basics needed for the taco filling.

Method

1. Set a 12-inch sauté pan over medium heat and add the olive oil.

2. Once hot, place the onions in the pan and sauté until translucent, 3 to 4 minutes. Add the garlic, ginger, green chilies, cumin powder to the pan and continue to sauté until fragrant, about 1 minute.

3. Add the beef or turkey to the pan and cook, breaking the pieces up as they cook, until the meat is browned, about 8 to 10 minutes.

4. Season with cayenne pepper, and garammasala and the salt. Add the broth and tomato sauce to the pan and bring to a simmer.

5. Cook the meat, stirring occasionally on medium heat until most of the liquid has evaporated, about 20 minutes. Remove from the heat.

6. Use this filling for the tacos by filling by placing 2 tablespoons of filling inside the fold of the taco and top it with a Tbsp each of diced tomatoes, green onions a pinch of minced peppers and desirable amount of shredded lettuce, guacamole, salsa and grated cheese and serve them with your favorite drink.

7. You can also let your company assemble their tacos to their liking and enjoy.

8. Serves 6-8.

Grilled Tilapia Fish Tacos

Ingredients

For Marinade
   Juice 1 lime
   1-Tbsp Ancho chili powder
   ¾- Cup Canola oil
   Salt to taste

For Tacos
   ¼-Cup Chopped fresh cilantro
      leaves
   1- Jalapeño coarsely crushed
   1-Lb Tilapia, Halibut, or any
      other firm white fish
   8-Flour tortillas
   Lettuce shredded
   Shredded white cabbage
   Chopped tomatoes,
   Chopped onion
   Cooked corn
   Grated cheese
   1-Cup Pica de gallo or tomato
      salsa
   Sour cream
   Hot sauce to serve
   Tortilla chips

There is anthropological evidence that the indigenous people living in the lake region of the valley of Mexico traditionally ate tacos filled with small fish. It is also documented that the first taco feast enjoyed by Europeans, was taco filled with fish. It is not clear why the Europeans (Spanish) used the word "taco" to describe this indigenous food.

In Mexico, authentic tacos are rather softer than the hard tacos that you find in fast food outlets here in the U.S. The ancho chili powder, jalapeno and hot sauce give these tasty fish tacos a real kick along with the use of all other fresh ingredients like cilantro, limejuice and the marinade. Traditional Mexican fish tacos do not come much tastier than this recipe. You can use any of the following fish Tilapia, Halibut, Mahi Mahi. Grilling gives wonderful flavor to both the fish and the tortillas. Tilapia is one of the most versatile and popular fish that is used for making fish tacos.

Grilled Fish Taco

Go ahead and serve all the ingredients separately, including the garnishes, or you can prepare the tacos with the ingredients in it and then serve it.

Method

1. Preheat the grill to medium high and whisk together the lime-juice, ancho chili powder (mildly hot), oil, salt, cilantro and jalapeno and marinade the fish in this marinate for 15 or 20 minutes.

2. Remove the fish from the marinade and grill it, flesh side down, for 4 minutes.

3. Turn it over, cook the other side for 30 seconds, and remove it from the grill.

4. Rest for 5 minutes then flake the fish using a fork. Grill the tortillas for 20 seconds each side.

5. Just before serving, warm the tacos and add 2 tablespoons of forked fish. Garnish with the shredded lettuce, cabbage, tomatoes, onion, corn, cheese, Pico de gallo or salsa, sour cream and hot sauce and serve with tortilla chips to make a meal.

6. Serves 4.

Chicken Quesadillas with Pico de Gallo

Ingredients

- 2- Tomatoes, diced
- 1-Onion, finely chopped
- 2- Limes, juiced
- 2-Tbsp Chopped fresh cilantro
- 1- Jalapeno pepper, seeded and minced
- Salt and pepper to taste
- 2-Tbsp Olive oil, divided
- 2- Skinless, Boneless chicken breast halves - cut into strips
- ½- Onion, thinly sliced
- 1-Green bell pepper, thinly sliced
- 2-Cloves Garlic, minced
- ½-tsp Cumin powder
- ¼-tsp Red pepper
- 4- (12 inch) Flour tortillas
- 2-Tbsp Butter Melted
- 1-Cup Shredded Monterey Jack cheese or Cheddar cheese
- ¼-Cup Sour cream, for topping

The quesadilla is a regional favorite in the Southwest United States where it is analogous to a 'grilled cheese sandwich'.

A quesadilla is a flour or corn tortilla filled with a savory mixture containing cheese and other ingredients such as cooked meat, refried beans, avocado or other vegetables. They are then folded in half to form a half-moon shape. This dish originated in Mexico and the name is derived from the Spanish word queso (cheese). Another preparation involves cheese and other ingredients sandwiched between two flour tortillas, with the whole package grilled on an oiled griddle and flipped so both sides are cooked and the cheese is melted. This version is often cut into wedges to serve. They have been adapted to many different styles. In the United States, many restaurants serve them as appetizers, after adding their own twist. Some variations in the fillings are, goat cheese, black beans, spinach, zucchini, or tofu. Even dessert quesadillas are made, using ingredients such as chocolate, butterscotch, caramel, and different fruits.

Method

1. In a small bowl, combine tomatoes, onion, lime-juice, cilantro, jalapeno, salt and pepper. Set aside. This is Pico de gallo (salsa)

2. In a large skillet, heat 1- tablespoon olive oil. Add chicken and sauté until cooked through. Remove chicken from skillet and set aside.

3. Put the remaining 1- tablespoon of olive oil in the hot skillet and sauté the sliced onion and green bell pepper until tender. Stir in

the minced garlic, cumin powder and red pepper. Mix in half of the Pico de gallo and chicken breast meat. Set aside and keep warm.

4. In a heavy skillet heat one flour tortilla after coating the both sides with a teaspoon of butter. Spread ¼- cup shredded cheese on the tortilla and top with ½- the chicken mixture.

5. Sprinkle another ¼- Cup cheese over the chicken and top with another tortilla coated with a teaspoon of butter. When bottom tortilla is lightly brown and cheese has started to melt, flip quesadilla and cook on the opposite side.

6. Remove quesadilla from skillet and cut into quarters. Repeat with remaining tortillas and ingredients. Serve quesadillas with sour cream and remaining Pico de gallo.

7. Serves- 4

Note: For Cheese Quesdilla prepare just with cheese and salsa and cook it similarly.

Southwest Quesadilla

Ingredients

- 4-Tbsp Olive oil
- 1-Bell pepper chopped
- ½- Red Onion, diced
- 1-tsp Minced garlic
- ¼-Cup Chopped tomatoes
- ¾- Cup Frozen corn thawed
- 2-tsp Cayenne pepper
- 1-tsp Cumin powder
- Salt and freshly ground black pepper
- A Pinch garammasala
- ½- Cup Freshly chopped cilantro leaves
- 4- 10-Inch Flour tortillas
- 2-Tbsp Butter melted
- 1- (16-Oz) Can Refried black beans
- 1-Cup Grated pepper jack or Cheddar cheese

The flavor combinations of these cheesy treats may come from all over the globe, but the quesadilla concept is pure Mexican. In addition to cheese, you can put practically anything in a quesadilla. My favorites are mushrooms, olives, tomatoes, and onions. You do not need to cook these ingredients first, but that is entirely up to your taste.

Method

1. In a large skillet, heat oil over medium-high heat. Sauté bell pepper and onion until soft, about 5 minutes. Add garlic, tomatoes, corn, cayenne pepper, cumin, salt and pepper to taste.

2. Toss to mix and sauté for another 3 minutes. Transfer to a bowl and add the cilantro and a pinch of garammasala.

3. Preheat cast iron griddle, or a large pan sauté over medium heat. Lay 2 tortillas on a work surface and spread each with melted butter and evenly with refried black beans. Place tortillas, bean side up, on the griddle. Sprinkle onion-bell pepper mixture evenly over the top of each, and then sprinkle evenly with the cheese.

4. Cover both with another tortilla coated first with melted butter and then with refried black beans and cook for 2-3 minutes. Flip quesadillas to toast the other side. Slice each quesadilla into 8 wedges, sprinkle with cilantro and serve with salsa and guacamole.

5. Serves 2-4.

Oven-Toasted Sonoran Quesadilla

Ingredients

- 2- Large (13-inch diameter) Flour tortilla
- 2-Tbsp Butter
- 1-Cup Grated cheddar cheese
- 1- Cup Picante sauce
- ¼- tsp Toasted green chilies
- ¼- tsp Toasted green onions

All you need is 20 minutes and four ingredients to make these tasty quesadillas, oozing with melted cheese and flavored with picante sauce and green chilies.

Method

1. Place the 2 tortilla on a large sheet. Spread butter all over the top of the tortilla, making sure to get the butter all the way out to the edges.

2. Cook for 2-3 minutes at 375°F in the conventional oven , or until the tortilla begins to visibly brown.

3. Remove from the oven, spread 2-tablespoons of Picante sauce and sprinkle the toasted onions and chilies and then cheese over the tortilla. Cover with the other buttered and toasted tortilla and return to the oven for an additional 2 minutes.

4. Serve immediately with salsa or Pico de gallo.

5. Serves 2.

> **Note: If you want to make them mild for small children then substitute the Picante sauce with mild salsa and omit the green chilies and they will be right.**

Nachos

Ingredients

2- Jalapeno peppers
10-Oz. Tortilla chips
1-Cup Refried beans
2- Cups Cheddar cheese, shredded
½-Cup Chopped green bell peppers
½-Cup Chopped green Onions
½ - Cup Chopped tomatoes
Shredded lettuce
2- Tbsp Sliced olives
2-Tbsp Fresh cilantro
1-Cup Salsa
1-Cup Guacamole
½- Cup Sour cream

Nachos are also one of the popular foods of Mexican origin more associated with Tex Mex Cuisine. It can be made quickly to serve as a snack or prepared with more ingredients to make a full meal. First created around 1943 by Ignacio "Nacho "Anaya. It is said that Anaya hurriedly put together a dish for his after hours American guests from Texas with whatever he had in his kitchen and called it "Nachos especiales". The popularity of the dish swiftly spread throughout Texas. As the word spread in Texas this Nacho especials became a very special dish in America. It got a special boost in a sporting event in 1976 as Ballpark Nachos. The chef passed away in 1975 but left his son Ignacio Anaya Jr a legacy and also fame and prosperity. The original nachos consisted of fried corn tortillas covered with melted cheddar cheese and pickled jalapeno peppers.

Sometimes nothing beats classic nachos with lots of cheese, spicy classic jalapeno peppers with lots of tasty toppings such as homemade guacamole, salsa and sour cream. This kind of food is perfect to serve with buffalo chicken wings, twice-baked potatoes and a nice crisp beer during a game or a movie.

In Mexico, they are just called totopos means Tortilla chips. Tortilla chips are served covered with shredded cheese and/or salsa. Sometimes French fries, potato chips or popcorn is used instead of tortilla chips.

Method

1. Slice the peppers quite thinly. Don't remove the seeds.

2. Using large baking pan, evenly distribute the tortilla chips on the bottom of the pan.

3. Layer half the refried beans. Spread about half of the shredded cheese on top of the beans and half of the chopped peppers and jalapeno peppers. Top with another layer of chips, then the rest of the refried beans, cheese and peppers.

4. Bake in a 400° F oven for few minutes or until the cheese has melted and is nice and bubbly.

5. Once out of the oven, sprinkle fresh, chopped onions, tomatoes, shredded lettuce, olives and chopped cilantro. Serve with salsa, guacamole and sour cream.

6. Serves 4.

> **Note: For making Non Vegetarian Nachos start with step 2, after the half the refried beans spread half the cooked and spiced ground beef and then spread shredded cheese. Top with another layer of tortilla chips and then the rest of the beans, ground beef, cheese, and peppers and follow the rest of the steps.**

America's Favorite One Dish Meals

One-Dish Meals are designed for the millions of health-conscious Americans who are always on the go. Many of these delicious dinners practically cook themselves.

Hamburger

Hamburgers

Ingredients

1-Lb Ground beef
1-tsp Chopped ginger
1-tsp Chopped garlic
1-Tbsp Green mildly hot chilies
1-Egg beaten
3-Tbsp Dry breadcrumbs
3-Green onions, chopped
1-Tbsp prepared mustard
1-Tbsp+1-tsp Cajun seasoning
¼- Cup Barbecue sauce
4- Slices Cheddar cheese
4-Large onion rolls
1- Red onion, sliced thin
1-Tomato sliced thin (optional)
1- Jar Roasted red peppers
2- Avocados

Nothing is more American than Hamburger among the favorite foods of America. If there was anything else it probably would be Apple Pie. The name "Hamburger" comes from Hamburg, a city in Germany. In Germany snacks are often named after the place of origin, like the Frankfurter, the Berliner, or Bratwurst. In Hamburg it was common to put a piece of roast pork into a roll and serve it warm. German immigrants brought this "Hamburger," to the United States where it was adapted into its modern form. U.S. Library of Congress, Local Legacies Project website credits Louis' Lunch of New Haven Connecticut as the maker of America's first hamburger and steak sandwich. Here the hamburger is still served today on two pieces of toast and not a bun. Burgers may be classified as two main types: fast food hamburgers and individually prepared burgers made in homes and restaurants. The latter is most always served all dressed up with lettuce, tomato, onion, and often sliced pickle, cheese with condiments such as Mustard, mayonnaise, ketchup, however salad dressings and barbecue sauce are also very common. Standard toppings may depend on the location and the region where it is prepared. Infact the variations will be hard to count and a entire book can be written on Hamburgers of America. Barbecuing hamburgers on National holidays, family and community get together or on stands at State and county fairs and sports stadiums are the most common sight and occurrence in America. Americans just thrive on hamburgers and hotdogs. There are many fast food chains that sell hundreds and hundreds of hamburgers each day. It is the most loved party and picnic food of American culture. An entire cook- book can be written on various types of hamburgers. Here is just one sample.

Method

1. Preheat grill on high heat. Mix ground beef, ginger, garlic, green chilies, egg, breadcrumbs, green onions, mustard, and 1 tablespoon Cajun seasoning in a large bowl.

2. Form mixture into 4 patties. In a small bowl, combine 1 teaspoon remaining Cajun seasoning into barbecue sauce and set it aside.

3. Lightly oil the grill and cook patties for 5 minutes per side, or to desired doneness and set them aside.

4. Coat the onion rolls with prepared seasoned barbecue sauce and place meat patty and top it with a slice of your favorite cheese.

5. Top the cheese with a slice of red onion, lots of roasted red peppers, and avocado slices and serve.

6. Serve the hamburger with French fries or onion rings or cole slaw with pickle and your favorite beverage. Makes an excellent on the go meal.

7. Serves 4.

Note: There are numerous variations to making hamburgers. Use the ingredients as you wish and enjoy.

Coffee Rubbed Cheeseburgers

Ingredients

1-Tbsp Freshly ground coffee
2-tsp Brown sugar
½ tsp ground coriander
2-tsp Freshly ground black
   pepper
½- tsp Ground roasted cumin
½- tsp Garamamsala
½- tsp Salt
8-Slices Bacon
2-Lb Ground chuck
1-Lb Ground sirloin
2-Tbsp of Onions
1-Tbsp Ginger, Garlic,
   Green-chilies/each
1-Egg beaten
¼- Cup Bread crumbs
8-Slices Smoked Gouda or
   Provolone cheese
8-Potato or Brioche hamburger
   buns, buttered and toasted
Bottled spicy barbecue sauce
Leaf lettuce/ sliced avocado
8-Slices red onion
8-Slices tomato

Give an extra zing to your hamburger with a spicy coffee rub and serve them with barbecue sauce for an outdoor picnic. It will make make your guests feel really special. Serve with grilled corn or coleslaw to accompany the delicious burger to complete the meal.

Method

1. Mix coffee, sugar, coriander powder, black pepper, cumin, garammasala and salt in a small bowl. This is your coffee rub. Set it aside.

2. Cook bacon in large skillet until crisp. Transfer to paper towels to drain. Break in half.

3. Gently mix chuck and sirloin in large bowl. Add Onions, ginger, garlic, green chilies, egg and bread crumbs. Form meat into 8 patties, each 3 ½- 4-inches in diameter and about ½-inch thick. Using thumb, make slight indentation in center of each burger.

4. Start the barbecue on medium high. Sprinkle 1-teaspoon coffee rub on top of each burger.

5. Place burger patties on grill rack rub side down.

6. Grill until slightly charred, about 4 minutes, turn. Place 2 bacon slices halves atop each burger. Cook 3 minutes.

7. Top each with 1 cheese slice. Cover and cook until cheese melts, about 1 minute.

8. Serve on toasted buns, rub the bun with barbecue sauce and top with, couple of leaves

of lettuce or avocado slices, slice of onion and tomato and serve potato chips, pickle or Cole slaw on the side with a beverage of your choice.

9. Serves-8

Note: Ground chuck and ground sirloin can be substituted with ground chicken or ground turkey, ground salmon or other fish that holds together well, textured protein or veggie burger mix, goat meat, ground buffalo or ground deer meat or elk meat. Provolone cheese can be substituted by sliced goat-cheese, crumbled goat cheese, blue cheese and feta cheese. Try any other cheese that crumbles and will mix well. Lettuce can be substituted by Arugula, Chicory, Mustard greens, Swiss chard, Kale, Dandelion greens, Collard greens.

Southwestern Turkey Burgers

Ingredients

¾- Cup Mayonnaise

2-Tbsp Extra-virgin olive oil

2-Tbsp Minced red onion

2-Tbsp Chopped fresh dill

1- Canned Chipotle chilies

1-Tbsp Capers, drained

Salt and pepper to taste

1½-Lb Ground turkey

½ -Cup Finely crushed tortilla chips

6- Tbsp Chopped cilantro

1-Egg

2-tsps Chili powder

1-tsp Ground cumin

½- tsp Garammasala

Pepper jack cheese slices

Whole-wheat hamburger buns, toasted

Red onion slices

Tomato slices

Arugula or shredded lettuce

Turkey meat is a great substitute to make Hamburger. Use lean turkey meat and flavor it similarly as a beef patty and you will have heart healthy, low fat, nutritious hamburger. Try flavoring the meat with some aromatic spices like ground cumin, chili powder and garammasla and you will be pleasantly surprised.

Method

1. Whisk first 6 ingredients in a small bowl. Season with salt and pepper. This is the sauce. Cover it and set it aside in the refrigerator.

2. Turn on the grill (medium heat).

3. Combine ground turkey, crushed tortilla chips, cilantro, egg, and chili- powder, ground cumin, garammasala and mix well.

4. Form into ½-inch thick patties. Grill burger patties until cooked through and place a slice of cheese on the top of the patty about 3 minutes prior to end of cooking.

5. Spread 1-tablespoon sauce on bottom half of each bun.

6. Top each with one burger patty and one more tablespoon sauce.

7. Top with onion, tomatoes and arugula or shredded lettuce and then top other half of bun.

8. Serve with your favorite chips and beverage. Makes a delicious hamburger to go.

9. Serves 4-6.

Veggie Burgers

Ingredients

1-7 Oz Container Plain Greek yogurt

2-Tbsp Fresh mint, finely chopped

2-Tbsp Fresh cilantro, finely chopped

1 ¼-tsp lemon peel

¼-Cup Mushrooms cleaned and chopped

2- Scallions chopped

2-Tbsp Red bell pepper chopped

1-Cup Chopped spinach

1-Carrot, peeled and grated

1-tsp Jalapeno pepper chopped

1-Tbsp Diced artichoke

½-Cup Black beans, drained

½ Cup Chickpeas, drained

½-Cup White beans, drained

¾-Cup Rolled oats

3-Tbsp Olive oil

2-Cloves garlic

1½- tsp Cumin

¼- tsp Cayenne pepper

1- Egg white

Salt and Pepper to taste

½-1 Cup Breadcrumbs

1-Cup Grated Mild cheddar cheese/or any cheese of your choice

6- Hamburger Buns, cheese slices, shredded lettuce, onions and tomato slices

Lately veggie burgers are also becoming very popular in America especially with people who are vegans. It is a hamburger-style, patty that does not contain animal products. The patty of a veggie burger is made from vegetables (like corn), textured vegetable protein (like soy), legumes (beans), nuts, mushrooms, or grains or seeds, And made right, they're delicious but some times fragile, if proper binders are not used. Even with binders like breadcrumbs, oats, egg whites, or farina, veggie burger patties tend to be delicate things that don't fare well on the grill and are usually prepared in a frying pan or baked in an oven.

Method

1. Mix together yogurt, mint, cilantro and lime peel. Refrigerate. This is the mint riata. Set it aside.

2. In a food processor, pulse together mushrooms, scallions and red bell pepper until finely chopped, but not liquefied. Separately pulse the spinach, carrot, artichoke black beans, chickpeas, white beans, rolled oats until fine and set each aside.

3. In a large skillet, heat one tablespoon of oil over medium high heat. Stir in both the mixtures, cooking for 3-4 minutes. Add garlic, cumin powder and cayenne pepper and heat it through. Remove from heat.

4. Add egg white and season with salt and pepper. Stir in enough breadcrumbs so that the mixture

holds together. Shape mixture into 6 disks and place on a plate lined with parchment or wax paper. Chill for a least 1-hour.

5. Heat remaining olive oil in a non-stick skillet and cook veggie burgers until golden on each side. Serve on a toasted hamburger bun, with the mint Raita as the dressing, top it with a slice of cheese, lettuce, tomato and onion slice or in a pita bread pocket garnished with lettuce, grated cheese and French fries or potato chips or any other munches on the side.

6. Serves 6.

Sandwiches and Sub Sandwiches

A sandwich is two or more slices of bread with meat or some sort of filling in between them.

America's love affair with sandwiches knows no bounds. There are many different types and styles of sandwiches in the United States alone. We have the more common grilled cheese, sloppy Joes, cheese steaks and then the hotdogs and hamburgers. America even has the National Sandwich month that is held every August and the grilled cheese sandwich month every April. In a nation of over 300 million approximately the same number of sandwiches are consumed in a single day!

In 1840, the sandwich was introduced to America as the industrial revolution was underway. When the bakeries began to sell pre-sliced bread the American public jumped at the ease of making a sandwich. The sandwich as an institution was born. Sandwiches are made many ways-we toast the bread or serve it plain; we pile high the sandwich with the maximum ingredients, or keep it simple with one or two. Need a quick bite? Make one.

If you were to assemble the most popular deli sandwich or sub in the United States, it would be ham with American cheese on freshly baked wheat bread. The five top-selling sandwiches with favorites are- Ham, Chicken, Roast Beef, Salami, Turkey Breast and Egg Salad staying on top with one of the following cheeses- American, Swiss, cheddar, Provolone and Muenster. In the five top-selling breads- wheat, white, wraps, Kaiser rolls and rye.

The Heros of sandwiches are Sub sandwiches that are sometimes made in foot long breads and look like a submarine. The oblong bottom half of the bread is typically loaded with various thinly sliced meats, lettuce, tomatoes and pickles. The French bread used is sometimes loaded with roast beef and shrimp and is sometimes smothered in gravy. From the simple peanut butter and jelly to the more sophisticated monte cristo, sandwiches will forever be a mainstay in American cuisine. They are delicious, easy to make and best of all, easily portable! Below is a recipe for a sandwich.

A roast beef sandwich is a sandwich that is made out of sliced roast beef or sometimes beef loaf. It is sold at many diners in the U.S. as well as fast food chains, such as Arby's and Roy Rogers' Restaurant. Roast beef sandwiches have been a specialty of the Boston area since the early 1950s, typically served on an onion roll with optional barbecue sauce and horseradish.

Ingredients

- 4-Tbsp Thousand-Island dressing, divided/Russian dressing
- 8-Slices Dark pumpernickel bread/or a salty kummelweck rolls /rye bread /Kaiser roll
- 8-OZ Corned beef or Roast beef sliced thin/turkey breast sliced
- ¾- Cup sauerkraut
- 1-Tbsp Dijon mustard
- 1-tsp Caraway seeds
- 4- Slices Swiss cheese
- Cooking spray

A roast beef sandwich on a Kaiser roll, seeded with caraway and topped with an abundance of chunky salt is everyone's favorite. This sandwich is usually served with horseradish, kosher dill pickle slices, a slice of cheese with French fries on the side. Sometimes you get a bowl or a cup of soup too that is if you really want to make it more of a complete meal. Roast beef sandwich on a kummelweck rolls is a unique staple of Buffalo, New York's bars and taverns. Few, if any, restaurants outside of the Buffalo area serve this sandwich or even know what it is. Here is a recipe for Ruben (roast beef with sauerkraut) grilled.

Method

1. Layer the sandwiches as follows:

2. Spread dressing and Dijon mustard on one side of each slice of the pumpernickel bread.

3. Place a turkey breast slice on the bread

4. Place Sauerkraut on the top of turkey slice or roast beef and sprinkle few caraway seeds and place cheese slice on this piece of bread.

5. Cover with a second piece of bread.

6. Heat a nonstick skillet to med-high; lightly coat with cooking spray.

7. Place sandwich in the pan.

8. Cook for one minute.

9. Spray topside of sandwich, flip and cook an additional minute until crispy and cheese is melted.

10. Cool slightly and cut in half. Serve with a soup or your favorite munchies.

11. Serves 6-8.

Note: Here are few of the most popular sandwiches of America; Grilled Reuben with coleslaw, Grilled cheese sandwich, Philly cheese steak, Chicken salad sandwich, Ham and cheese, Egg salad sandwich and many more.

Ingredients

- 8, Oz Package crème cheese
- ¼ Cup Milk
- 2-tsp Olive oil
- 1-Cup Spinach leaves
- ½-tsp Chopped garlic
- ½ tsp Salt
- ½-tsp Red pepper
- 10-12 Slices Calabrese bread
- 2-Cus Cooked chicken or Turkey or Shredded roast beef
- 1-Cup Shredded Mozzarella or mixture of Italian cheeses

'Panini' is the Americanized version of the Italian word panino, which means little sandwich and refers to a class of sandwiches that became popular in the United States in the late 1990s. Flavor is the key to Panini, which is based on high-quality Italian artisan breads like focaccia or ciabatta. The sandwiches are layered, but not overstuffed, with flavorful combinations of cheeses, meats, or roasted

Panini Grilled

vegetables. Various dressings or condiments are added, and the sandwich is pressed and lightly grilled. Panini-style sandwiches are popular in trendy restaurants throughout the United States. Food historians generally agree Panini, as we know them today, originated in the panintecas (sandwich shops) of Italy, perhaps as early as the 1960s. A survey of newspaper articles confirms Panini origin caught American consumer attention in the mid-1970s. As time progressed, Panini evolved from upscale fare to trendy sandwiches for the masses. Industry experts credit both novel flavor texture and also the fact that they can be made ahead of time, for Panini's success. You may use any type of bread you want, but it is important to use relatively dense bread that will hold up well on the grill. Foccacia, ciabatta and sourdough breads are popular, along with herbed loaves of breads. A Panini sandwich is a delicious and filling meal that is simple and quick to make, and can be customized to your heart's content. Some popular additions to Paninis include spinach, roasted red peppers, basil, olive oil, olives, tomatoes, garlic, balsamic vinegar and oregano.

Panini is always grilled, so most restaurants and cafes have invested in professional grooved sandwich presses that flatten and heat the sandwich while creating a crunch, buttery outer crust. If you do wish to grill the sandwich, the outsides of the bread may or may not be buttered or brushed with extra virgin olive oil to give it a crispier texture. In Italy, sandwich shops traditionally wrap the bottom of the panino in a crisp white paper napkin, providing a practical solution to drips while enhancing aesthetics.

Method

1. Heat Panini grill if you have one.

2. Whip together milk and crème cheese to make crème cheese crème. Set it aside.

3. Heat oil in large skillet on medium heat. Add spinach; cook and stir 1 to 2 min. or just until wilted. Add salt pepper and garlic and stir to mix. Cook for 2 minutes.

4. Add ½ of the crème cheese creme, chicken and shredded cheese; cook and stir 5 minutes or until chicken mixture is heated through and cheese is melted.

5. Spread chicken mixture onto bread slices; cover with remaining bread slices. Spread outsides of sandwiches with other half of whipped crème cheese.

6. If using grill then spray grill with cooking spray. Add sandwiches, in batches; cook 2 min. or until golden brown. If you are using cooking pan then spray each sandwich on both sides with remaining crème cheese crème and transfer them to the warm skillet. Press it hard with a turner and cook till brown on both sides and the cheeses melt. Serve it hot with warm soup.

> **Note:** Thick slices of Italian or French bread will also work well. Strongly flavored meats such as salami and prosciutto are often used with cheeses such as mozzarella, provolone or asiago. You can swap out the meat and make a vegetable Panini and use eggplant or zucchini, or any other vegetable you like.

7. Serves 5.

Gyros

Ingredients

Meat Mixture
1 Lb. Ground lamb (or
    Beef)/1-Lb Chicken breast
¼- Cup Minced red onion
2- Cloves garlic, minced
2- tsp. Salt
1- tsp Black pepper
1 ½- tsp Cumin
¼- tsp Nutmeg
1- tsp Dried oregano
2- tsp Fresh lemon juice

Sandwich
4- Rounds flat bread or pita.
Lettuce
Tomato; sliced
Tzatziki Sauce
1-Cup Plain yogurt
1-Cucumber peeled and grated
1-Minced garlic
1-Minced green chili
1-tsp Olive oil
1-Tbsp Lemon juice

Gyros are tasty and popular Greek-American sandwiches that you don't need to be able to pronounce to enjoy. Americans today are more experimental and are eager to try flavors and cuisines from around the world and Gyros provide a taste sensation everyone craves. To make Combine savory meat with flavorful sauce, and top it with tomato slices, onions, French fries and wrap it in pita or sandwich bread. Traditional Greek gyros are usually made with whole pieces of thinly sliced marinated pork skewered in a large stack on the rotisserie before being cooked and shaved. The outside of the meat is sliced vertically in thin, crisp shavings when done. Greek-American gyros are made from meat shaved from a large, sausage-like cone of seasoned minced lamb and beef (pressed into a cylinder and cooked on a spit) topped with onions and tomatoes. Tzatziki, the white creamy sauce that is usually added to gyros, is made with strained yogurt, cucumbers, salt, pepper, garlic and dill. Lemon juice, parsley and mint are additional add-ons. Some places opt for sour cream-based tzatziki or just sour cream in place of yogurt. A gyro is similar to Turkey's doner kebab or shawarma, invented in the 19th century.

It is generally served in an oiled, lightly grilled piece of pita, rolled up with various salads and sauces. The pita and gyro meat themselves are the only obligatory ingredients. Gyros sandwiches are called pita gyro or psomaki gyro depending on the type of bread used.

George Apostolou says he served the first gyros in the United States, in the Parkview Restaurant in Chicago, in 1965, and nine years later opened a 3,000-square-foot manufacturing plant, Central Gyros Wholesale.

"The response to the product was tremendous," Mr. Apostolou said. "My two brothers and I, became millionaires in two years' time."

Gyros

Method
Meat mixture

1. Thoroughly combine ground meat with all the marinating ingredients in a bowl. Do the same with the chicken breast if using chicken breast.

2. Divide into ground meat four equal portions and shape into oblong patties about 3" wide, 6" long and ½- thick. Refrigerate for an hour. Similarly do the same with the marinated chicken breast also.

Tzatziki sauce

1. Chop the cucumber in a food processor or shred. Squeeze to remove as much water as possible.

2. Mix together with the yogurt, shredded cucumber, garlic, white wine vinegar, salt and pepper to taste, and lemon juice. Drizzle lightly with olive oil.

3. Refrigerate for at least 30 minutes before serving so the flavors can meld.

Sandwich

4. Grill patties over a hot fire for 3 - 4 minutes per side. Similarly grill the chicken breast and cut into small pieces.

5. Spread tzatziki sauce down the center of flat bread round, add a lettuce leaf, and add some diced tomato. Add the patty, or the chopped grilled chicken and fold the bread over the meat and enjoy.

Note Warm pitas in the microwave. Top with chicken, tzatziki sauce, diced tomatoes and onions. Serve immediately.

6. Serves 4.

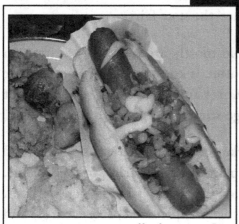

Hotdog on a Bun

Ingredients

1-Gallon Peanut oil
1- Cup Yellow cornmeal
1 ½--Cup All-purpose flour
2-tsp kosher salt
2-tsp Baking powder
½-tsp Cayenne pepper
2-Tbsp Jalapeno pepper, seeded
    and finely minced
1- 8.5 Oz Can Cream-style corn
1/3- Cup Finely grated onion
¼-Cup Oil
2-Eggs
1½- Cups Butter milk
4-Tbsp Cornstarch, for dredging
8- Beef hot dogs
A set of chopsticks

Totally an American creation, Coney Island's most iconic Emblem hot dogs were created nearly 100 years ago. Around 1870. German immigrant Charles Feltman started selling sausages in rolls on Coney Island and called it Frankfurter. Claim is that use of dog meat was common in Germany in early 20th century so Americans named it as dog meat frank and called it hot dog. A hot dog is a sausage served in a sliced bun. It is very often garnished with mustard, ketchup, onions, mayonnaise, relish, and/or sauerkraut.

Hot dogs have many different names. They can be called Wieners, Franks, Sausages, Corn dogs, Bratwursts or Frankfurter. Whatever you call them they are an integral part of American culture and Cuisine. It is one of those foods that are always there whether it is a baseball game, football game or it may be a some kind of a fair or a social get together. They are prepared and are served in a variety of ways. They may be boiled, grilled, fried, steamed, broiled, baked, or microwave. The cooked wiener may be served on a bun (usually topped with condiments), or it may be used as an ingredient in another dish. They may be served plain on a bun but are commonly served with a variety of condiments, including ketchup, mustard, Chile con carne, pickle relish, sauerkraut, onion, mayonnaise, lettuce, tomato, cheese, and chili peppers. Condiments served do vary across the country.

Hot dog or a sausage coated in a thick layer of cornmeal batter and deep-fried in oil is called a corn dog although some times they are baked too. Almost all corn dogs are served on wooden sticks, though some early versions had no stick. There is some debate as to the exact origins of the corn dog; they appeared in some ways in the US by the 1920s, and were popularized nationally by Carl and Neil Fletcher who laid such a claim, that they introduced their "Corny Dogs" at the Texas State Fair sometime between 1938 and 1942. America's greatest food inventions have all originated in one place-the state fairs.

In Argentina they are called panchukers and are sold mostly around train stations, In Australia, a hot dog sausage on a stick, deep fried in batter, is known as a Dagwood Dog or Pluto Pup or Dippy Dog, in New Zealand and South Korea and Japan as an "American hot dog". In Canada, corn dogs may be referred to as "pogo sticks", or "pogos" and so on.

Corn dogs can also be found at almost any supermarket in North America as frozen food that can be heated and served. Corn dogs may be eaten plain or with a variety of condiments, such as ketchup, mustard, relish and mayonnaise. Hot dogs, corn dogs and sausage on a bun are as much a fixture of baseball stadiums as the bleachers, pennants, scoreboards, and organ music. They are also sold at many outdoor events or fairs because they are easy to walk around and munch, as all you have to do is hold the stick (in case of corn dogs) and keep walking. Serve them at home at your child's Birthday party and they will be equally popular.

Method

1. Pour oil into a deep fryer or large heavy pot and heat to 375 °F.
2. In a medium size-mixing bowl combine the cornmeal, flour, salt, baking powder, and cayenne pepper.
3. In a separate bowl, combine the jalapeno, corn, onion, oil, egg and buttermilk.
4. Add the dry ingredients to the wet ingredients all at once, and stir only enough times to bring the batter together. There should be no lumps. Set batter aside and allow it to rest for 10 minutes.
5. Spread the cornstarch into a dry pie pan. Roll each hot dog in the cornstarch and tap well to remove any excess.
6. Transfer enough batter to almost fill a large drinking glass. Insert chopstick into each hot dog and quickly dip them in and out of the batter.
7. Immediately and carefully place each hot dog into the oil, and cook until the coating is golden brown, about 4 to 5 minutes.
8. With tongs, remove to cooling rack, and allow it to drain for 3 to 5 minutes. Serve them with relish, ketchup and mustard.
9. Serves 4-8.

Frankfurters Stuffed with Chili

Ingredients

- 1-Lb Large frankfurters (6-8)
- ½-Lb Ground beef
- 1-Tbsp Olive oil
- 2-Tbsp Sliced green onion
- ½- tsp. Chili powder
- ½-tsp Cumin powder
- 1-Cup Can chili beans, drained
- ½-Cup Chili sauce
- ½-Cup Cooked rice
- 1- Egg beaten
- 1- Cup Shredded Monterey Jack cheese
- Corn chips

Hot Dogs with chili stuffings are very popular at the state and county fairs. There are several variations in the stuffings. The chili stuffing can be with meat or without meat, either way these frankfurters are heart and soul food of a county fair. They are cut lengthwise and stuffed with chili stuffing and then placed in a shallow baking dish. Cook them covered until heated through and then top it with cheese sauce. Heat them until cheese melts. Then serve with or without chips.

Method

1. Cut frankfurters lengthwise, cutting to but not through opposite side. Place them in a shallow baking dish.

2. Brown the ground meat in a frying pan and drain the fat. Set the meat aside.

3. Add one tablespoon of olive oil in the same pan and cook the green onion till it is transparent. Add chili powder, cumin powder, canned chili beans, chili sauce, cooked rice, beaten egg and the cooked meat and mix it.

4. Mound mixture into cut frankfurters.

5. Cook covered, in microwave until heated through. Sprinkle cheese over top.

6. Cook again uncovered, on high heat for 1-2 minutes or until cheese is melted. Serve the frankfurter with ketchup, relish, mustard, salt and pepper.

7. Place corn chips around outer edge of serving dish.

8. Makes 3-4 servings.

Falafel Hamburger

Ingredients

1-16 oz. can of chickpeas or garbanzo beans or Fava beans cooked (drained and washed

1-Cup Frozen and thawed green peas

1- Medium Onion, chopped

2- Cloves of garlic, chopped

1-Tbsp Chopped ginger

1-Tbsp Chopped green chilies

3-Tbsp Fresh parsley or cilantro leaves chopped

1-tsp Coriander powder

1-tsp Cumin powder

½- tsp Cayenne pepper (optional)

Salt and Black Pepper to taste

2- Tbsp Lemon juice

4-5 Tbsp Flour

½-tsp Baking powder

For serving

Oil for frying

6- Mini Pita buns

Lettuce leaves

1- Cup Tomatoes chopped

1-Cup Chopped cucumbers

½ Finely chopped onion

1-Cup Shredded Cheddar or Mozzarella cheese

Tahini sauce bought from the store

The famous Sphinx, with a pyramid in the background, Egypt

Falafel is one of the most widely consumed and recognized foods of the Middle East. Fried balls or patties of chickpeas with spices make falafel both tasty and easy to prepare. Falafel is found all over the Middle East and is a delicious part of a Mediterranean meal. It is more common in countries like Israel, Egypt and Syria. It is regarded as a "fast food" here and sold like hot dogs of America by street vendors. Falafel is also the national dish of Israel. It first made its way into America in the 1970's, as Middle Eastern Immigrants started to settle down in America. They introduced it into the local cuisine and it is gaining popularity ever since. It gained popularity especially among the vegetarian crowd of America because it is rich in proteins and it is quite pleasing to the pallet. Serve it on pitas, with your favorite sauces and toppings, or on buns like a burger. This recipe below is good when accompanied by any Middle Eastern dish such as tabouleh or even roasted potatoes. As a main dish, it is served as a sandwich, stuffed in pita bread with lettuce, tomatoes, and Tahini. As an appetizer, it is served on a salad, or with humus and tahini.

Method

1. Combine chickpeas, peas, onion, garlic, ginger, green chilies, cilantro, coriander powder, cumin powder cayenne pepper, salt and pepper (to taste) in medium size bowl.

2. Process ingredients in a food processor. Add lemon juice and mix well. Add flour and baking powder mixture to make dough that can be made into balls or patties. Keep the dough fluffy not too solid.

3. Form the mixture into small balls, about the size of a ping-pong ball. Flatten them slightly into patties.

4. Fry them in oil about 2 Inches deep or bake at 350°F until golden brown (5-7 minutes). Serve hot.

5. Stuff a pocket of a-pita bread with couple of falafel patties and top them with lettuce, chopped tomatoes, cucumbers, onions and some shredded cheese and Tahini sauce to make a meal.

6. Or serve them with humus as an appetizer if you like or you can serve them as snack with Tahini sauce, Mint chutney or ketchup.

7. Serves 2-4.

Delightful Chili Con Carne

Ingredients

1 ½- Lb ground turkey
1- Lb Ground beef
½- Lb Ground veal
3-Cans Red kidney beans
    drained and washed
1- Stick butter melted
2-3-Large onions chopped
4-Large green peppers hot or
    mild according to taste
2-Tbsp Ground fresh ginger
1-Tbsp Ground fresh garlic
2-small sticks of cinnamon
2- Crushed green cardamom
½-tsp of cloves
3-Cans Tomato sauce
1-Small can of tomato puree
2-Cups Water
1½-Tbsp Sugar
1½-Tbsp Salt
1- tsp Red pepper or hot chili
    sauce.
½- tsp Black pepper
½-tsp Garamamasala
2-Tbsp Chopped cilantro

In Spanish the "Chile" refers to Chile pepper and "carne" means meat. In 1880s, brightly dressed Mexican women known as "chili queens" began to operate around Military Plazas and other public gathering places in downtown San Antonio Texas. Then at the 1893 Columbian Exposition in Chicago San Antonio Chili-stand was in operation and it helped people from other parts of the country taste and appreciate chili. San Antonio was a significant tourist destination and helped Texas-style chili con carne spread throughout the South and West. This dish now has become the official dish of Texas in U.S.

Chili con carne (chili with meat) or more commonly known as simply "chili" is a spicy stew containing chili peppers and meat. Traditional versions are made using Chili peppers, garlic, onions and cumin-powder along with chopped or ground beef. Beans and tomatoes are frequently included. Variations, both geographic and personal, may involve different types of meat as well as a variety of other ingredients. The variant recipes provoke disputes among the culinary experts, and that makes chili a frequent dish for Cook Offs. Chili is also used as an ingredient in a number of other foods.

Once again, there are many claims to the home of Chile con carne, including Tijuana in Baja California or Juarez, Mexico, but we will have to go with San Antonio Texas. If it were not for state of Texas in America, there would be no chili. There are many different types of chili, with meat, without meat, with beans, without beans, turkey chili, venison chili you name it and you will find it in the Chili. Here is my own version that won several awards. This recipe is made with keeping the minimum calories intake in mind.

Method

1. Fry ground beef, ground turkey and ground veal one by one in a skillet until just turned brown, drain the fat every time.

2. Mix it with beans in a Crockpot (beans have to be drained and washed under tap water in a colander). Set it aside.

3. Cook the chopped onions and green peppers, chopped ginger, garlic in melted butter until lightly brown and add the whole sticks of cinnamon, cardamom and cloves.

4. Add the tomato sauce, tomato puree, and water and cook it on low heat for about 10 minutes.

5. Add sugar, salt, red pepper and black pepper.

6. Add this mixture to the beans and ground meat mixture in the Crockpot and cook and simmer on a low heat for 45 minutes to an hour. Add garamasala and chopped cilantro and stir it well. Give it more time if you want the flavors to penetrate. Add a little more water if you need to.

7. Discard the whole spices and serve it with your favorite bread, rice or couscous.

8. Serves 6-8

Korean Tacos

Ingredients

Bulgogi Filling
3-tsp Red pepper powder
2-Tbsp Soy sauce
1-Tbsp Sugar
2-Tbsp Sesame oil
2-Tbsp canola oil
1-tsp Roasted cumin powder
1-Tbsp Minced garlic
1-Tbsp Ginger
2-Tbsp Mirin (Japanese rice wine)
Pinch of black pepper
1-Lb Pork shoulder, thinly sliced

Kimchi Fried rice filling
4- Strips bacon, cut into ½-inch pieces
2-Cups Napa cabbage Kimchi, diced
4- Cups Cooked rice, cooled and chilled in refrigerator
1-Tbsp Butter
2-tsp Sesame oil
Salt to taste
Sesame seeds, for garnish
Sliced scallions, white and green parts, for garnish.

Salad Mixture
1-Cup Shredded Cabbage
2-Tbsp Shredded carrots and green onions /each
1-Avocado chopped
2-Tbsp cilantro chopped
2-Tbsp of marinade

Korean tacos are a fusion dish popular in United States mainly the State of California. They are served as a street food here topped with Korean style fillings, such as Bulgogi, Kim chi and Ramen noodle salad. Korean burritos are a similarly themed dish, using large flour tortillas as a wrap. Korean taco trucks can be seen now in Portland, Oregon (the "KOI Fusion" truck), Austin Texas (the Chi'Lantro BBQ truck) and Seattle, Washington ("Marination Mobile", whose spicy pork Korean tacos earned them 'Good Morning America's Best Food Truck' award. In San Francisco the dish was popularized at the farmers market food stand at the San Francisco ferry building. The dish's popularity is leading fast food chain Baja Fresh to test and market Korean tacos as a menu item in California and with plans to introduce the dish to hundreds of locations nationwide.

Below are recipes for several different fillings used in tacos and burritos like Bulgogi, Kim chi fried rice and Ramen Noodles.

Bulgogi is made from thin slices of sirloin or other prime cuts of beef. Before cooking, the meat is marinated to enhance its flavor and tenderness with a mixture of soy sauce, sugar, sesame oil, garlic, pepper and other ingredients such as scallions, onions or mushrooms especially white button mushrooms Shitake. Sometimes cellophane noodles are added to the dish but that varies by region and specific recipe. It is listed at number 23 on World's 50 most delicious foods readers' poll compiled by CNN in 2011.

Method

1. Combine soy sauce, red pepper, sugar, sesame oil, minced garlic, ginger, mirin and black pepper and marinate the meat in it for at least 2 hours or up to 24 hours.

2. Cook the meat on grill till nicely browned. Shred it and set it aside.

3. Mix the salad ingredients and set them aside.

4. Fill the Taco shell with the shredded meat and top it with salad mixture and serve.

Kimchi Fried rice filling

1. Cook the bacon in a large skillet or wok over medium heat. Add the Kim chi and cook several minutes.

2. Raise the heat to high, add the rice and stir-fry several minutes, until rice is beginning to brown.

3. Stir in the butter and sesame oil. Season with sesame seed and salt to taste and garnish with scallions. Serve as a filling for Tacos or Burritos. It can be served as a side dish in a regular meal.

4. Top it with mixed salad and serve.

5. Makes about 5 cups, enough for 4 burritos or tacos if you wish.

Jambalaya

Ingredients

¼-Cup Butter
1- Medium size onion, chopped
1-small Green bell pepper, chopped
½--Cup Chopped celery
2-Bay leaves
2-Clove garlic mashed
½-Lb Skinless, boneless chicken breast halves - cut into 1-inch cubes
½-Lb Andouille sausage, sliced
1-tsp Cumin powder
2-tsp Dried oregano
2-tsp Cajun seasoning
1-tsp Cayenne pepper
½-tsp Dried thyme
1-Cup Freshly chopped tomatoes
1-15Oz. Can Tomato sauce
2 ½--Cup Chicken broth
1-Cup Bansmati rice
¾-Lb Frozen cooked shrimp without tails
Salt and pepper to taste
Pinch Saffron
2-Tbsp-Chopped cilantro

It probably originated from the French settlements of New Orleans, in the original European sector. It seems that an attempt was made by the Spanish to make paella in the new world, where saffron was not readily available due to import costs. Tomatoes became the substitute for saffron. As time went on, French influence became stronger in New Orleans, and spices from the Caribbean changed this new world paella into a unique dish. In modern Louisiana, the dish has evolved along a variety of different lines. Creole jambalaya, or red jambalaya as it is called by Cajuns, is found primarily in and around New Orleans, where it is simply known as' Jambalaya' and it includes tomatoes whereas Cajun jambalaya does not.

Cajun Jambalaya originates from Louisiana's rural, low-lying swamp country where crawfish, shrimp, oysters, alligators, duck, turtle, boar, venison and other game are readily available. Any variety or combination of meats, including chicken or turkey may be used to make jambalaya. Cajun jambalaya is known as 'Brown jambalaya' in the New Orleans area. To Cajuns it simply means 'jambalaya.' Cajun jambalaya has more of a smoky and spicy flavor than its cousin Creole jambalaya. The French Creoles introduced jambalaya to the Cajuns, but since tomatoes were rarely used in Cajun cooking, they omitted them, browning the meat for color instead.

Jambalaya experienced a brief jump in popularity during the 1920s and 1930s because of its flexible recipe. The dish was little more than the rice and vegetables that people could afford, but the recipe grew out from these humble roots.

During the third term of President Franklin D. Roosevelt, the dish caused a feud between the president and friends of the Presidential family, the Richardson's of Virginia because the family sent a dish to FDR, but the president had to refuse it, because he was allergic to crawfish. In 1968, Louisiana Governor John J. Mckeithen proclaimed that the town of Gonzales in the state of Louisiana be declared as the Jambalaya Capital of the World and now every spring an annual Jambalaya festival is celebrated there.

Method

1. Melt 3 tablespoons of butter in a slow cooker or a heavy bottom pan and fry the onions, green bell pepper, celery, bay leaves and garlic.

2. Add the chicken, sausage and fry a little. Season with cumin powder, oregano, Cajun seasoning, cayenne pepper and thyme.

3. Add the tomatoes and tomato sauce. Cook till oil separates from the sauce.

4. Add the broth and let it come to simmer and add the rice. Let simmer and cook until the rice is tender.

5. Panfry the shrimp in remaining one tablespoon of butter until it is transparent and season with salt and peeper.

6. Add the shrimp during the last few minutes of cooking time and gently stir them in.

7. Sprinkle saffron and cilantro and serve it with your favorite salad, French bread, and green beans.

8. Serves 4 or more.

The famous Gaudi Church, Barcelona, Spain

Classic Goulash

Ingredients

15-Oz Package elbow macaroni
2-Tbsp Olive oil
1-Large onion, chopped
½-Red bell pepper, chopped
5-Mushroom caps, diced
2-Lb Ground beef
1-Lb Ground turkey
28-Oz. Can Tomato puree
15-oz. Can Diced tomato, with
    juice
3-Tbsp Soy sauce
¼-Cup Sugar
3-tsp Garlic powder
1-tsp Anise seed
1-tsp Paprika
1-tsp Ginger powder
1-tsp Cayenne pepper
2-tsp Dry basil
Salt/pepper to taste
2- Tbsp Chopped cilantro
Sour cream

American goulash refers to a stew-like dish, sometimes baked as a casserole that has many variants. Though Goulash originally hails from Hungary the only real connection seems to be the name, and the usual inclusion of beef and paprika.

American goulash is mentioned in cookbooks since at least 1914. Originally the dish of American goulash has core ingredients cubed steak, seasoned ground beef or hamburger, tomatoes in some form (canned whole or tomato sauce or tomato soup) and/or tomato paste. It is usually served as a simple lunch or supper dish or as a main (or only) course. It is a delicious dish that can be made in a variety of different ways, its versatility and popularity lies in its ease of preparation - it requires only one pot to prepare and it uses relatively few common, inexpensive ingredients. Some variants resemble the southwestern stew chili.

Other ingredients that might be added by regional tastes include corn, bell pepper, onions, celery, kidney beans, or chili peppers and cheese, either grated or melted.

Every European country had their own version of Goulash. The Austrian recipe includes dumplings, the German recipe includes potatoes, and in the Netherlands they sometimes include fish. This great recipe for American goulash is sure to tickle every taste bud! American goulash differs from its European counterpart because it calls for ground meat, whereas European goulash uses stew meat. This tasty dish is really easy and relatively inexpensive to make and cooks in no time.

Method

1. Cook the macaroni in a dutch oven, 2 minutes less than the directions. Drain and set aside.

2. In the same pan cook the onion in 2- tablespoon oil until transparent and then add the bell pepper, and mushrooms. Cook 2 more minutes and set it aside.

3. Cook the beef and turkey in another frying pan until it is little brown and drain the fat. Add this turkey mixture to the onion and bell pepper mix and stir to mix.

4. Add the tomato puree, diced tomatoes with the juices, along with the soy sauce, sugar, garlic powder, anise seeds, paprika, ginger powder, cayenne pepper, dry basil, salt and pepper and mix well. You can vary the spice amounts to satisfy your particular taste.

5. When sauce is heated through, add the macaroni and heat it 10-15 minutes more until it is ready to be served. Serve with your favorite vegetable with a sprinkle of cilantro and dollop of sour cream on top and a green salad and dark bread on the side.

6. In some European countries it is served with mashed potato, polenta, dumplings or with spatzle (German noodles) or alternatively as a stand-alone dish with bread.

7. Serves 6-8.

Lentil/Quinoa Pilaf

Ingredients

3-Tbsp Melted butter
1-Cup Chopped onions
1-Tbsp Minced ginger
1-Tbsp Chopped Anaheim
    peppers
1-tsp Cumin seeds
1-tsp Minced Garlic
1- Medium Zucchini, diced
1 Medium Potato diced
1-Cup Fresh tomatoes diced
Salt and pepper to taste
½-tsp Turmeric powder
1-tsp Coriander powder
1-tsp Cumin powder
½-tsp Red pepper
4- Cups Vegetarian broth
1 ¼- Cup Lentils (washed split
    mung beans or washed well
    soaked and drained
¾- Cup Quinoa washed several
    times, soaked and drained
2-Tbsp Lemon juice
½-tsp Garammasala
2 –Tbsp Cilantro chopped

The dish is of middle-Eastern origin and they in turn picked it from Indian Cuisine. In Indian Cuisine similar dish is prepared with lentils and rice instead of quinoa. Protein is a key component in building strong muscles and maintaining a healthy immune system. Both vegetarians and nonvegetarians alike can benefit from eating recipes that feature protein packed lentils and rice or quinoa. The recipe below combines lentils and quinoa with vegetables (in this case, yellow squash and zucchini) in a dish that would work well not only as a side dish but that is also hearty enough to stand on its own as a meal.

Americans have recognized that quinoa is a powerhouse of healthful nutrients. It is gluten free and low in carbohydrates. The ancient Incas called it mother grain and considered it sacred as it has perfect balance of 8 amino acide and it iis a great complement to legumes.

Method

1. Cook onions, ginger, and Anaheim chilies in 3 tablespoons of melted butter on medium low heat in a heavy 4-quart saucepan until transparent.

2. Add a teaspoon of cumin seeds and let them pop. Add the garlic, all the vegetables, and stir to mix.

3. Add the spices, turmeric, coriander powder, cumin powder, red pepper, salt and black pepper. Stir to mix. Add the vegetable broth. Mix well.

4. Add the drained mixture of lentils and Quinoa.

5. When the lentil-quinoa mixture has almost completely absorbed the broth, add lemon juice and stir. The vegetables should be tender. If not add couple of tablespoons of broth and turn the heat low and let it simmer for 5-10 minutes until everything is tender.

6. Sprinkle with garammasala and chopped cilantro. This recipe will serve six. It can be served warm immediately after cooking, or it can be stored in the refrigerator overnight and warmed and served the next day with chutney, raita (yogurt with grated cucumber) or some curry.

7. Serves-4-6 or more.

> **Note: Serve as is or better still with chicken curry, tofu curry, or any other meat entrée you desire. You can substitute the Squash and Zucchini with frozen peas.**
>
> **Mung beans can be bought at Indian or oriental food store or any other major grocery store.**

Fried Rice Dinner

Ingredients
4-Tbsp Vegetable oil
1-Tbsp Fine chopped ginger
1-Fine chopped green chilies
1-Tbsp Fine chopped garlic
3-Cups -Shredded Cabbage
1 ¼-Cups Shredded Carrot
1--Large onion chopped
1-Tbsp Sesame oil
1 ½-Cups Chopped cooked
    chicken pork or any
    luncheon meat
Salt and pepper to taste
3-Cups Cooked rice
¼-Cup Soy sauce
½-Cup Green onion
3-Eggs beaten
1-tsp Black pepper and salt to
    taste
½-tsp Red pepper
2-Tbsp Chopped coriander leaves

Fried rice is a popular component of Asian cuisine, especially in Southeast Asia, like Indonesia, Burma, Thailand, Malaya, Vietnam, Singapore and Philippines where it is almost their staple food. It was brought to America by the Chinese immigrants in the early 19th century. These early settlers created their own typical fried rice version it is based on their own techniques and tastes. There are various types of fried rice recipes available in U.S. The main ingredient is always rice, cooking oil, sweet soy sauce but many other extra ingredients have been adapted ranging from vegetables, meat, chili, sauces and fried eggs. Chinese, who do not like cold food prepared this home food with the leftover cold rice by frying it back to serve at the table. The dish is very popular in the West African nations of Nigeria, Ghana and Togo both as restaurant and as street food. Ready in mere minutes, fried rice is the perfect weekday dinner. Leftover cooked rice is the key to delicious fried rice and is always the most popular item in Chinese restaurants. It is a versatile dish and one can add any meat or seafood (shrimp) or any chopped vegetables to it, plus it's a great way to use over night rice and make it into an appetizing, cheap, and flavorful meal. It has kind of become a common staple of American Chinese cuisine.

Method

1. Heat 2-tablespoons of the oil in a deep wok and add the ginger, green chilies and garlic and fry till transparent while stirring constantly. Cook 2 minutes. Then add one more tablespoon of oil and add the cabbage, carrots and onions into it. Stir-fry until crisp tender. Remove the vegetables to a bowl.

2. Add the sesame oil to the wok and stir fry the chicken pieces and season with a little salt and pepper. Cook till it is no longer white and seems cooked. Add the vegetable mixture to the wok.

3. Reduce heat to medium and add the rice and try to breakaway any clumps. Add the soy sauce. Cook 3 minutes without stirring. Add the green onions and stir to mix and heat it through.

4. Heat the remaining 1-tablespoon of oil in the center of the wok and add the eggs to make omelets. Coarsely chop it and mix it into the cooked vegetables, chicken, soy sauce. Add salt and peppers to season. Toss 1 minute to heat through. Sprinkle and Coriander leaves Add serve.

5. Servings- 4-6

Peking Hot Pot

Ingredients

20-Oz Homemade or Canned chicken broth

2-Scallions chopped

1-tsp Minced Ginger

1 tsp Minced Garlic

2 ½- Cups Water

1-Lb Beef sirloin, sliced thin

1-Lb Boned chicken, sliced thin

8-Oz Uncooked, cleaned, medium shrimp

1-Lb Fresh mushrooms, sliced (enoke)

1-Lb Fresh spinach, washed, drained

1-Lb Celery and /or cabbage, cut into 1-inch pieces

2- 8-Oz. Cans Water chestnuts, drained, sliced

2- 6-Oz Pkg. Frozen pea pods, thawed

Lemon juice drowned 8- oz. can bamboo shoots.

Chinese Bok Choy (baby) whole leaves

2-Oz. Fine egg noodles, cooked

Chopped parsley or green onion

Any of 4 or all of these sauces can be served

Sweet and sour sauce soy sauce

Hot Chinese mustard sauce

Chinese Sesame paste

Oyster sauce

Chinese Hot Pot is a popular, interactive, winter dish for family and friends that is enjoyed around the table all over America and in the modern world. There are restaurants that only specialize in serving Chinese firepot. Unlike the western oil-based fondue, the Hot Pot recipe can be made with water or with any kind of stock that will cook both meat and vegetables. Hot Pot (huoguo in Chinese) is a traditional Chinese social meal. The literal Chinese translation is fire pot, as huo means fire, while guo refers to pot. The Chinese hot pot consists of a simmering metal pot of stock at the center of the dining table. You can call it a Chinese Fondue. While the stock is simmering, thinly sliced pieces of meat, fish and vegetables are simmered and cooked in it and served right on the table. This type of cuisine is also referred to as "steamboat". In Western cooking, the fondue is used in a similar way, although usually with different ingredients.

Method

Preparation prior to cooking

It is not necessary to use all ingredients listed here but as long as you offer an interesting blend of meats, fish and vegetables, it will work. Place beef, chicken and fish in freezer and chill until firm to touch but not frozen. Slice beef and chicken in strips one inch thick and about two inches long. Cut fish into 3/4-inch cubes. Shell and devein shrimp. Chop cabbage into bite-size chunks. Clean mushrooms. If using forest mushrooms, remove and discard stems. Slice mushrooms and sprinkle with lemon juice. Cut off and discard root portion of enoki mushrooms and separate clusters as much as possible.

Rice wine vinegar
Peanut butter sauce
Ginger Soy sauce

Ginger Soy Sauce
2-Tbsp Ginger minced
2- Tbsp Honey
1-tsp Sesame oil
½- Cup Soy sauce

Peanut sauce
¾- Cup Peanut butter
3- Garlic cloves, minced
3-Tbsp Hoi sin sauce
1- Tbsp Sugar
2- Tbsp Soy sauce
1- tsp Chili powder
2-Tbsp Lime Juice
1-tsp Sesame oil
¼-warm water

Wash, trim ends and string pea pods. Clean green onions and cut in halves lengthwise, including green portion. Cut into 2-inch lengths. Clean spinach and discard thick stems. To serve, arrange beef, chicken, fish, shrimp, cabbage, forest mushrooms, enoki mushrooms, snow peas, green onions, spinach leaves, water chestnuts and bamboo shoots in individual rows on large platters or serving plates. Bring broth to boil. Place heating unit under Chinese hot pot and pour boiling broth into hot-pot bowl. When it starts to boil the guests dip whatever ingredients they desire into hot broth to poach with Chinese wire ladle and chopsticks or fondue forks. When cooked (this will take only a few moments) each guest can then dip the pieces into sweet-and-sour sauce, soy sauce or hot mustard (each guest is served these condiments before hand) as desired, and eat with noodles. Add cilantro to the broth to garnish if you wish. Now follow the steps below:

1. Heat chicken broth, minced chopped scallions, garlic, ginger and water to simmer in a deep electric cooking pot placed in the center of the table.

2. Arrange meats and vegetables on large individual platters around the electric cooking pot. Arrange the dipping sauces on the table around the simmering broth

3. Each guest should have their own bowl, a small plate, chopsticks, sauces to dip and a spoon.

4. With slotted spoons, forks or Chinese wire ladles, each diner drops food into the simmering broth to poach to individual taste turn by turn. Then dip cooked food into sauce and eat.

5. When all food is cooked, stir noodles into the broth in the main pot and serve in soup bowls. Garnish with parsley or green onions. Serve with the sauces. Soy sauce, and honey mustard can be purchased at the grocery store. Below recipes for 2 major sauces that are needed.

6. Makes 6-8 servings

Ginger Soy Sauce
1. Wisk the above ingredients together and serve with hot pot ingredients.

Peanut sauce

1. Wisk the peanut butter, garlic cloves, hoi sin sauce, sugar, soy sauce, chili powder, lime juice and sesame oil once in a blender adding the warm water during processing.

2. Serve it with the hot pot ingredients.

Note: The special pot needed can be purchased at a Chinese grocery stores.

There are many varieties of Hot Pots. Vietnamese have this delicious chrysanthemum Hot Pot. (It is traditionally seasoned with the petals of white chrysanthemums but is not safe to do so here in U.S. as the flowers are sprayed) In Mongolia it has resulted in Mongolian Hot Pot (the dipping broth is highly seasoned by hot bean sauce, fermented rice wine, shaoxing wine, ginger, hot chilies and peanut oil). It is spicy and very delicious. Sukiyaki and Shabu shabu are the typical hot pots of Japan. In Thailand it is called Thai suki. In Singapore and Malaysia it is called Steamboat.

Swiss and Gouda Curry Fondue

Ingredients

For Fondue
- 1- Cup White grape juice
- 1-Clove garlic, minced
- 2- tsp Curry powder
- ¼- tsp Nutmeg
- ½- tsp Salt
- 2- tsp Cornstarch
- 2-Tbsp Dry sherry /German Brandy
- 2-Cups (8Oz.) Shredded Gouda cheese
- 2-Cups (8Oz.) Shredded Swiss cheese
- ¼-Cup Lemon juice

For dipping:
- Bite - Size pieces of cooked chicken or turkey
- Lettuce, Fresh vegetables cut into bite size pieces
- Carrot sticks cut into matchstick shape
- Apples, plums and pineapple

Fondue is very popular in America. Swiss villagers invented fondue in the 18th century as a means of survival with only stale cheese and stale bread to eat during harsh winter months. They began to melt the cheese down and add flavors to improve their meals. As the years progressed, fondue recipes evolved to the creation of gourmet dishes and lent themselves to international mediums for flavor experimentation. The name fondue is of French origin, meaning -melted therefore it is not certain if it is of French or Swiss origin or somewhere else.

There are many kinds of fondue, each made with a different blend of cheeses, wine and seasonings mostly depending on where it is made. For a serving of four you need a pound of cheese, a pint of white wine, a clove of garlic, two teaspoons of cornstarch, lemon juice, nutmeg and a small glass of kirsch (German Brandy). There are a variety of cheeses to choose from. Heat the whole mixture to a boiling point while stirring with a wooden spoon or wire whip until smooth and creamy. Care must be taken to get the right consistency. Here you have a complete meal, needing no entrée and no dessert. Each person is given a special fondue fork on which small bite-size piece of French or brown bread or toast is placed. After dipping and twisting until drip free, one has a mouth-watering morsel that is a real treat. While eating if fondue thickens, add a little hot wine. Should it curdle, return it to the stove and whip in a little lemon juice or vinegar.

There are many variations on this fondue theme. For example, use curry or paprika instead of pepper or season with mustard, cumin, dill or basil or you can even use various spices to suit your taste and fancy. If there are side dishes of cooked mushrooms, small meatballs, shrimp or olives, these can be dunked along with the bread. Side dishes of lettuce, celery, carrot sticks or other fresh vegetables are enjoyable and help to heighten interest in the fondue.

Method

1. In a medium-size heavy-bottomed saucepan, heat the grape juice, garlic, curry powder, and nutmeg and salt until it just starts to simmer.

2. Each guest is given a plate, fork and French bread or a bread of your choice. Serve also meat pieces, lettuce, fresh vegetables, carrot sticks and fruits of your choice.

3. In a cup, dissolve the cornstarch in the sherry. Add this to the boiling juice mixture, stirring until slightly thickened.

4. Add the cheeses, a handful at a time, stirring until all the cheeses are melted before adding more. Gradually stir in the lemon juice.

5. Transfer the fondue to an enamel or ceramic fondue pot and keep warm over a fondue burner. Serve immediately.

6. Dip your pieces and enjoy. If it thickens add more grape juice.

7. Makes 10 servings.

> **Note:** Many different types of Fondues are available. Apple cider, cheddar cheese, nutmeg and cinnamon flavored fondue for meats like pork sausages and cooked chicken, red bell pepper and dill flavored fondue for raviolis, multiple juices of berries and mint flavored used for dipping dessert items like lady fingers, cookies etc and many more.

Lo Mein Noodles

Ingredients

2-Qts-Water
1-Tbsp chicken bouillon powder
1-16 Oz Package thin spaghetti
¼ -Cup Soy sauce
2-Tbsp Teriyaki sauce
1 ½- tsp Chinese five-spice
  powder
1/8-tsp White pepper
¼- Cup Vegetable oil
½- Cup Thinly sliced onion
1-Cup Fresh bean sprouts
1-Red bell pepper, seeded cut
  into matchsticks
½-Lb assorted mushrooms
  (shiitake, straw, enoki, or
  oyster), coarsely chopped
1-Tbsp ginger root minced
1-Tbsp minced garlic
1-Cup Fresh snow peas
½- Cup Chopped green onions
Toasted Sesame oil as needed

Lo mein noodles are popular as a take out food in American Chinese restaurants. Traditionally this is a variation of wonton noodle soup. The soup is simply separated from the noodles and other ingredients and then these noodles are served on the side of the soup separately as Lo Mein Noodles.

Lo mein noodles are usually prepared in America by stirring them with a sauce made from soy sauce and other seasonings and vegetables such as Bok Choy, mushrooms, bean sprouts, cabbage, snow peas and then mixed with meats like roast pork, beef or chicken. There are several variations of this dish depending on what kind of meat we are using and they are named by the meat you use, like shrimp lo Mein, lobster lo Mein, vegetable lo Mein, and "House" lo Mein (more than one meat). Chicken Lo Mein is one of the most popular take-out items you can find on the menu of Chinese restaurants worldwide.

In Hong Kong Lo Mein is a popular noodle dish where noodles are boiled, drained and then stirred in with clear broth or served on the side or with a house special soy sauce. The 'stirred noodles' are served with vegetables, wontons and meats such as BBQ pork, Cantonese beef stew, etc.

Method

1. In a dutch oven, bring water and bouillon to a boil. Add spaghetti. Return to a boil.

2. Cook, uncovered, for 6 minutes or until almost tender. Drain, reserving ¼ - Cup cooking liquid. Set spaghetti aside.

3. Add soy sauce, teriyaki sauce, five-spice powder and pepper to reserved liquid and set aside.

4. In a large nonstick skillet or wok, heat oil until hot. Add onions, bean sprouts, bell peppers, mushrooms, ginger and garlic and sauté for 2 minutes. Add peas, sauté 2 minutes longer. Stir in cooked spaghetti. Add reserved (spaghetti liquid +soy sauce+ spice mixture) liquid to the pan. Simmer, uncovered, for 3-4 minutes or until liquid has evaporated.

5. Sprinkle with green onions and toasted sesame oil and serve.

6. Serves 4-6.

California Pizza

Ingredients

1-Tbsp Honey
1-Cup Warm water
2-tsp Active Dry yeast
3-Cups All-purpose flour
1-tsp Salt
2-Tbsp Olive oil
10-Oz Chicken breast - boned and skinned
2-Tbsp Barbecue sauce
1-Cup barbecue sauce/Tomato sauce
2-Cups Gouda cheese/ Mozzarella or Cheddar cheese
½-Onion cut into rings
2-Tbsp Cilantro chopped
2-Tbsp Bell pepper chopped
2-Tbsp Fried mushrooms
½-Tomato Sliced

Pizza has become popular as a globally accessible dish in the latter half of the 20th century after its invention in Naples Italy. It is an oven-baked, flat, round bread typically topped with a tomato sauce, cheese and various toppings.

Pizza may have started life in Italy, but since its adoption by United States it has been nurtured and created in so many different ways that we can call it as another American classic. Due to the wide influence of Italian immigrants in American culture, the US has developed regional forms of pizzas, some bearing only a casual resemblance to the Italian original. There are so many varieties with so many different types of crusts and so many different types of toppings that it has become a dish with a new idea every day, not only in America but also all over the world. Here in America there are many state specialties like New York style, Chicago style, St Louis style and many many more. Here is a recipe of California style Pizza.

Method

To make the dough

1. In a small bowl, dissolve the honey in the warm water.

2. Sprinkle the yeast over the water and stir until it dissolves. Let the yeast mixture stand for 5 minutes, until a layer of foam forms on the surface.

3. In a large bowl, combine the flour and the salt. Make a well in the center of the flour mixture and pour the olive oil and the yeast mixture.

4. Stir the flour into the wet ingredients, until all the flour is incorporated. If it's too dry, add more water.

5. On a lightly floured surface, knead the dough for 15 minutes, until it is smooth and elastic.

6. Shape the dough into a ball and put in a well-oiled bowl. Cover with a moist towel

7. Let rise in a warm place until double in bulk about 1½ hours.

Prepare the chicken

1. In a large frying pan, heat the remaining olive oil on medium high heat. Add chicken pieces. Sauté until cooked (6 minutes). Chill.

2. Coat chicken with 2 tablespoons barbecue sauce. Set aside in the refrigerator.

Pizza

1. Heat the oven to 500 ° F.

2. Punch the dough down, and divide into 2 equal portions. Roll out each portion into a 6-8 inch flat circle.

3. Spread ¼ cup barbecue sauce over the surface of the dough.

4. Distribute ½- of the cheese over the sauce. Distribute ½ of the chicken over the cheese. Place half of the onion rings, bell pepper, mushrooms and tomato slices over the chicken pieces.

5. Place the pizzas in the oven (on top of pizza stones). Bake until crust is crispy and cheese is bubbling (8-10 minutes). Remove pizzas from the oven and sprinkle each with cilantro and serve.

6. Serve both the Pizzas.

7. Makes 4-6 servings

Macaroni and Cheese

Ingredients

- 8-OZ. Elbow macaroni
- 6-Tbsp Butter, divided
- ¼- Cup Flour
- 1-tsp Salt
- ½-tsp Dry mustard
- ¼-tsp Pepper
- 3-tsp Hot pepper sauce
  —optional
- ¾-tsp Worcestershire sauce
- 3-Cups milk
- 1-Small Onion, grated
- ¾-Lb Shredded sharp Cheddar cheese+ 2 ½-Cups Mixture (1 cup of shredded pepper jack + 1 cup of sharp pepper jack + ½ cup of grated Parmesan cheese)
- 1-2-Tbsp Chili powder (Optional)
- ¾- Cup Soft breadcrumbs

There is nothing more American then Macaroni and Cheese. Macaroni and Cheese, also abbreviated as "mac and cheese" in America, Canada, Australia and New Zealand or "macaroni pie" in Caribbean Islands, is a dish consisting of cooked elbow macaroni and white sauce with some cheese added.

Macaroni ("Maccheroni" in Italian) is mentioned in various medieval Italian cookbooks, though it is not always clear whether it is a pasta shape or a prepared dish. "Macaroni" with various sauces was a fashionable food in late eighteenth century Paris. The famous American president Thomas Jefferson encountered the pasta in both Paris and in northern Italy. He drew a sketch of the pasta and wrote detailed notes when he was leaving Paris. In 1793, he commissioned American ambassador to Paris, William Short, to purchase a machine for making it. Jefferson later imported both macaroni and Parmesan cheese for his use in Monticello. In 1802, Jefferson served a "macaroni pie" at a state dinner. It is clear that Thomas Jefferson did make it popular in America. Since that time, the dish has been associated with America and especially the American South. In those times pasta was still made by hand –a laborious process that often exploited slave labor and servants. Traditionally, the cheese sauce was prepared as a Mornay sauce - a classic French sauce of butter and flour cooked into a roux, to which milk and cheese were added. Soon pasta factories came into existence between 1914-1919 and that brought a halt to past import as well as making it by hand. Paralleling this was the introduction of cheese making factories. With the lowering of price of the factory-produced product, macaroni and cheese lost its cachet. Even fashionable Italian restaurants in New York and other places have stopped serving it as a gourmet dish. Though it has lost its status as a sophisticated dish but it is still a darling dish of children and is still served for lunches and as a side dish.

When the cheese sauce and cooked macaroni are added together with a crunchy topping and baked as a casserole dish it still becomes an unbeatable delicacy. Here is a classic macaroni and cheese recipe, made with sharp cheddar cheese and topped with breadcrumbs. In United States July 14 is celebrated as a National Macaroni and Cheese Day.

Method

1. Preheat over to 375 °F (190° C).

2. Cook the macaroni according to package direction and drain.

3. In saucepan over medium low heat melt 4 tablespoons butter; blend in flour and seasonings and sauces. Keep stirring until smooth and bubbly. Gradually stir in milk; cook and stir until thick and smooth. Stir in grated onion and cheeses and set it aside.

4. Place cooked drained macaroni in a buttered 3-quart casserole. Pour prepared sauce over macaroni and gently mix to blend.

5. Melt remaining 2 tablespoons of butter +chili powder and toss with the breadcrumbs.

6. Sprinkle breadcrumbs over the macaroni. Bake at 375°F for 30 minutes, or until golden brown.

7. Serves 4 to 6.

Crunchy Fried Chicken

Ingredients

2½ -3 lbs Frying chicken, cut up
2-Cup All purpose flour
¼-Cup Fine bread crumbs
1 ½-tsp Italian herb seasoning
2-tsp Salt
1-tsp Garlic powder
½-tsp Black pepper
½-Cup Parmesan cheese
1-tsp Cayenne Pepper
3-Eggs
¼-Cup Water
Vegetable Oil to fry the chicken

Fried chicken (also referred to as Southern fried chicken) is a dish consisting of chicken pieces that have been floured and/or battered and then pan fried or deep fried or pressure fried. The coating of breadcrumbs or flour adds a crisp coating or crust to the exterior. What separates fried chicken from other fried forms of chicken is that generally this chicken is cut at the joints and the bones and skin left intact. Crisp well-seasoned skin, rendering fat, is a hallmark of well made fried chicken.

No American recipes list would be complete without fried chicken. America has taken fried chicken and elevated it to an art form. It has its origins in the rural American South, starting as a Scottish tradition, but as the African household cooks straight from Africa started frying the chicken after coating it with seasoned flour. This became a practice that spread through the African American community. After the civil war, rural southern blacks continued the tradition since chickens were the only animals they could afford to raise. Moreover fried chicken could keep for several days, it travelled well, and it gained favor during segregation when people had difficulties finding places to eat and had to carry their own food. People in south picked up this tradition of frying chicken and it became popular with everyone especially those who were on limited budget. Made famous worldwide by a chain of popular restaurants fried chicken has hundreds of variations and some of them have become very famous chicken recipes. There are several fast food chains of restaurants like "Kentucky

Fried chicken" that serve just fried chicken meals (with mashed potatoes, rolls and coleslaw) in America and worldwide.

Method

1. Wash chicken pieces and pat dry.

2. Mix flour, breadcrumbs, seasonings, Italian herb seasoning, salt, garlic powder, black pepper and cheese in a thick plastic zip lock bag and shake well. Coat the chicken pieces, few at a time, inside the bag and set them aside.

3. Beat egg with water and dip coated chicken pieces in beaten egg. Coat the chicken pieces again in the flour mixture in the bag and set them aside.

4. Fill an electric fry pan or large, heavy skillet with vegetable oil, no more than 1/3 its depth. Heat oil to 375° F and fry the coated pieces skin side down until brown and crispy.

5. Turn chicken and fry slowly at this temperature only for 10-15 minutes and let stand at least 5-7 minutes before serving.

6. Serve with mashed potatoes with gravy, cole slaw, rolls or any other sides you   prefer. It makes a great meal.

7. Serves 4-6.

Note: Increase the amounts of seasonings as needed

The Author